Center for
Creative Leadership

The Leader's Edge

Charles J. Palus and David M. Horth

The Leader's Edge

Six Creative Competencies for Navigating Complex Challenges

JOSSEY-BASS
A Wiley Company
www.josseybass.com

Center for
Creative Leadership
leadership. learning. life.

Published by

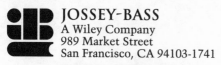

JOSSEY-BASS
A Wiley Company
989 Market Street
San Francisco, CA 94103-1741

www.josseybass.com

Copyright © 2002 by John Wiley & Sons, Inc.

Jossey-Bass is a registered trademark of John Wiley & Sons, Inc.

No part of this publication may be reproduced, stored in a retrieval system, or transmitted in any form or by any means, electronic, mechanical, photocopying, recording, scanning, or otherwise, except as permitted under Sections 107 or 108 of the 1976 United States Copyright Act, without either the prior written permission of the Publisher or authorization through payment of the appropriate per-copy fee to the Copyright Clearance Center, 222 Rosewood Drive, Danvers, MA 01923, (978) 750-8400, fax (978) 750-4744. Requests to the Publisher for permission should be addressed to the Permissions Department, John Wiley & Sons, Inc., 605 Third Avenue, New York, NY 10158-0012, (212) 850-6011, fax (212) 850-6008, e-mail: permreq@wiley.com.

Jossey-Bass books and products are available through most bookstores. To contact Jossey-Bass directly, call (888) 378-2537, fax to (800) 605-2665, or visit our website at www.josseybass.com.

Substantial discounts on bulk quantities of Jossey-Bass books are available to corporations, professional associations, and other organizations. For details and discount information, contact the special sales department at Jossey-Bass.

We at Jossey-Bass strive to use the most environmentally sensitive paper stocks available to us. Our publications are printed on acid-free recycled stock whenever possible, and our paper always meets or exceeds minimum GPO and EPA requirements.

Jossey-Bass also publishes its books in a variety of electronic formats. Some content that appears in print may not be available in electronic books.

Library of Congress Cataloging-in-Publication Data

Palus, Charles J.
The leader's edge : six creative competencies for navigating complex challenges / by Charles J. Palus and David M. Horth.—1st ed.
p. cm.
"A joint publication of the Jossey-Bass business & management series and the Center for Creative Leadership."
Includes bibliographical references and index.
ISBN 0-7879-0999-8
1. Leadership.   I. Horth, David M., 1945–   II. Title.
HD57.7 .P354 2002
658.4'092—dc21

2002003578

FIRST EDITION
HB Printing   10 9 8 7 6 5 4 3 2 1

A Joint Publication of

The Jossey-Bass

Business & Management Series

and

The Center for Creative Leadership

Contents

Preface   xiii

Acknowledgments   xv

The Authors   xix

Introduction: Navigating Complex Challenges   1

1. Paying Attention   11
   Shifting Between Modes of Attention   12
   Understanding Left-Mode and Right-Mode Attention   14
   Using Kinesthetic Attention   17
   Paying Attention to Negative Space   19
   Asking Powerful Questions   21
   Developing the Competency of Paying Attention   29
   Cautions   34

2. Personalizing   37
   Learning Begins with the Personal Connection   39
   Practicing Assessment for Development (A4D)   41
   Practicing Exploration for Development (E4D)   46
   Tapping Into Your Passion   50
   Knowing When to Let Go of Your Personal Side   56
   Developing the Competency of Personalizing   58
   Cautions   68

3. Imaging   71
   Making Imagination Tangible   72
   Seeing Organizational Vision in a New Light   84

Exploring Scenarios		87
Making and Using Metaphors		91
Making Poetry in the Face of Complexity		95
Developing the Competency of Imaging		98
Cautions		104

4.   Serious Play | 107 |
Play Enhances Learning amid Turbulence		109
Play Is a Community Activity		114
Play Is the Heart of Science and Technology		117
Developing the Competency of Serious Play		121
Cautions		125

5.   Co-Inquiry | 129 |
Building Creative Leadership Communities		130
Creating Spaces for Group Work		133
Conducting Dialogue		136
Putting Something in the Middle		142
Crossing Boundaries		149
Developing the Competency of Co-Inquiry		153
Cautions		156

6.   Crafting | 161 |
Thinking in Wholes		162
Crafting Decisions		164
Building Scaffolds for Learning		169
Developing Leadership as Science and as Art		172
Learning from Artists		177
Developing the Competency of Crafting		184
Cautions		189

7.   Creative Leadership in Action | 193 |
Case Study 1: Task Force Collaboration		194
Case Study 2: Leadership in New Media		198
Case Study 3: Individual Leadership Coaching		202
Case Study 4: Creative Product Innovation		204

Case Study 5: Executive Interdependence 206

Case Study 6: Inventing a New Manufacturing Paradigm 211

Appendix A: The Leading Creatively Program 217

Appendix B: Our Research Methods 221

Appendix C: A Reflective Assessment of
C2 Competencies: Competencies for Making
Sense of Complex Challenges 223

Appendix D: The ORC Star-Mapping Process 227

Notes 233

Bibliography 255

Index 265

About the Center for Creative Leadership 271

For Beth, Brooke, and Shannon

—Charles J. Palus

For my family and friends with love.
You are all such talented artists in your own right.
Remember, "Hot chocolate, drinking chocolate"
for rainy days.

—David M. Horth

Preface

During the last two decades many of those who study and practice leadership have come to this important realization: *shared understanding* is a powerful force—even the essential force—for navigating an organization through turbulence and uncertainty. This shared understanding takes many forms. It may be manifested as, for example, knowledge management, organizational learning, corporate vision and mission, self-organization, or culture building.

Our special interest for over ten years has been how people create shared understanding, how they invest their work with *sense* and *meaning*.[1] It seems to us that now more than ever, in this time of rapid change and complexity, sense and meaning are part of the bedrock for culture, knowledge, social learning, and leadership. Making sense of complexity appears to be the key to developing successful solutions to complex challenges. It is a key to innovation.

But what exactly are sense and meaning, and how are they discerned? Do people and organizations create (or *make*) and share meaning? How do leaders apply sense making and meaning making in practice as they face and resolve complex challenges?

In 1994, we and our colleagues at the Center for Creative Leadership embarked on an R&D initiative to investigate these questions. A key component of the initiative was the Leading Creatively program (LCP). There are now over six hundred alumni of this intensive five-day experience. They are managers, leaders, and professionals from all levels and from a wide variety of settings, and all have had a role in our research and are represented in this book. Each of them used the program to explore the leadership issues around a particular complex challenge he or she was facing. We have followed over two hundred LCP alums back to work through a variety of means—site visits, interviews, surveys, and an annual conference. Invited, we have listened, watched, conversed, and occasionally joined in as their newly sharpened leadership competencies were tested by all kinds of new challenges. This book tells *what* we have learned from these individuals and *why* the lessons matter.

We outline six Complex Challenge (C2) Competencies that were identified in our research and practical experience. These sensibilities and skills are unique means that leaders, teams, and organizations can use to make sense of rapid change and complexity.

Our purpose in writing this book is to help you improve your ability to lead creatively in three ways. First, this book will help you recognize that you already have C2 Competencies, and it will assist you in developing them further. Second, it will give you a practical understanding of how these competencies, when integrated with traditional skills, are vital to the essential process of making sense of a seemingly chaotic reality. And third, you will discover ways to help your organization and community develop and use these competencies to create shared understanding and thus to better navigate and resolve complex challenges.

This book is for executives, managers, leaders of cross-functional teams, strategists, research and development groups, and anyone working in the fast-moving organizations that are emblematic of today's unpredictable, turbulent, and changing times. It is our hope these competencies will help people of all kinds achieve their leader's edge.

March 2002   Charles J. Palus
                                     Philadelphia, Pennsylvania

                                     David M. Horth
                                     Greensboro, North Carolina

Acknowledgments

The Leading Creatively Project, culminating (for now) in this book, has enjoyed the efforts of many people. We are deeply indebted to the alumni of the Leading Creatively program. This book is about their work and would not have been possible without them. We offer our special thanks to the companies we worked with and to the participants in our annual co-inquiry at the Airlie Conference Center.

The project could not have reached this point without the vibrant community of the Center for Creative Leadership and the generous support of the Smith Richardson Foundation.

Special thanks are also due to those who played major roles in starting or sustaining this work. Suzanne Merritt is a founder of the project and discerning seeker of aesthetic competence in organizational theory and practice. Pam Mayer is a founder of this project; she knew just where to look, and what to do with what she saw. Victoria Guthrie is a project founder, skillful designer of experiential learning, constant teacher and mentor, and curious student. Cheryl De Ciantis is a founder of this project and a master educator, administrator, and inspiring artist. Stan Gryskiewicz is a champion of creativity in all its forms and has been instrumental in nurturing this project. Talula Cartwright is a fine teacher and researcher who helped us weave ideas together and test them. Sharon Rogolsky shared her compassionate, creative mind and guided us amid the turbulence of co-inquiry. Wilfred H. Drath gave us the sweeping vista of leadership as meaning making in a community of practice and has been an all-around excellent boss, colleague, and friend.

We and our colleagues have drawn on the work of a number of scholars whose theoretical and practical ideas allowed us to dare to design a program in creative leadership. Peter Vaill has been a primary inspiration with his ideas about learning and navigating in permanent whitewater. Bernice McCarthy helped immeasurably with her 4MAT model and her spirited encouragement. David Hurst showed us the place of creative leadership in the organizational ecocycle and how the embodied mind really swings. Ralph Smith validated our explorations into the realm of the arts and devoted a special issue (30[4]) of the *Journal of Aesthetic Education* to "the aesthetic face of leadership." Betty Edwards taught us to draw, taught us to teach the art of seeing, and opened the door to the power and rigor of R-mode. Susanne Cook-Greuter in her gentle, yet incisive wisdom connected visual literacy to higher stages of human development. David Whyte showed us what poetry means for soul, navigation, and everyday life. Colin Funk shared his remarkable gifts for improvisation and community theater. And through their groundbreaking research and writings, David Perkins and Howard Gardner showed us the textures, forms, and meanings of creative intelligence.

Many names should share the top of this list of additional project members, angels, and architects; to resolve this dilemma, we have made the list alphabetical. Our thanks to Kevin Asbjornson, Betsey Baun, David Berke, Cynthia Bower, Robert Burnside, Carl Davison, Barbara Demarest, Lynn Fick-Cooper, Jim Francek, Heidi Gailor-Loflin, Leslie Hiatt, Kenton Hyatt, Linda Lemar, Jim MacDonald, Laurie Merritt, Glenn Mehltretter Jr., Kate Panzer, Jill Pinto, Albert Selvin, Lee Stine, Walter Tornow, Michael Wakefield, Dan Weeks, and Yolan Williams.

We are deeply grateful to our sterling editors: Lisa Lee and Byron Schneider at Jossey-Bass and Marcia Horowitz and Martin Wilcox at CCL. We are also indebted to Martin for over ten years of editorial magic in supporting and shaping the ideas presented here. Laurie Merritt has been a wizard at organizing all the little details that really matter. We also thank Elspeth MacHattie for her excellent and instructive copyediting.

Finally, we wish to thank the people who gave us insightful feedback on earlier drafts of this book: Eva Beck, Laura Davis, Judith Diaz-Myers, Beth Dixon, Donald Filer, Marilyn Gannon, Sally Helgesen, Steve Kelsey, Cathy King, Sylvie Labelle, Cheryl Lison, Bud Martin, Martin McCarthy, David McGehee, Rebecca Neff, Nick Nissley, Janie Page, Lori Painter, Sonya Prestridge, Jodi Sansonne, J. Mike Smith, Cathy Tyler, Michael Wakefield, and Arthur Zbrozek.

Chuck's Acknowledgments

Bob Kaplan profoundly shaped the ways in which I understand how people develop. More than that, Bob shaped me and, by extension, this book.

Several guides at Boston College have been essential to my navigation of complexity. Randy Easton opened the domain of cognitive science and gave me a long look at the ecology of perception. Marc Fried shared with me the adventure of social science and profoundly shaped my understanding of the transformative potential of stressful experiences. Ali Banuazizi and Ramsey Liem taught this engineer how to think about psychology and how to pursue its messages across cultures. The remarkable educational vision of Peter Gray provided a foundation for what I know about learning and for how I came to learn it.

The Hurricane Island Outward Bound School supported my early research on experiential education, fed my passions, and taught me how to teach.

The Center for Creative Leadership has been a constantly supportive and challenging environment for exploration, research, and development for me and for a rich network of collaborators and colleagues.

The members of my family, Beth, Shannon, and Brooke, have been a constant source of love, support, and inspiration, for which I am forever grateful.

David's Acknowledgments

I first want to thank all my friends at ICL, an information technology company based in the United Kingdom, where I served my apprenticeship as a creativity practitioner—initially as an engineer and later as a marketer and strategist. I especially want to recognize Cliff Wright, Bob Beard, and Hugh Macdonald—all of whom contributed greatly and warmly to my understanding of the creative process. The late Robert Burkhart helped me reconnect with my own artistry so that in the process I could help others do the same.

My heartfelt thanks goes to those at CCL who gave me space to play seriously with concepts and ideas that eventually led to the development of the Leading Creatively program; Bob Dorn artfully practiced leadership of the highest order; Victoria Guthrie—an extraordinary program designer—encouraged me to contribute my own knowledge and experience to the program.

I am eternally grateful to Betsey Baun. Betsey, you are an artist with a huge scope. Your mentoring when I doubted my own ability to make something of difficult concepts helped me connect my passion for art with my passion for leadership education.

The Authors

Charles J. Palus (Chuck) is a research scientist, faculty member, and project manager at the Center for Creative Leadership in the practice area of Leadership for Complex Challenges. Chuck's current focus is individual and organizational competencies for addressing complex challenges, with a special interest in the role of aesthetic competencies in relational leadership. He is lead researcher and codesigner of the Leading Creatively program and lead researcher and codesigner of Facing and Solving Complex Challenges, a custom program that helps intact groups apply leadership to their most pressing issues. Chuck began his career as a chemical engineer with E. I. DuPont de Nemours and subsequently transitioned into the area of adult development. He has served with the Hurricane Island Outward Bound School in the areas of professional development, leadership, team building, and adolescent development. He is the coauthor of several CCL reports and magazine articles and the lead developer of *Visual Explorer: Picturing Approaches to Complex Challenges*, a CCL product used to support group sense making. Chuck has a Ph.D. degree in social psychology from Boston College.

David Magellan Horth is a senior faculty member in the Leadership for Complex Challenges practice area at the Center for Creative Leadership. His responsibilities have included management of various CCL programs, including the Leading Creatively program, for which he was one of the chief architects; the Innovation Assessment Process (IAP); and Targeted Innovation. He also codesigned

Facing and Solving Complex Challenges, a custom program that helps intact groups apply leadership to their most pressing issues, and he instructs in many other open-enrollment and custom executive development programs. An active member of the international community of creativity practitioners, David presents regularly at international creativity conferences. He began his career as a research and development engineer and emerged twenty-one years later as a strategist specializing in creativity and innovation. David has coauthored several reports and articles in the leadership and creativity field and is coauthor of *Visual Explorer: Picturing Approaches to Complex Challenges*, a CCL product used to support group sense making. He holds a B.Sc. degree from the University of Surrey in England.

The Leader's Edge

Navigating Complex Challenges

The challenges faced by leaders and organizations today are increasingly complex. The words *volatile, multidimensional,* and *unprecedented* are just a few of the descriptors leaders use when discussing these challenges. They often find themselves beleaguered on all sides as the pace of scientific discovery accelerates, deregulation increases, mergers and acquisitions alter goals and systems, demographics shift, business models are adjusted, and the economy fluctuates.

Consider the following cases. (We use pseudonyms for some of the people—referred to by first names—and companies we discuss; these pseudonyms are italicized the first time they are used in a chapter.[1]) A cross-functional task team at *Chemstar, Inc.*, a high-tech chemical products company, is formed to address a serious quality problem in the manufacture of the firm's flagship product, a medical analyzer. The team observes that the problem has been recurring in various forms for five years. It appears likely that fundamental limits inherent in the underlying technology are driving Chemstar's customers to new products. There is a climate of fear in the organization—a fear that a root-level solution to this challenge will bring radical changes, an ending of the company as employees have known it.

The research and development (R&D) department at *Orion, Inc.*, an office solutions company, is seeking better ways to strategically select and prioritize company projects. The team of scientists and technologists staffing this department has been given the task of "picking winners"—high-return projects that match corporate strategy and capabilities. Team members feel a sense of urgency because Orion's competitors are picking winners at an accelerating pace. The team attempts to analyze all relevant data but runs into a wall: the inputs are too complicated and incomplete to produce clear decisions. To make matters more challenging, the team has just been asked to help management evolve corporate strategy rather than simply apply it.

The *Johns River Station* is a coal-fired power plant scrambling to remain competitive in a deregulated market. The station management team faces environmental compliance issues, a strong and conservative union, planned and unplanned power outages, and increasing pressure for operational efficiency. An attitude of "just punching the clock" is widespread among employees. On top of all this, the team members have just been told that the plant is up for sale and their own jobs are vulnerable. The executive who directs their work recognizes that the company and its management are up against a wall and gives them license to create new approaches to their work. The team asks itself how its members can be creative and effective in light of all these challenges.

To many people, such challenges may seem insurmountable. And they may very well be—if people respond to them using only traditional leadership, management, and technical competencies. Traditional management by itself simply isn't equipped to cope with the scope and number of such challenges. Why? Because the critical factors that drive these challenges are often not measurable or quantifiable by traditional methods. Often the complexity of these situations renders them unpredictable or unprojectable.

Leaders facing such situations—what we at the Center for Creative Leadership call *complex challenges*—need more information and ideas than those that are traditionally mustered. Complex challenges do not have prescribed or tried-and-true approaches or solutions. They are central in importance and demand quick and decisive action. Yet organizations, teams, and individuals do not know how to act in these cases. In fact, instead of taking immediate action, they feel a need to slow down and reflect. The tension arising from this paradox calls for a different approach to development—organizations and individuals must tap into a wider array of resources, and acquire a larger framework for leadership.

In the past eight years, we have worked in depth with several organizations and several hundred individual leaders from a variety of industries and disciplines. We have seen that when leaders can use *all* the resources available to them, their organizations can not only *survive* turbulent environments but *thrive* in them. In our work and research, we have sought to identify the insight, skills, techniques, and wisdom that separate true leaders from effective managers. What do these leaders know, and more important, how do they know it? We found that six interrelated competencies give leaders the edge they need when they have to act in a seemingly unactionable situation.

The keys to creative leadership take the form of what we call *Complex Challenge Competencies*, or *C2 Competencies* for short. These competencies are

1. *Paying attention:* using multiple modes of perception to understand a complex situation.

2. *Personalizing:* tapping into your and others' unique life experiences and passions to gain insight and create energy to tackle group challenges.

3. *Imaging:* making sense of complex information, constructing ideas, and communicating effectively by using all kinds of images, such as pictures, stories, and metaphors.

4. *Serious play:* generating knowledge through free exploration, improvisation, experimentation, levity, and play.

5. *Co-inquiry (or collaborative inquiry):* dialoguing within and across community boundaries of language, culture, function, and professional discipline.

6. *Crafting:* synthesizing issues, objects, events, and actions into integrated, meaningful wholes.

Coordination of the six C2 Competencies can be understood as an artistic endeavor. Organizational scholar Peter Vaill says, "Art is the attempt to wrest coherence and meaning out of more reality than we ordinarily try to deal with."[2] Leadership, especially today, has to rely on more and better ways to wrest meaning from difficult challenges.

Historically, leaders and organizations have neglected the C2 Competencies or even actively discouraged them. Among the reasons for this neglect is the mistaken assumption that only quantification and analysis are worthy of professionals. Even when the value of these competencies has been glimpsed, the artistry they embody has been viewed as too mysterious to teach, too difficult to grasp. Moreover, practicing these competencies may involve questioning the established order of things, and this process can be misused (one of the important cautions we address throughout this book). Finally, of course, times have changed. When challenges weren't so mercurial and multifaceted and the established order was more reliable, the C2 Competencies were perhaps less necessary and thus less valued. Today, however, they are crucial.

In short, leadership today must be a blend of the traditional management methods of measurement and control and the C2 Competencies.

Making Sense of Complex Challenges

All the C2 Competencies are elements of the human *sense-making* process. We believe that deliberate and effective sense making within and among communities is the essence of creative leadership. But what does it mean to *make sense?* Why is it vital during times of change and complexity? And how can it be done systematically?

When we humans are faced with confusion, our instinct is to repair it with order. Consider this simple sequence of thoughts: "What was that noise? I think it was just the cat. Put her out. Go back to sleep." The process of making sense occurs when we encounter a disturbance. We filter it through our minds. We run our senses over it. We examine it viscerally. We analyze, imagine, and check our intuitions, looking for logic, until we can say: "Aha, I know this. Now I know what to do." That, in a nutshell, is the sense-making process.

As members of organizations we do the same thing, both individually and collectively. We encounter disorder and repair it. We make it make sense: "What is this noise? This is just the third-quarter earnings data. Write the report. Go back to sleep." Usually making sense is rapid and automatic—quite a gift in a world filled with cats, night noises, third-quarter earnings, and so forth. Like most gifts, however, automatic sense making is not the answer to all our needs. It relies on ingrained assumptions and past experience to produce quick answers. In the realm of complex challenges, quick answers are valuable, but they are never enough and are often dangerous by themselves.

To make effective sense of a complex challenge we must have a grasp of the whole of the situation, including its variables, unknowns, and mysterious forces. We must examine more than just the surface. This requires skills beyond everyday analysis. Although they are not easily managed, we need to attend to those valuable professional resources we call *heart* and *guts*. We grasp events through intuitions and personal passions as well as through mission statements and standard operating procedures. We also use our imaginations to figure things out. Because these ways of making sense tap unique resources and reveal additional information, they are highly useful when we are trying to make sense of complex challenges in a way that leads to effective action. Creative leaders use the C2 Competencies to engage as effectively as possible in these powerful ways of making sense.

The best way to conceptualize the C2 Competencies is as a cycle, or sense-making loop (Figure I.1). Leaders do not use them formulaically and individually but creatively and in concert to grasp and handle complex challenges.

Figure I.1. The Sense-Making Loop.

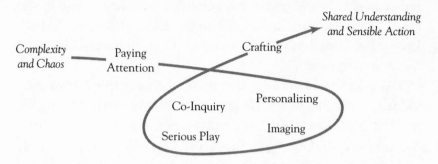

Paying attention is the starting place for sense making in the face of complex challenges. This is a resource that you can harness and enhance to aid your search for patterns in the chaos. Paying attention begins with slowing down, temporarily, in order to be more deliberate in grasping the situation. You must also take note of your own reactions and how they contribute to the complexity.

The second step in the sense-making loop is to *personalize*, to access personal resources that you might otherwise overlook or discount. Great energies lie at the confluence of avocation and vocation, the personal and the professional. Your personal side is, for better or worse, a powerful filter for your attention and how you can pursue your craft. The timely letting go of the personal side is thus also part of this competency. There are dangers as well as rewards in personalizing—as there are with each of the other competencies—so heeding a few cautions is important.

Once you have developed new perceptions of your challenge and gained a stronger sense of who you are and what you bring to the table, *imaging* helps you process this information. Words by themselves are usually not enough for making sense of complexity, even though organizational habits often assume otherwise. When something strange comes along—an opportunity? a threat? a piece of a larger puzzle?—imagery is a very good way to take it in and make sense of it. Imaging can be understood as an activity that combines *imagination* with *intent*.

The fourth step in the sense-making loop is what we call *serious play*. One pitfall of everyday sense making is that it can become a rigid process. Overcontrol amid complexity is an all-too-frequent and crippling stance. Making sense of what you may never have seen before requires play with a serious intent: experimentation, improvisation, and imaginative exploration. Bend some rules, have some fun—and harvest what you learn in the process. Play becomes serious when it is contained within the constructive purposes of co-inquiry.

Co-inquiry (or collaborative inquiry) refers to sustaining an effective dialogue with and between the individuals or within and among the communities who have a stake in the reconciliation of a complex challenge. Variety among the stakeholders is usually the source of much of the complexity of the challenges faced at all levels of society—and the source of much opportunity. But how do you make shared sense of complexity when you are separated from the other stakeholders by culture or language or both? Collaborative inquiry occurs when a group accepts its leadership role and group members, despite their deep differences, commit themselves to collaborative sense making as a way of tackling one or more challenges. The momentum that develops from co-inquiry turns the gears of the larger context and makes things happen.

Crafting, the sixth competency, is the synthesizing of issues, objects, events, and actions (including the results of your work with the first five competencies) into integrated, meaningful wholes. Organizations too often fail to recognize that it is creative synthesis, or artistry—and not simply the heaping together of parts—that shapes order out of chaos. A key to successful crafting is that it dwells not in isolated individuals but in communities dedicated to making great products and services. The ability to produce artistry of this kind is a practically universal human trait and is surely present within your own organization—but it may be hiding.

Basically, then, competent sense making in the face of a complex challenge comes down to this. Grasping the challenge with fresh eyes. Enlisting personal passions. Exercising disciplined imagination.

Improvising and experimenting amid turbulence. Making diverse perspectives work for the whole community. People engaged in competent sense making have better conversations about things that really matter. They conduct open and heartfelt dialogue well leavened by critical thinking. They craft sense, with an eye for the elegant and a feeling for the whole. They artfully shape the forms of work and life in periods of turmoil.

Understanding this sense-making loop and putting it into action is an essential part of making sense of complexity. Creative leadership cannot be accomplished without it.

Developing Both Individual and Community Competencies

There are two facets to the C2 Competencies: each can be exercised as an individual leadership competency and as a community leadership competency.

Individual competencies. Almost everybody has some natural ability in each of these six creative areas and can use them to make sense of complexity. Therefore you can work individually to refine your skills and aptitudes in these competencies as part of your leadership development. You can apply these competencies to the challenges you face at work and in life.

Community competencies. But leadership development today is about much more than the individual leader. Leadership must also reside within and be developed by the organizational community.[3] As former president of the World Academy of Art and Science Harlan Cleveland points out: "National states, big business, and computer networks are all becoming nobody-in-charge systems."[4] Each of the six competencies is something that groups of people do together to make shared sense of the complexity they face as a community. Successful communities come to share a robust and dynamic *common sense* about complex challenges. They have ways in which individual members participate in sense making, problem solving, and mutual action. Leaders can craft successful communities by helping groups practice the skills and abilities of the six competencies—by helping others participate in leadership. Leaders can grow communities with strength, creativity, and resilience in the face of turbulence.

Putting This Book to Use

Each of the first six chapters of *The Leader's Edge* is devoted to one of the six distinct but interrelated C2 Competencies. We begin each chapter by explaining the characteristics of the competency and why and how it works during times of complexity and challenge. Then we provide specific suggestions and activities for developing that competency on both the individual and community levels. Last, we offer important cautions to keep in mind as you develop and employ the competency. Like any good tool, each one has specific uses and thus can be mishandled.

Throughout these chapters, we illustrate the discussion with real-life stories and case studies from a number of companies. Some are taken from the business literature. Many concern the collaborators in our research that we call Chemstar, Orion, and Johns River Station, the companies with which we distilled much of our knowledge about navigating complex challenges. These stories and studies illustrate the organic and varied processes by which groups develop and employ the C2 Competencies.

In Chapter Seven, we present case studies that illustrate how individuals and communities have applied the six C2 Competencies as a series of activities, together with traditional leadership and management skills, to deal effectively with complex challenges.

The four appendices supply background information on the work we did in developing our ideas. Appendix A, "The Leading Creatively Program," describes the five-day program that is playing a key role in our research on how people practice creative leadership in the workplace. Most of the members of the three groups featured in our main case studies, for example, attended the program.

Appendix B summarizes our research methods. Appendix C, "A Reflective Assessment of C2 Competencies," contains a self-assessment tool for both individuals and groups. Appendix D, "The ORC Star-Mapping Process," explores the technique developed by Orion to combine analytical analysis with the C2 Competencies for the purpose of strategic project selection.

We encourage you to read this book with pen in hand. Make notes, flag activities, highlight what's useful, and write in the margins. Approach this material thinking about how it can work best for you and your organization. Remember, you are your own best expert. If you find ideas in here that you have doubts about, organize your own best ideas and continue. A participant in one of our programs had what seemed to us to be the right attitude for our readers too. In response to a point we were presenting, he said, "Not proven—but carry on." One key to practicing creative leadership is discovering ideas and activities that resonate with your situation. The strength of the C2 Competencies increases as you find the best ways to work with their tools in your unique circumstances. From here on there are no formulas. Take what you find in this book as raw material for your own inventions.

Chapter One

Paying Attention

The increasing pace of work today often demands that people scan information quickly and make rapid judgments. To do this, they typically take mental shortcuts, acting on what they expect to see. When work is routine or only incrementally novel, the ability to make quick judgments based on historical experience is a valuable skill. In situations of high complexity or chaos, however, making quick judgments can be disastrous. A different way of evaluating the circumstances, making decisions, and taking action is called for. This is where the mastery of Complex Challenge (C2) Competencies comes into play.

As Harlan Cleveland notes in *Leadership and the Information Revolution*, revolutions in many fields are spreading, overlapping, and interacting at such an increasing pace that unprecedented *complexity* is the hallmark of our age. Whereas in the Industrial Age leadership tended to be concentrated in central leaders who were able to present a simple and clear organizing vision, Cleveland warns that today "we had better not neglect . . . those bits of messiness that interfere with a neat picture. . . . Those bits of messiness are often near the center of the leadership function in a complex society."[1]

In our general experience at the Center for Creative Leadership (CCL), managers faced with a complex problem typically spend about 90 percent of their time solving the problem and only about 10 percent examining the problem and its context—with the typical result that they end up solving the wrong problem. Complex problems—even really wicked ones—often begin to crack and shift when you spend more of your time looking at the problem. In problem-solving sessions, clients often tell us that their problem has either "gone away" or dramatically shifted after careful attention. What has happened is that the client has come to see past the facade of the presenting problem to its underlying issues. Often upon such deeper examination the solution pops out as an integral part of the landscape.

One key to achieving real solutions to complex challenges is the critical skill of *paying attention*. A person competent in paying attention has the ability to selectively use multiple modes of perception when taking in a situation. We consider paying attention the master C2 Competency because it precedes and organizes the others.[2]

Paying attention has five components:

- Shifting between different modes of attention
- Understanding left-mode and right-mode attention
- Using kinesthetic attention
- Paying attention to negative space
- Asking powerful questions

Shifting Between Different Modes of Attention

Everyone has a variety of modes, or gears, of perception—quick, slow, intellectual, intuitive, rational, and emotional. In work situations, people tend to emphasize some modes and neglect others because their professional environments encourage and reward some modes more than others. Therefore the first step in paying attention is twofold: becoming familiar with the full range of your modes of perception and learning how and when to shift from one to another.

What you might think of as *high-gear attention* gives you speed over smooth terrain. It quickly and efficiently chunks the world into familiar categories and allows you to make snap judgments. Consider it a hit-and-run way to take in information. Working in high gear, you place a series of bets that the world is a familiar place. You skim the surface, assuming you can accurately grasp what is underneath. In familiar situations, high-gear attention can be very effective. David Perkins, scholar of human development at the Harvard Graduate School of Education, estimates that for people with a solid base of experience in the issue they have at hand, high-gear attention is effective roughly 90 percent of the time.[3] In an environment of rapid change, however, people are likely to lack such experience in the issues they confront. If the people in your organization pay attention to complex issues the same way they pay attention to routine information, you've got a problem.

Arie de Geus, former Royal Dutch Shell strategist, observes that the average life span of a company is less than that of a person.[4] The reason, he believes, has to do with perception: people will not see that which is foreign to their experience or which calls forth unpleasant emotions. In business this trait gets expressed as the corporate one-track mind: companies plan only one path into the future and then see only signals relevant to that path. *Donna*, the team leader at *Chemstar*, for example, has told us about getting stuck in exactly that rut: "This company is famous for collecting more data. My team would collect the data and look at it with the same set of eyes all the time and ask the same questions and get the same answers. We learned to look at the same data in a different manner. Once we learned that, it opened up other avenues to looking at different sets of data that the team wouldn't even have considered before."

Perkins offers an antidote for the same-set-of-eyes syndrome: the discipline of what we call *low-gear attention*. Low-gear attention, a core perceptual component of human intelligence, requires taking the time to observe in depth, breadth, and detail; it means temporarily suspending the assumption "I already know what I see." We see it as the discipline of discerning both the unfamiliar in the familiar and the familiar in the unfamiliar.

The different modes of attention used in a coordinated way provide individuals and communities with a full set of perceptual options in complex territory. In addition to specifying the speed of attention, these modes specify *how* people employ their attention. Such expanded options for paying attention are needed when facing complex challenges—when the need for action is urgent but the lack of adequate formulas requires reflection and new perspectives.

Understanding Left-Mode and Right-Mode Attention

In recent years, much has been discovered about how people perceive and process information. One important finding is that the mind is modular. People have multiple *processing modules* that organize their thoughts, feelings, and behavior and provide diverse options for perceiving and making sense of experiences.[5] Two basic modes of perception are *right-mode* and *left-mode*, or *R-mode* and *L-mode* for short (in the terminology of educator Betty Edwards, whose work we examine further in Chapter Six).[6]

It is theorized that for most people left-mode perception is driven predominantly by the left side of the brain and is heavily associated with language. L-mode is logical, analytical, and verbal. It clocks the passing of time. It breaks things down into named pieces, assigns symbols to represent them, and then strings them into sequences. L-mode provides individuals with very powerful, symbolic shorthands to use in paying attention—for example, financial definitions, time management concepts, and written standard operating procedures. L-mode offers powerful tools, and most organizations are skilled in at least the basic use of this mode.

Right-mode perception, related primarily to the right side of the brain in most people, is associated with images and patterns. It is synthetic and intuitive, it works in terms of wholes rather than pieces, and it favors concrete sensations over abstract ideas. R-mode complements the high-gear capacity for representing things symbolically. More specifically, L-mode traits and R-mode traits complement each other, as outlined in Table 1.1.[7] Everyone uses both modes of perception, but for most people, one tends to dominate. People with a dominant L-mode prefer thinking analytically and conceptually. Those with an R-mode preference draw more on their emotions and intuition. In organizational life, L-mode tends to dominate the means people use to perceive, analyze, and communicate.

Anytime you fly on a jet aircraft, for example, you are surrounded by the triumphs of L-mode thinking—relentless analysis, planned execution—all of it relying on precise numbers and words. Any sense of suspended time that the passengers might enjoy is forbidden to the pilots and controllers. Organizations have analogous

Table 1.1. Complementary Traits of Left-Mode
and Right-Mode Attention.

L-mode	R-mode
Word	Image
Convergent	Divergent
Intellectual	Visceral
Deductive	Inductive
Logical	Metaphorical
Abstract	Concrete
Sequential	Parallel
Historical	Atemporal
Successive	Simultaneous
Verbal	Non-verbal
Parts	Wholes
Analysis	Synthesis
Propositional	Narrative
Elements	Patterns

Source: Adapted from S. P. Springer and G. Deutsch, *Left Brain, Right Brain* (New York: Freeman, 1981), p. 186.

needs for flawless planning and execution. And yet we all know there is more to both airplanes and people.

Not surprisingly, organizational life can be hostile to the use of R-mode attention, to the detriment of creative leadership. R-mode is often thought of as *irrational*, but this is a misunderstanding. In actuality it draws on a different kind of rationality—what scholar and former steel-industry executive David Hurst calls *values-based rationality*. Whereas L-mode is formal and fact-based, R-mode taps into your values and subjective experiences. Because R-mode involves all your sources of knowledge, it offers you a more complete rationality to draw on when you face complex challenges.

R-mode and L-mode are characterized by different but complementary ways of experiencing time. Hurst compares the two notions of time through the metaphor of surfing: "When in R-mode we are surfers on a wave of time, the trough of which is the perpetual now. Here the time is always *now, now, now* as the past recedes and the future approaches. In the analytical L-mode we are outside the situation, watching the surfers from the shore as it were, noting the chronology of their travel."[8]

When your R-mode is dominant and you are engaged in the "now now now,"[9] you enter a flow state, as described by Mihaly Csikszentmihalyi.[10] To be in a *flow state* is to be engrossed in the complete, unhindered awareness that allows you to achieve peak performance. Flow states can be experienced by everyone, from athletes to musicians to scientists. In our experience, people in organizations must experience flow or R-mode dominant perception at least occasionally if they are to adequately reflect on and make sense of complex challenges.

As individuals and groups sense the need for flow and try to find its rhythms, there is much that can go awry. Consider the perils of what Microsoft researcher Linda Stone calls *continuous partial attention*. Let's say you're working at home, doing email, talking to your kid, and the phone rings. Your attention is continuously split. "Being fulfilled is about committing yourself to someone else, or some experience, that requires a level of sustained attention," said Ms. Stone. "And that is what we are losing the skills for, because we are constantly scanning the world for opportunities and we are constantly in fear of missing something better." Stone suggests that the negative consequences are spiritual as well as cognitive in nature.[11]

Many among the large number of scientists and engineers we have worked with tell us that both their education and their work environment stress the conceptual and analytical competencies of L-mode attention. This bias is continually reinforced by legitimate needs for verbal communication. Yet despite this L-mode emphasis, these scientists and engineers maintain a strong appreciation for the powers of R-mode attention: visualization, pattern recognition, an eye for fine details, and the wordless intuition of a passionate mind. As one scientist explained: "I'm interested in adhesion to different surfaces. One of the things that I routinely do now is . . . actually visualize what the molecules are doing. It's helped me to develop a hypothesis for why certain things stick. We've yet to prove it completely, but visualization helped me develop this hypothesis."

Using Kinesthetic Attention

Attention is more than just brain stuff. It is deeply connected to what goes on in the body: heart and guts, hands and feet. *Kinesthetic attention* is the knowledge you gain through hands-on work and physical engagement. For example, with the now-traditional technique of *management by walking around*, managers take advantage of physical movement—of choosing to operate physically *in* the environment rather than from above or outside—to literally and metaphorically see and grasp what is going on from different angles.[12]

In our experience, people process their feelings and intuitions in more useful ways once they engage their kinesthetic attention. Recent work by brain researcher Antonio Damasio and his colleagues indicates that human thought processes are structured like a layer cake. Good decision making, for example, has been shown to be dependent on connections to feelings and underlying emotions, which are in turn rooted in the alertness of the body. The notion that complete understanding requires heart and guts is proving to be more than a metaphor.[13]

Henry Mintzberg, organizational scholar and author of the classic text *The Nature of Managerial Work*,[14] illustrates the value of kinesthetic knowledge by telling the story of some modern-day Inuits who froze to death when their snowmobiles broke down. Having traded physical intimacy with their environment for modern prosthetics, the Inuits became disconnected from knowledge of their landscape, at great cost. Mintzberg writes, "Our machinery, in the broadest sense, not just our organizations, has likewise dulled our senses, driving out our intuition and making it increasingly difficult to find our way out of our problems."[15]

Sharpening your kinesthetic awareness will increase the wisdom of both your body and your mind. The knowledge gained from this awareness can have crossover benefits, as Arthur P. Bollon, chief executive of Cytoclonal Pharmaceuticals, learned when he took up karate as part of his personal fitness program. He discovered that this activity also makes him more fit as a leader. For some practice sets, he must memorize and execute more than fifty movements while visualizing an imaginary attacker. This takes considerable concentration and focus and complements his creative nature. Karate training is "invaluable" in keeping everything organized and on track, he reports. "It gives me more discipline and developed that part of myself that . . . wasn't necessarily obtainable through conventional training."[16]

As philosopher Mark Johnson points out, "We are *rational* animals, but we are also rational *animals*, which means that our rationality is embodied."[17] Information resides not only in the brain but also in the body—and that's where you should look for it. Intuition is the practice of tapping into the wordless, tacit knowledge you feel in your bones. In Chapters Five and Six we will discuss how leaders and communities critique and properly assimilate such information.

Paying Attention to Negative Space

A profound aspect of attending to information is an awareness of *negative space*. This term from the visual arts refers to the so-called empty, or white, space among the objects in a scene. This space is almost never really empty or white although exactly what it is defies easy categorization. Because people's conscious attention is naturally attracted to positive spaces, they easily pick out the figures in the foreground. The key to understanding negative space is to pay attention to the background in which the figures are set. When you focus on the foreground, or positive space, your vision may be clouded by a symbolic representation of what you see, a mental generalization rather than the specifics and nuances of the actual event or thing you are encountering. Engaging negative space means paying attention to the complexity of an unrecognizable shape in order to sharpen the outline of the ultimate object of your attention. Once the shapes surrounding the object engage your eyes, you can discern the foreground more clearly.

In our work at CCL we have found that the activity of drawing is a powerful device for understanding negative space. For example, drawing a picture of a specific tree can be difficult when your preconception of a tree—your L-mode symbol for tree, perhaps just a stick figure—gets in the way of your ability to see the real, individual tree. But you have no preconceived symbols for the shapes between the branches of a tree. So if you faithfully attend to and draw these negative spaces, the real tree gradually emerges. By your focusing on and drawing the negative space, the tree appears as if "for free." Your drawing will accurately illustrate your particular tree, not your symbol for one; in addition, the tree will appear woven into its context, not abstracted from that environment. Likewise when paying attention to organizational turbulence, people need to see and replicate more than the all-purpose stick figures they carry in their minds. They must be mindful of particulars, attending to the question, What is *this?*

Attention to negative space can be learned, practiced, and used to engage all kinds of complex scenarios. Many of the concepts and practices in the rest of this book are extensions of this basic idea. Paying attention to negative space makes you aware of how you have framed an issue and thus defined the boundaries of your consideration. By focusing on the complexity at the edges of the issue, you can more clearly and accurately define what the issue really is.

One of us, David Horth, was recently engaged on assignment to coach *Erica*, the senior manager of a group of scientists. Erica sought to determine where her leadership would have maximum value for her organization in the short and long term. David interviewed Erica's coworkers for feedback on her current effectiveness and the major contextual issues of the organization. Then Erica and David mulled over the consolidated interview data, searching for patterns and themes. David introduced the notion of negative space, and they turned their attention from what was *said* to what was *not said* in the picture that was emerging of Erica's leadership and the challenges facing her team. By looking at this negative space, David and Erica discovered that an issue they had previously placed at the periphery of Erica's leadership challenges was in fact a major concern. The interviewees had consistently *not* said anything about where the organization was headed in the long term. The concurrent absence of both a vision for the organization and a shared sense of what the organization was all about was the key issue hindering the performance of Erica's team. Thus remedying this absence became the major focus for Erica's leadership development.

Asking Powerful Questions

The scientist William Beveridge once remarked that "the effect that questioning has on the mind might be likened to the stimulus given to a fire by poking; it disturbs the settled arrangement and brings about new combinations."[18] Have you ever had someone ask you a question that took your breath away, that made you stop in your tracks? A question that in some way fundamentally shifted your perception and therefore your understanding of the issue at hand?

A few years ago David was working with a group of executives from a large, international organization that financed development projects around the world. Their aim was to figure out the key strategic leadership issues facing the organization. David posed this question to the group: "If your organization was not able to supply capital, what would it provide?" Immediately the group members answered, "New knowledge." So David asked another question: "What if a country wasn't able to pay off its loans or new knowledge through financial means?" The members of the group sat silently for what seemed an eternity. Then someone ventured, "Payment must be something tradable on the stock market." Another reflective silence followed. The questions and their responses sparked a productive dialogue about the core leadership values they shared and the mission of the organization. They were led to ask of themselves, "How do we reconcile our altruistic mission with our fiscal imperatives?"

Powerful questions take aim at the roots of people's issues and assumptions. Asking such questions can disrupt perceptual shortcuts, helping people notice details, patterns, or movements that they have previously overlooked. A powerful question can be as simple as, What's missing? Or, it can be as confrontational as, How can an apparently irreversible trend reverse? The personal computer industry was founded on powerful questions. Steve Jobs and his cohorts asked, What if computers were small and personal? As a result, they identified the essence of Apple Computer, Inc. An important shift for leaders, then, is to supplement their role of answer finder with the role of question asker. As one manager we worked with said: "For a long time my whole frame of reference was that I had to have all the answers. Now I'm finding out that it's better to have the good questions." A colleague at Chemstar echoes this sentiment: "We really weren't asking the right questions to begin with. We were asking a lot of technical questions, but the really powerful ones we weren't asking. In order to do big picture stuff, you have to find the right questions."

What Is a Powerful Question?

Powerful questions in the service of creative leadership typically have three characteristics: they invite exploration, they resist easy answers, and they invoke strong passions. Powerful questions pull people's attention to unnoticed places. They are offered as an open door, not as a criticism of how things are. When asking powerful questions, you must be careful not to use them as weapons. On many occasions we have seen leaders use questions to intimidate their colleagues. Attending to trust and tone is essential. Depending on the context, an exploratory question such as, Why do we do it like this? may spark defensiveness in people. The group we worked with at Chemstar, for example, developed trust among group members before asking that question repeatedly as a team. Posed in that trusting context, the question led team members to profound insights about their operations.

Powerful questions resist easy answers. They slow your attention at crucial times so you notice more. They do not look for a final answer immediately but resonate within you and your colleagues over time in a way that feeds collaborative inquiry. The creative leader's task is to devise contexts in which both asking and responding to powerful questions are invited and supported. We have seen such contexts created during strategy retreats, peer coaching sessions, conversations with invited controversial experts, and impromptu brainstorming meetings. These contexts can also be established through something as simple as consistently asking people where the work could get blindsided and consistently listening to the responses—and the negative spaces in the responses. One leader we know keeps a short list of the best, most provocative questions facing his team, then refers to these questions when he thinks things are stuck. It has become a point of honor on his team to pose a question that makes this list.

Questioning is more powerful when the questions can and do come from anywhere without inhibition—from workers, customers, partners, competitors, even chance encounters on the fringes of your usual business. Cultivating this openness is an ongoing process for leaders. One leader who succeeded in making it legitimate to ask powerful questions in his organization, says: "To be creative, you've got to keep asking *why* and *what* and *where*—and there's always more. So I did that and I gave my people the freedom to do that, and I think as a result, we are much more productive. We come up with better ideas; we don't just accept the first idea. People generally feel better; they participate more."

How does one make powerful questions legitimate? In this last case, the leader made questioning acceptable by changing his attitude. Previously he expected his people to "always exhibit control and to always have the answers." Although that expectation hasn't disappeared, it has been tempered. He has another mode now that opens the door to the exploration of questions without quick answers. His leadership has become less about proclamation and more about skilled conversation.

L-Mode and R-Mode Questions

Leaders can easily limit their ability to make sense of complex issues by the mode in which they gather information. Organizational effectiveness tends to be measured in terms of the answers to analytical or L-mode questioning. However, asking for and inviting information from yourself and others that derives from R-mode attention rounds out your understanding of complex scenarios.

R-mode questions ask about patterns, emotions, and intuitions. Here are some examples:

- *What are the patterns?* Seek patterns as you look for the lessons of the past. Create group histories by asking long-standing members to reflect on episodes and themes. Use this information to ask questions about possible, emergent patterns facing the group.

• *What's interesting, unique, beautiful, or unusual about this?* A Buddhist sage once said his constant question was, "What is *this?*" L-mode answers the question abstractly. R-mode explores and synthesizes particulars and is thus especially useful in conditions of newness or change.

• *What is one hope you have going into this? What is one fear you have going into this?* Emotions and feelings carry a lot of the implicit knowledge in a group. L-mode and co-inquiry can be encouraged to come back in once the hopes and fears are, as one leader put it, "on the table, in the air, not so hot anymore." Ask these kinds of questions when mobilizing your people to pursue a new venture.

• *How do you feel about this at a deep down gut level? What does your intuition tell you?* We often run into situations in which questions that call for intuition are considered illegitimate; questions that elicit facts are the only questions allowed. Legitimizing intuition means occasionally injecting, into the organizational rhythm of questions that ask people to "prove it," questions that ask people to "offer hunches about it."

• *What is this like?* R-mode attention is more *analog* whereas L-mode attention is more *digital*—and because human perception is largely analog, R-mode questions can accentuate key aspects of attention. They can invite sometimes flamboyant comparisons of one thing to another—modeling, simulating, comparing. The question, What's a metaphor for this? quickly leads to the question, What's the story behind this? People begin to notice more things and then to share what they notice in sustainable and meaningful ways. R-mode questions are key to navigating what organizational scholar Peter Vaill calls the *permanent whitewater* of organizations.[19]

• *What questions are we neglecting to ask?* Negative space questions complement inquiry by looking at the spaces between what is known: What are we missing? What could blindside us? How would a Martian describe this?

What-If Questions

By posing surprising scenarios and inviting imaginative responses, leaders can break out of the rut of a traditional analysis. What-if questions turn a usual line of questioning on its head. They are daring and can be confrontational. They are intriguing and may lighten a dialogue and get the creative juices flowing. Here are some examples of what-if questions:

What if we deliberately tried to make this problem worse?

What if we asked people why they did it this way in the first place? What would they say?

What would happen to our customers if our business [or industry] simply went away?

What if all our employees became free agents?

What if our CEO got hit by a bus tomorrow?

What would be the negatives if our dream came true?

What would be the positives if we failed?

What would we do if the roles were reversed?

What if we couldn't invent anything new and just used what we had at hand?

What if key assumption X is wrong [or backward]?

How would we do this if we had unlimited resources? If we had no resources?

What if I disappeared for a month and my team handled this?

Wild Cards

Futurist John Petersen, president of the Arlington Institute, uses the term *wild cards* to describe changes with very low probability but extremely high impact that could drastically affect the way people live, do business, and think. Among his examples of wild card changes, Petersen lists human cloning, a large asteroid hitting the Earth, and time travel. He says, "In the coming years, wild cards will only be wilder and come faster, and people who recognize and learn to make sense of them will have a real advantage."[20]

Petersen offers several questions leaders can ask to increase their awareness of wild cards:

What are the most important wild cards for me, my organization, and my customers?

What would really wipe us out?

How can I anticipate these things?

What are the early indicators?

What can I do about my wild cards?[21]

So-What Questions

Questions are powerful when they get at underlying assumptions about purpose and value: Why do we value this? Why is this more valuable than that? What is the essence of what we're trying to achieve? What deeper purpose and meaning does this serve?

A favorite line of questioning for strategists and marketers consists of a series of so-what questions. For example:

So what's great about this new product?
Our new product has more bells and whistles on it.
So what?
This will enable the customer to play more music on it while she works.
So what?
She will feel happier working.
So what?

If she's happier working, she will be more productive.

So what?

If she's more productive, the company will value her more.

And so on. By probing your assumptions about purpose and value, you uncover all the nuances of your context. And the key to your solution, strategy, or campaign may lie in this context.

Appreciative Questions

Appreciative inquiry is an organization development approach that begins with appreciative questions rather than looking for problems: What are we doing right? What are our strengths? Where have we been? Where are we going? To what do we aspire?[22]

Jane is a division director presiding over aging legacy IT systems still needed to serve critical customer needs. She describes it as an unglamorous pursuit, the quaint stepsister of the sexy new technology. However, Jane had a breakthrough with her own mind-set and then with her unit when she changed her focus to the positives. Needing first to identify those positives, she started asking appreciative questions: "Why do some customers prefer the legacy features?" "What is well built or even beautiful about the older IT architecture?" "What did programmers know when they built this that we now seem to be forgetting?" As a result of this inquiry, Jane's division was better able to leverage the small but numerous advantages inherent in the legacy systems. One result was a boost in morale that clients noticed, saying in one instance, "They believe in the services they provide."

When we ask powerful questions without easy answers, they often leave responses that didn't exist before in their wake. Appreciative questions sustained over time can create a whole nuanced web of appreciation and comprehension as they give a clear focus to attention that was previously shapeless and ineffective.

SCAMPER *Questions*

Alex Osborn, a founder of the modern field of creative problem solving, has devised a series of categories for powerful questions that generate new ideas.[23] The series is often referred to by the acronym SCAMPER, from the first letters of the categories. Use questions from these categories to take existing ideas and transform them into a new set of specifications or to power up a group that has stalled while working on a set of promising but as yet incomplete solutions.[24]

Substitute: Who else? What else? Other ingredient? Other material? Other process? Other place? Other approach? Other tone of voice?

Combine: A blend? An alloy? An assortment? An ensemble? Combine units? Combine purposes? Combine appeals? Combine ideas?

Adapt: What else is like this? What other idea does this suggest? Does the past offer a parallel? What can we copy? Whom can we emulate?

Modify: Change meaning, color, motion, sound, odor, form, shape? Add a new twist?

Minify: Make it smaller? Make it condensed? Make it lower, shorter, or lighter? Subtract? Omit? Streamline? Split up? Understate?

Magnify: Add something? More time? Greater frequency? Extra value? Another ingredient? Stronger? Higher? Longer? Thicker? Duplicate? Multiply? Exaggerate?

Put to other uses: New ways to use? Other uses if modified?

Eliminate: What can we get rid of? Omit? Do without? Sacrifice? Give away?

Rearrange: Interchange component parts? Use another pattern? Another layout? Another sequence? Transpose cause and effect? Change pace? Change schedule?

Reverse: Transpose positive and negative? How about opposites? Turn it backward? Turn it upside down? Reverse roles?
Change shoes? Turn tables? Turn the other cheek?

Developing the Competency of Paying Attention

Now that we have explored techniques for paying attention, let's
consider how to deepen the ability to pay attention. Where does
competence in paying attention come from? There are three main
sources, all of which suggest opportunities for development: biology,
culture, and experience.

Biology predisposes all of us to pay attention in certain ways and
affects our capacity for discernment. We are wired to pay less attention to that which is in front of us all the time. Our reflexes and
perceptual systems therefore have trouble grasping the novel when
it is enveloped in what appears to be familiar.

Our attention also tends to follow the grooves our culture offers.
People typically pay more attention to group consensus than to what
is in front of their noses. Television has inculcated several generations with the habit of passive attention; the Internet favors more
active forms of attention but also encourages "surfing" and brevity.
Culturally, we are facing an increasing staccato of information—
from school, the Internet, television, work, and community life.
Not surprisingly, many professionals feel they suffer from *attention
overload* and continuous partial attention.

In today's world, cultivating an ability to winnow out and listen
to various indicators will bring you the insight and understanding
necessary for flexible, effective, creative leadership. Everyone has
life experiences that train his or her perceptions. Our own research
since 1994 with the CCL Leading Creatively Project suggests that
developmental experiences in paying attention can come from all
parts of people's lives, not just their formal expertise. One manager,
for example, has learned to listen "in a room where several conversations are going on." He says, "I can ferret out the one I want to
hear and pick up subtle distinctions of inflection and emotion in

people's conversation." Where did he learn this? "From ensemble singing and musical comedy, which trained him to make seamless contributions to performances."[25]

Developing Individual Competence

To develop means "to grow outward," and the word attention similarly carries the idea of a "stretch out to" something, which implies that you must expand yourself in order to develop your competence of attention. In R-mode you become absorbed with what is at the limits of your attention, and wind up growing in that direction. You strive toward the edges of who you are in order to better attend—more objectively *and* more subjectively—to the world.

To appreciate also means "to grow larger." Paying attention creates care and appreciation, the ability to grow larger. Appreciation is more than just liking or approving. To appreciate is to immerse yourself in sensing and experiencing something in an open way. Eric Booth, in *The Everyday Work of Art*, and Mary Catherine Bateson, in *Composing a Life*, have explored in depth the nature of attentive, personal growth.[26]

Deep attention, as one leader has described it to us, involves listening at many levels: "When I am facilitating groups, I find myself paying deep attention to the process and interaction of the group. I pay attention to the sounds, to the nonverbals, to the faces, at a heightened level." Another leader we know describes listening as something profound to offer others: "I have experienced the gift of the silence of others, special people who have given me the incredible grace of their full attention. There have been people in my life who have put aside their own agendas and created safe and hospitable spaces in which they have literally listened me into my own truth. I have begun to consider how I might learn to give others the same gift."[27]

Here are some specific suggestions for developing the competence of paying attention in yourself:

Stand in Different Places. Shift perspective by radically changing your point of view. If you are a marketer, become the customer. If you are a coach, become the trainee. If you are outside something, look at it from the inside, and vice versa. Turn the problem upside down so that all the familiar parts look strange—then look again.

Use the Lenses of Other Domains. For example, if you are an artist, import the lens of science. If you are a scientist, import the lens of artistry. The ability to use different lenses may already exist within you as an individual leader or within your group's collective experience. Seek these lenses out. (Checking the veracity of alternative lenses is a matter of co-inquiry, which is explored in Chapter Five.)

Go Against the Grain. Attention has preferred directions, like wood grain. An experienced sculptor of wood will work both with the natural direction, or grain, of the wood fibers and against it—but working against the grain is more difficult and feels unnatural to the novice. Paying attention in different modes may likewise feel uncomfortable initially. Figure out what your own grain is (curly or straight? how many rings?). Practice sculpting your attention in small ways at first.[28]

Involve Others in Forums for Shared Attention. The enterprise of addressing a complex challenge, as the story of the blind men examining an elephant illustrates (What is *this?*), requires the coordination of multiple perspectives. This kind of kaleidoscopic attention is more characteristic of communities than of individuals.

Developing Community Competence

The Xerox Palo Alto Research Center (PARC) is exemplary in using multiple modes of paying attention. PARC is famous for inventing devices and concepts key to personal computing, many of which have blossomed only in the hands of individuals and organizations elsewhere. (Creative leadership can be *leaky* in generative ways.) PARC, perhaps learning a lesson from having good ideas leak away, now pays deliberate attention to what Director John Seeley Brown calls "strong and weak signals." Brown says that the PARC senior team wants to keep asking, What are the big signals? At the same time, it keeps tuned to the weak signals so team members know which are fading and which are growing.[29] One way PARC keeps tuned to these signals—in and across cultures, in technology, and in potential markets—is through PAIR, the PARC Artist-in-Residence program.[30] PAIR matches Xerox technologists with San Francisco Bay Area artists to look at the future of digital technology. The pairs are matched by their interests; for example, a vocal artist is paired with a digital sound technologist. The artist pays attention to what is negative space for the scientist, and vice versa.

As a leader, you can foster competent attention in your community in the following ways:

Share Information Widely and Reward Perception. Encourage the free exchange of information and constantly ask group members how they perceive it. Don't accept the view from any one point as a complete picture. Ask, What do you see? Pay attention to the reply. Verify perceptions analytically (*after* or *between* flurries of paying attention and imaging) so that your attention and the group's can become more accurate and less naïve.

Recognize the Value of Different Styles of Paying Attention. For example, as we have discussed throughout this chapter, attention to intuition and emotion have an important role alongside attention to "just the facts, please." Acknowledge and reassure your colleagues when they demonstrate various styles of attention. Alternate attention that is focused inward—feelings and intuitions—with attention that is focused outward on observable data.

Foster New Knowledge. Send members out of your organization and into the market, among customers, constituencies, competitors, and others. Make sure they regularly spend time in places where they can gain new perspectives.

Support Honest and Open Feedback About People and Ideas. One director we know, managing in a time of great upheaval in her organization, held a series of meetings that she called *open kimono sessions*—a metaphor for getting a little bit "naked," or frank, with each other. She found it was better to do this publicly, with her support and structuring, than to have it happen behind her back.

Attend to the Periphery. Create time or a structure for asking the group: What is on the edges of our awareness? What is on the fringe of what we do? Our colleague Stan Gryskiewicz has written about using the turbulence that occurs within and at the periphery of an organization.[31] He recommends inviting in guests with unusual viewpoints that might trigger alternative views and ideas.

Recognize the Aesthetics of Attention. Attention gravitates toward that which is relevant, meaningful, interesting, dynamic, inspiring, well designed, and beautiful. Stacks of spreadsheets will be ignored by all but committed specialists. Identify and emphasize the compelling stories and the big pictures so that people will love to have a look and will look twice.

Change the Pace of Attention. If the group you are leading likes to surf quickly through issues, schedule retreats for what David Perkins calls *slowing looking down*—letting questions emerge, shifting positions, letting your eyes work, noticing interesting features, comparing perceptions.[32] If your group naturally prefers ponderous analysis, practice taking intuitive scans of the data or hold short, rapid-sensing forums on fast-breaking issues.

Cautions

There are some dangers of course to paying careful attention: seeing things that aren't really there, seeing things intended to be hidden, jumping at noises, glimpsing scary things. The experiences and lessons collected in this book push your perception to the limits. Competent leadership will provide good navigation, but some perils remain and may even intensify as your individual and community competence at paying attention increases. The trick to navigating these waters is not to shut down your attention but to exercise caution around the hazards.

You need to exercise caution in three specific areas: dealing with the flood of information and emotions, mistaking patterns, and seeing undiscussables.

Dealing with the flood of information and emotions. Taking in information these days can be like drinking from a fire hose. In addition, you and your colleagues inevitably have emotional involvement in the issues and these emotions become part of the stream as well. As a leader, you can increase or decrease the volume of the stream by selectively using the concepts and techniques in this book. Decrease the volume by focusing your group on the critical few items that need immediate or sustained attention. You can't dam the stream indefinitely, however, so periodically it is wise to face the flood deliberately, in a structured way. When the volume is increased—and you invite in the full complexity of people's attention—be careful to allow ample time and space to deal with the results. Resolve to extract meaning from the information flood, finding what Oliver Wendell Holmes called the "simplicity on the other side of complexity." Finally, make sure you have a plan for follow-up so that people trust the threads they discover will be pursued and acted on. And make sure that your plan cares for all modes of your group's attention, from analytical to intuitive.

Mistaking patterns. The human brain is designed to look for patterns, but pattern recognition can go awry. Not all or even most intuitive perceptions are correct. Intuition likes to say, "Here is a pattern," but seeing the pattern is not a verification of it. For example, humans are hard-wired to see human faces. This is an indispensable asset for infants as they develop, but the tendency to see faces also means that people often see faces in randomness—like the man in the moon, the face of Jesus in the wood grain, and so on. The competency of co-inquiry involves checking patterns for their veracity.

You can employ traditional analytical skills as checks and balances for perceived patterns. Don't be afraid to check intuitions against numbers, demographics, the bottom line, and similar data points. Both the C2 Competencies and technical competencies are essential to making sense of complex challenges. Using multiple modes of attention at repeated points in time will also help you test the accuracy of patterns that you have discerned. No one stream of information should be ranked above all others.

Noticing the undiscussables. Paying attention gets particularly interesting when it means attending to things that aren't meant to be seen, what organizational learning expert Chris Argyris calls *undiscussables:*[33] uncomfortable truths, deep-rooted conflicts, maverick points of view. Although you may feel it is perilous to discuss these issues openly, it is also dangerous to ignore them. The team of managers at Chemstar, for instance, had to deal with an undiscussable that was actively blocking a solution to their challenge: "As we were exploring this challenge together people started to see fear as a big blocker and then our job was to kind of get under what was the fear. The fear basically turned out to be the fear of solving the technical problem because the technical problem was one that kept a lot of people busy and employed. And also made careers at Chemstar."

Re-vision can threaten corporate vision. In environments lacking an honest commitment to open inquiry, people may interpret powerful questions as betrayal. At Sandoz, oncologist Athos Gianella-Borradori had doubts that a new gene replacement therapy would work. He told his superiors of his doubts even as he worried that his concerns would be interpreted "as a betrayal of our cause."[34] It is easy for people to interpret concern as resistance, and doubt as a betrayal.

Inquiry must be robust enough to face such concerns and doubts without flinching. As a leader, you must protect the people around you who are paying attention. Take pains to give them a safe place and methods to explore their perceptions without having those perceptions construed as disloyalty to the company vision.

Paying competent attention indicates your care, carefulness, and caring. It is a form of recognition. Attention is also a tool to use with caution: *be aware* and *beware* are twins.

Once you have developed a strong competency in paying attention, you can leverage this skill across the other C2 Competencies: personalizing, imaging, serious play, co-inquiry, and crafting. The next competency we discuss, personalizing, draws on paying attention to and selectively applying your individuality—your personal perspectives, life expertise, and leadership style.

Chapter Two

Personalizing

People working together require ways of thinking that are as broad and complex as the challenges they face. Not surprisingly, times of turbulence and change require broader, deeper leadership approaches. Who people are and what they know as individuals are the richest, and perhaps most important, frames of reference they have for leading creatively. To deal most effectively with the level of complexity characteristic of contemporary organizations, it is imperative that you muster all your personal resources and bring them to bear on the issues at hand.

In our work at the Center for Creative Leadership, we have discovered that executives passionately engage in an extraordinary range of talents outside the workplace: we know a medical research executive who modestly calls himself a gardener but whom others consider a gifted landscape architect; a bank executive who plays the bagpipes; a marketer who is a lauded poet; a systems architect who plays jazz piano; a software designer who throws pots. All too often, however, individuals fail to use these talents to enhance their leadership effectiveness; they exhibit an unconscious gap between these huge personal resources and the resources they typically draw on as leaders.

It used to be that a potted plant and a family photo on one's office desk were as far as people allowed the personal to enter the professional workplace. But just as the nature of professional challenges has evolved, the context in which this old rule held true has shifted dramatically. The poet David Whyte now counsels that just because you're earning a living you can't check your personal destiny at the door. If you do, you'll have a personality split for which you'll pay very dearly.[1]

The second C2 Competency, *personalizing*, is about tapping into your unique life experiences to gain insight into and energy for shared challenges. Personalizing is consciously bringing the thinking processes you use in extracurricular activities to the business of doing good work. Personalizing uses what we think of as *collateral skills*: unique competencies and perspectives from the various facets of your past and present life taken as resources for making sense of the complexity of your work.[2]

Successfully mobilizing these crossover resources in yourself and others is an essential part of moving from a management to a creative leadership mind-set. To make this shift you must understand how "who you are" is woven into the fabric of the complexities you face. As one manager we worked with remarked: "The connections between leadership and who you are as a person are deep. The more responsibility you assume and the more people you touch from a leadership perspective, the more critical the connection becomes."

Creative leaders personalize effectively in two ways: They create a climate in which people can make creative connections between personal passions and work, and they make these same connections for themselves. To bring more of who you are into the work setting is a courageous act. Yet once begun it promotes a climate in which people can be more adaptable to organizational challenges. That is why one senior manager we know has declared that her primary leadership task is "connecting people with their passions."

No one gives the best and deepest of herself or himself lightly. In this chapter we talk about what it takes to reach the fullness of what people have to offer. We explore what is required to personalize successfully while addressing complex leadership challenges. Our discussion is organized around these key ideas:

- Learning begins with the personal connection
- Practicing assessment for development (A4D)

- Practicing exploration for development (E4D)
- Tapping into your passion
- Knowing when to let go of your personal side

Learning Begins with the Personal Connection

In our training and co-inquiry work, we describe the initial step in the learning process as *meeting people where they are*. This goes further than the notion of *buy-in* commonly used in business. We see the process as *reaching out*, because this is how it is viewed from the perspective of the colleague, client, or customer. Rather than selling an idea, proposed change, or learning agenda that we have dreamt up, we first engage the stakeholders: their perspectives, their desires, their level of familiarity with the subject at hand.

Effective learning begins for individuals when they establish a personal connection to the issue at hand. People with a personal connection feel themselves to be part of the fabric of the situation and thus important to its solution. Their connection is powered by both their implicit emotional and intuitive knowledge and their explicit factual and analytical knowledge. According to organizational learning expert Bernice McCarthy, people best approach complex situations, "Not as strangers in a strange land, but rather as those who can say, 'Ah yes, I already understood some of this. . . . I knew that in some small, other way.'"[3]

Craig Wynett, manager of new ventures at Procter & Gamble, deliberately lets his people pursue their unique interests and passions in order to "increase the surface area" for new ideas to form. Surrounding issues with a diversity of unique perspectives leads to what he calls "unlikely expertise." For example, one of his group members was interested in the psychobiology of stress. Fine, said Wynett; "Now overlay that interest on consumer interests." The result? Promising new products in the P&G pipeline have been informed by the psychobiology of stress reduction.[4]

We don't mean to imply that the first idea someone brings to the table will be the final word but rather that a personal spark is often the most viable starting point. However, in the rush to make sense of the hurly-burly of contemporary organizational life, it is easy for people to extinguish and overlook these sparks of energy. You need to connect personalizing to the competency of paying attention, to slow looking down, in order to discover resources within yourself and your colleagues. By doing so, you can connect with the hidden resources of those who can help you make collective sense of complexity. For example, one leader holds what she calls *freewheel* sessions with her team, in which she asks team members to open up and let fly with their concerns, feelings, and hunches about the issues they are working on. She learned the hard way that it is useful to practice such freewheeling from the start of a project, rather than using it only as a venting mechanism later on. Many other leaders use an off-site or retreat setting to ensure plenty of airtime for hearing where everyone is coming from. For effective freewheeling, it is critical to establish an atmosphere of trust within your group; personalizing successfully around low-key issues is one way to establish a foundation of trust and openness that you can rely on later when you confront situations with a greater impact.

So, how do you make personal connections? Begin by asking people *where they are* with an issue. Wherever they are is where you should start, even if where you need to end up is very different. By personalizing challenges at the outset, you defuse hidden personal agendas that have the potential to blow up the process later on. People have two main communication channels: the intuitive and emotional gut and the rational intellect. Although we all purportedly do business with our intellects, quite a lot of business gets snagged by our gut. If you don't acknowledge emotional issues, they can create roadblocks or white noise on the intellect channel.

Successful personalizing requires a well-founded sense of who you are and where you are going. This sense does not come for free. The next sections of this chapter look at ways to solidify your knowledge and understanding of your personal identity.

Practicing Assessment for Development (A4D)

Personalizing effectively requires you to make the effort to know and develop yourself. A good way to begin your personal leadership development is by applying the Center for Creative Leadership's ACS model. This model sets out three basic elements for developing leadership style in yourself and in those who work for you: assessment, challenge, and support.[5]

Assessment

The first element in the model, *assessment,* focuses on gathering information that tells you:

- What your current strengths are
- What your development needs are
- What your level of effectiveness is in your current situation
- What your level of effectiveness would be in any future situation to which you aspire (for example, a specific leadership position)

The basic guidelines for assessment are:

- Assess yourself and your situation.
- Use formal and informal assessment techniques.
- Balance self-assessment with data from other sources.

The following list suggests the kinds of questions that can guide an accurate self-assessment.

Powerful Self-Assessment Questions

What significant challenges or learning experiences have I had in my life and my work?

What lessons did I learn?

Have I leveraged and applied these lessons adequately?

What patterns emerge from how I go about learning these lessons? Are there new patterns I want to develop?

What new challenges should I seek out?

Can I experience these challenges in my current position? If not, where can I gain such experience?

Does my organization offer well-validated, 360-degree feedback programs so that I can get feedback from supervisors, peers, and direct reports and compare their perceptions of me with my own? If not, how might I get such feedback?

What three adjectives might significant others, friends, and coworkers use to describe me? What three adjectives would I use to describe myself? Are there differences? Why?

What information can I gather from my responses to recent climate or culture surveys conducted in my organization?

What and how can I learn from someone I know who has been in a similar situation? What questions would this person ask?

In what areas am I rated highly by others?

Where do others think I need to develop?

How do others' ratings of me compare with my own assessment?

What is my most pressing development need?

As I reflect on my leadership experience and style, deep down where only I can see, what is driving me? What sustains and guides my leadership?

How do I need to develop in order to meet the needs of my next leadership assignment?

Self-assessment implies identifying and embracing your personal style of leadership. It is about finding your unique voice—the signature way that you make things, shape ideas, craft your work. Self-assessment unearths what is really important for you. An ef-

fective A4D process clarifies your personal standards of achievement and success. It helps you to be less dependent and to be more
*inter*dependent, in a healthy and balanced way. Although assessment solicits information about you from other people, it is not
about caving in to what others expect from you.

Solicit assessment feedback within a supportive structure, such
as ongoing coaching or a leadership development program. Seek
multiple forms of feedback: for example, on-the-spot feedback as
you perform a task; multirater surveys (also known as *360-degree
feedback*); and psychological styles data about your personality and
preferences, such as results from the Myers-Briggs Type Indicator.

For assessment to be truly useful, you must value the feedback
you are being given and believe the data and sources to be credible.
Psychometric data, for example, must be accompanied by docu-
mentation demonstrating that the instrument used measures what
it purports to measure and that it does so with statistical reliability.
In addition, feedback will be most useful when it is centered on behaviors or characteristics linked to the organization's needs. Finally,
feedback should be geared toward informing you about what is required for taking action and discerning the steps that will help you
grow in your ability to lead.[6]

One critical function of assessment is to help you identify and
embrace your strengths—and note how these strengths might be
overextended. An example of a strength being overextended can
be seen in the highly intelligent executive who relies solely on her
intellect. Her usual way of getting things done is to use her intellect to analyze and propose highly creative solutions to challenges.
In the process she often becomes frustrated with her coworkers because they "just don't get it." Her frustration damages her ability to
collaborate effectively with her coworkers in implementing solutions. Her intellectual strength works against her when she uses
it to bulldoze the people she needs to implement her solutions
and inhibits them from finding new solutions for other complex
challenges.

Challenge

Experiences that are new to you call for skills and perspectives you may not currently have available. Developmental *challenge* stretches you to learn and grow, to become more than what you currently are. The optimal level and kind of challenge is different for each person. Too much challenge might overwhelm a person or cause him to withdraw and remain entrenched in old habits. A work situation with few new challenges can lead to boredom and burnout. Courageous leaders find ways of stretching themselves within their existing roles, either in some new area of the organization or outside the organization. The courageous organization accommodates the potential of a drop in performance and even of failure as its people step into challenging assignments.

Here are four ways to introduce challenge into your and others' work:

- Change to a job with a higher level of complexity: for example, one with broader or different responsibilities.
- Add new tasks, responsibilities, or goals to the existing job.
- Seek developmental opportunities outside work, such as leadership roles in the local community or in recreational activities.
- Seek to work with people who have different and diverse perspectives.

Support

Leadership development requires *support,* a climate that enhances self-confidence and acknowledges new behaviors. Even as people are challenged, they need to be reassured about their strengths, current skills, and established ways of thinking and working. When a person is working on a high wire, she needs a safety net underneath. You probably have support networks in your personal life, but you and your colleagues also need them in the professional sphere. A professional support network can help you as you structure or re-structure your world during the disequilibrium of challenge and change.

When considering the people who might be available as sources of support, think of the qualities they display that suit them to one or more of the following roles.

Support as counseling: Who might give you emotional support and let you vent your feelings? Who will avoid becoming embroiled in any negative feelings you are experiencing and instead encourage your can-do attitude?

Support as cheerleading: Who is willing to express confidence in your current abilities and to cheer you on when you try out new behaviors or hit roadblocks?

Support as reinforcing: Who finds ways of recognizing and re-warding your progress?

Support from cohorts: Who is in a similar situation and can therefore empathize with you and offer lessons from similar experiences?

Support as mentoring: Who can provide long-term support and guidance based on experience, example, and ability to co-inquire and solve problems with you?

Support as coaching: Who can provide support that is much like mentoring but geared toward a specific new skill you seek to acquire?

Leadership development also involves offering these kinds of support to others, like the leader who reports, "I find myself work-ing with, coaching, and supervising people ten, fifteen, twenty-plus years younger than I am. I find that I can offer experience, a sense of the big picture, [a sense of] ebb and flow, a sense of the patterns—and a strong voice in support of *their* creative selves."

The ACS model is a simple and useful tool for revealing gaps in your personal development. To develop your personalizing competency, make sure the elements of this model are present in your career, and as a leader, conscientiously make them available to those around you. Be aware, however, that the ACS model works best when you have fairly well-defined metrics for assessment and templates for growth. When the turbulence around you increases and you face more uncertainty, we recommend you adopt the strategy of exploration for development.

Practicing Exploration for Development (E4D)

The well-worn paths of leadership development are not as reliable as they once were. Career maps just a few years old are now outdated. New paths and maps must be made by new experiences. People have little choice but to take charge of their own careers and improvise in this rapidly changing world. Organizations are beginning to realize this and are expressing it in their hiring practices. Avery Dennison Inc. recently put its understanding of the qualities it wants in employees in this notice:

Wanted: a new breed of individual for the new organization:

Inquisitive, Innovative, Visionary, Conceptual, Entrepreneurial, High Energy, Competitive, Flexible, Team Player, Empowered, Global Thinker, Responsive, Broad-based Experience, Multi-Project Management, Business Acumen, Open Communicator, Comfortable with Diversity, Creative Self Starter.

Deliberately orchestrating your career and life paths requires an activity that we call *exploration for development:* you create opportunities for growth by probing in depth the complex challenges you face as a leader. Exploration for development has five main components:

- Seeking out and engaging adaptive challenges
- Seeing yourself as part of the challenge
- Realizing that exploration is both individual and collective

- Using all possible resources for making sense of challenges
- Creating maps and compasses to navigate complexity

Seeking Out and Engaging Adaptive Challenges

Ronald Heifetz at the Kennedy School of Government distinguishes two types of leadership challenges: technical and adaptive.[7] *Technical challenges* can be solved using existing techniques. Because the standards for success and the developmental opportunities they present are fairly well understood, these challenges lend themselves to assessment for development. *Adaptive challenges* are those that require something quite beyond people's present levels of expertise. Solving adaptive challenges, or what we call complex challenges, requires people and systems to change in fundamental ways. To solve adaptive challenges, you must create a new path through the proverbial thicket.

A danger in tackling complex challenges is defaulting to known techniques. Old maps (ways of looking at things and how they fit together) don't always fit the new territories being created everywhere today by forces such as biotechnology, telecommunications, deregulation, and globalization. Exploration for development therefore begins with paying attention to a complex challenge in fresh ways and enjoining others to do the same. To become adept at E4D, practice identifying and engaging adaptive challenges by working with others to create new maps, starting first on a small, local scale. Then locate yourself on the map you have drawn. Most people, especially early in their careers, become proficient at following the maps others have made. As leaders they must become mapmakers, and that takes practice.

Seeing Yourself as Part of the Challenge

Although technical challenges can be treated impersonally, complex challenges engage who you are as an individual. Because you are part of the fabric of the challenge, you must adapt in order to successfully address the challenge. One leader told us, "I have learned to look at a challenge and ask more questions in order to understand how the challenge relates to me—such that I can discover another part of myself, and the challenge becomes less intimidating."

While exploring complex challenges, people often discover that they have multiple selves. A person's signature as a creative leader is not monotonous and static. It has many facets. Exploring the points of connection among these selves builds personal integrity and resilience. Exploring the distinctions among them builds creative vitality, and the chance for higher levels of integrity. All this can benefit your work, as *Elsa*, a director in a consulting firm, explains: "The rules say to separate work from personal life. But I couldn't do it. I began to look for ways to bring my lifelong passion for dance and choreography to my work. Choreography tells me what it is like for twenty people to relate on stage—or in a conference room—and what it means to dance solo as well. I still see things best as paisley, circles, and rhythms rather than as lines."

Self-exploration also opens the door to exploring the potentials of those around you. *Pam,* who manages a group of research scientists, says, "By understanding myself better I am more appreciative of the differences and contributions of others."

Realizing That Exploration Is Both Individual and Collective

The exploration process is, paradoxically, an intensely personal activity pursued collectively. The educator Ira Progoff calls it "this solitary work we cannot do alone."[8] It is not enough to focus solely on yourself, nor is it enough to focus on your team and work issues. These avenues of investigation must be brought together. Realizing your group's potential will come when you connect people's passions with something wonderful they create together, with shared passion. Creative leadership means becoming adept at enlisting and developing the personal energies of those around you.

Complex challenges spill across all kinds of traditional boundaries. Communities of exploration often consist of people from diverse walks of life: customers, designers, seniors, juniors, marketers, Generations X, Y, and Z, and so on. In the Arthurian legends, King Arthur's rule was made powerful by his knights. Though Arthur was king, he dined equally with his knights, at a round table. Each knight also had his own quest, and each had to find his own way through the forest before any could find the Grail. Thus it is with creative leadership: strong and seasoned individuals join around a table, each bringing personal strengths to the fore, to better face shared leadership challenges.

Personalizing means recognizing that others hold unique, individual points of view and that they use these views to make sense of their work. Effective personalizing legitimizes these subjective experiences, bringing them into a dialogue to mitigate their biases. As a leader, take time to explore the personal qualities of those around you. Notice other people's stories, their passions, their images, and the ways they pay attention.

Using All Possible Resources for Making Sense of Challenges

In responding to technical challenges, a narrow range of expertise is often sufficient. Complex challenges bring neglected capacities to the surface. People suddenly find new meanings for old patterns. They reveal their *black-market knowledge*—skills and abilities that are not viewed as legitimate by the formal organization but that are nonetheless valuable and that may facilitate a new way of doing things. We find that sensibility and meaningful responses, even wisdom, may arise from unexpected sources. When the path disappears, everything that expands your available options is important.

Creating Maps and Compasses to Navigate Complexity

Ralph Stacey, in *Managing the Unknowable*, writes that "it is becoming clearer why so many organizations die young. Recent studies increasingly make the point that managing by existing maps leads to imitation, repetition, and excess."[9] The old rules were about following maps. The new rules are about making the maps—and often the compasses as well. In his chronicle of exploration in the Arctic, naturalist-historian Barry Lopez contemplates the significance given to maps: "I traveled everywhere with maps, no one of which was entirely accurate. They were the projection of a wish that the space could be this well organized. You cannot blame the maps of course; nor can you travel without them. . . . Even a good map . . . masquerades as an authority. What we hold in our hands are but approximations of what is out there. Neatly folded simulacra. . . . The orderliness, simplicity, and clarity of the presentation, of course, is often seductive."[10]

Exploration for development uses the metaphor of exploring unknown places. We have noticed how strongly people crave maps for new territory—yet by definition any maps for these uncharted plains will inevitably be proven inadequate or even perfectly wrong. David Hurst suggests that managers simply select and use existing maps, whereas true leaders create and employ compasses to find their way.[11] We believe that when transformation is under way, you must actually construct your compass first, out of whatever materials you have at hand.

Where do you find a compass when navigating new and murky waters?—in shared values, organizational visions, and essential stories. New business principles can be compasses. In the 1980s, one compass was *quality*; in the 1990s, *first mover*. For many now, the principle that acts as a compass is *always on*. To build your own compass, ask: What navigational tools are right for my unique challenge? Where can I get them? How can I build them?

Throughout the rest of this book, you will see how the six C2 Competencies help leaders build shared meaning—the metaphorical maps and compasses that will steer organizations through complex, turbulent times.

Tapping Into Your Passion

People are at their most creative and productive when they do work for the love of it. According to Harvard Business School professor

Teresa Amabile, sustained creativity in the workplace depends primarily on intrinsic motivation, that which comes from within the person.[12] When people are passionately engaged and believe in what they're doing, they have intrinsic motivation.

To have passion is to see and feel with the heart. One manager we work with says: "Leadership really begins with the heart, and I'm checking in with my heart. I've been opening my eyes and my heart, and now I can see and speak with both."

Passion at work is not all or nothing. Nor does it come quietly. Passion at work must be sculpted so it fits with the flow of people's lives. Another manager told us: "I choose to enjoy this work. And I want to be a soccer coach and be with my kids. Now if that means I can't stay and do the macho thing and work until nine every night then I'm making that choice. It doesn't mean that I'm failing. . . . I opened up my eyes and said, 'Do I want that bigger job?' Probably not. I think I want my life to look different. By asking those questions, you change the potential of the people in the workplace."

Often people come to realize that they are not finding a place for personal passion at work. Having that realization and then choosing to live one's life in accordance with one's own vision and values has been a critical turning point for many of the people we have worked with in our studies. "Life is about fit," said one, "and if it's not a good fit, it's just mental struggle, and it's not worth it. I've spent so much of my life working hard and achieving but not always having a good time. Now after changing jobs I care more about the people with whom I work, more about the clients." Similarly, *Barbara*, a software engineer, had always kept her love of making pottery and her career separate. Then she had the insight that designing software is like making pottery and that the two tasks draw on the same reserves of creativity: "Being a programmer is like being a potter. Both are about building. You can pursue each with the same inner aims, the same deeper sense of craft. And my joy is not from the pot itself. The pot, the program, become a symbol of the love and the crafting I have used to make the finished product." Indeed, pottery making in this example has become a collateral skill for software design.

The Passion of the Amateur

The word *amateur* comes from *amare*—"to love." An amateur is a person who works at something for the sheer love of it. Amateurs suffer a bad reputation, generally speaking. When was the last time you had a problem and called in an amateur? But every organization needs the passion of amateurs. It needs them to speak up about their love for what they do. It needs amateurs who can contribute their expertise to tackling complex challenges in fresh ways.

Consider the case of Mark Ptashne, the Harvard biologist whose work led to the discovery of the long-sought mechanism— the repressor molecule—through which a genetic DNA code is turned on and off. The solution, Ptashne sensed, would be found in the borderland between genetics and biochemistry. With a contrarian spirit, he declared himself "an amateur, that is, neither geneticist nor a biochemist. Most geneticists would not do the messy biochemistry that was required, and on the other hand, most biochemists would not consider doing these outlandish experiments" by the principles of genetics. Moreover, the problem of the repressor molecule affected him "deeply and aesthetically."[13]

Experts are prone to assume they are so aware of what happens in their field that if they haven't heard of an idea then it can't possibly be valid. Sociologist Ron Westrum calls this the *centrality fallacy*.[14] Formal expertise is frequently conservative—or to put it slightly differently risk averse—in just this way. Ptashne's amateur passions let him go places that experts wouldn't or couldn't: "The fact that so many people were working on it, fancy people, was grounds for asking what basis an amateur like me has to attack the problem. But as I looked into it more . . . it became clear that the others were willing to take risks only to a certain point."[15]

As amateurs people have a naïveté that invites exploring, asking questions that haven't been asked by the experts, and creating outlandish ideas that might provoke creative solutions from others or be solutions in themselves. Amateurs don't know the rules of engagement so they don't know when they're breaking the rules. They don't know what they're not supposed to know.

David Horth loves to tell the story of how he learned to play the didgeridoo a few years ago. An ancient instrument of the native Australian people, the didgeridoo requires mastery of the complicated technique of circular breathing. David bought the instrument and an audiotape to get him started. As he listened to the tape he worked through each learning step along with it. By the end of the tape he was circular breathing. After a few months of playing he met other didgeridoo players on the Internet. The first thing they asked was whether he could circular breathe, and they were astonished when he answered yes. No one had told him it is supposed to take a year to learn this technique. Now he jokes that the instrument must have found him rather than the other way around.

We are all experts, of a certain kind, in the domain of our own experience. That is, we are all experts in the areas in our lives where our experience, sharp perception, intuition, and passion come together. Some find they have expertise that does not lie in any formally recognized field. The trick is to first figure out your niches of expertise, then to develop and practice them without judgment.

Black-Market Knowledge

Explore your personal experience, make it explicit, and claim it as expertise. Expert-knowledge researcher Beth Crandall calls this "unpacking what you know." She studies the ways skilled people make decisions: "Often the story [of how they use what they know] contains examples of intuitive reasoning, points where they 'just knew' what was going on, or what to do. As we probe for details, and sift through the experience with them, they become aware of the components that underlie or comprise that sense of intuition. They come out of these interviews pleased with themselves, in part because they have made contact with what had been mysterious, outside of consciousness."

Some of this is what one of Crandall's informants calls *black-market knowledge*. As we mentioned earlier, black-market knowledge and abilities have value but lack organizational legitimacy. "When people come in contact with these building blocks that allow them to perform automatically but wonderfully," says Crandall, "suddenly the intuitive *is* legitimate, grounded in experience, skill and an extensive knowledge of the world in which they function. No longer magic, black-market knowledge can be identified, documented, shared, and owned."[16]

Your personal expertise is your ticket to be a free agent in the new workplace. But as an amateur, or as a person working with black-market knowledge and abilities in the cracks between recognized fields, what you are good at often has no universal name. So the name of your expertise is your *own* name. William Bridges calls this phenomenon Me, Inc.[17] You are your own product, research department, and marketing function. What new domains can you enter? What areas have you wanted to stumble around in? What is the essence of your personal expertise that can be abstracted and applied in new fields of endeavor?

Having Guts

Making the connection between the leadership challenges you face and who you are takes guts. One senior vice president we interviewed told us: "Corporate America is so fragmented. What we need are people that have *the guts to be whole people at work*."

Having guts means possessing both the mental quality of courage and the visceral knowledge of one's flesh and bones. It is having a body-based intuition laced with adrenaline, endorphins, and emotions. Your guts are grounded in your personal values and experiences. Courage and visceral knowing reinforce each other. It takes guts to create and to lead. It takes guts to be fully who you are.

For example, *Pam*, station manager at *Johns River Station*, was an open-enrollment participant in the Leading Creatively program. Pam experienced a shift in her leadership toward R-mode perception and personalized frames of reference, which she summarized as "confidence to go with my gut":

> For me that transformation was that I did have a right side, and there was a place in business for that right side. I think that trans-

formation gave me courage. It gave me courage, and it gave me confidence in that right side to pay attention to it, to trust it, and to use it. I now have the guts to do things differently and to say things when people are not sure where I'm coming from. I'm a better manager and a better person. I am braver.

Donna, the team leader at *Chemstar*, found that

the key learning is that leadership requires courage and a leap of faith. There is power in having the courage to speak the truth. I believed in it intuitively but I knew I was really pushing against the tide and there was more than one time that I was afraid of asking these people to commit so much time to something I wasn't sure was going to work. The leap of faith is, you don't see results right away. I mean it's not something that you do and you get something for it immediately. There's a long incubation period. People aren't always as willing to sign up for that. They want the silver bullet.

One of Donna's direct reports had a similar perception about her: "I think it's a tough role to be so far ahead of the curve because you end up dragging people along with you until they get it. So it's difficult but I appreciated that she stuck with it. That's certainly a lot of courage on her part. When she's got something, she tenaciously hangs on and goes with it."

Vulnerability

Exploring who you are in the context of the leadership challenges you face will leave you more open and, at times, vulnerable. Leaders today do well to show vulnerability in times of challenge. According to human development specialist Kerry Bunker, there is great power in vulnerability. However, "most leaders wear protective masks of invincibility that they don't remove easily or lightly."[18] Many leaders would rather be, or at least appear to be, invincible.

David, for example, was brought up in the United Kingdom, a culture known for the standard of "the stiff upper lip." Our work with organizational leaders who are in the midst of major organizational transitions has shown David the surprising power of vulnerability. At the simplest level it builds trust—people who see you as a leader also need to see you as human. Letting others realize the complexity of who you are engenders compassion and respect along with trust. For David, having a stiff upper lip just doesn't cut it anymore.

To comment on his own imperfection and attendant vulnerability, a vice president of a consulting organization told us that he began to notice over time that his weaknesses actually helped him see the way forward, rather than just immobilizing him. This recalled for him a bit of wisdom he once heard about the cracks being the places where the light can come in.

Knowing When to Let Go of Your Personal Side

Personalizing is a leadership tool to be wielded skillfully—not something to be pushed to its limit in any and all situations. Competence at personalizing is a two-step dance. The first step is experiencing something in deeply personal terms—hot passions. The second is moving to personal detachment and a cooler head. Effective personalizing requires knowing when to let go of the personal side of things, with respect to other people as well as yourself. It means knowing which aspects of yourself to invest in an issue and which to rein in.

People fool themselves if they think they can be totally objective and bias free. The trick is to develop enough flexibility to move between the poles of subjectivity and objectivity. These poles are places no one can fully reach and the middle ground is always an amalgam. Science, art, and creative leadership are disciplines that seek leverage and motion in this middle place between the poles. Objectivity ultimately comes from knowing your own subjectivity very well and from understanding how subjectivity works in others.

Here are several approaches for finding the right balance between personal engagement and letting go:

Assessment for development. Seeing yourself more objectively as a result of assessment, even if in partial, momentary, and imperfect ways, is a means to *enlarge* the ultimate scope of your subjective reach. This is a paradox that brings much power to the competency of personalizing. Learning how to give good feedback to others is a way of exercising objectivity in thoughtful balance with subjectivity.

Checks and balances. High-performing groups have a common attribute: they balance personal freedom with collective interdependence. Each side of this dynamic is a check on the other, making its opposite more reliable and thus more potent. High-performing groups welcome and support the personal views of their members while providing a challenging environment and critical testing ground for those views. Good coaching and mentoring does the same. Dialogue, which we discuss in Chapter Five, is a way to put your intuitions and assumptions *in the middle* of a discussion to invoke the checks and balances that well-functioning groups provide.

Philosophical or spiritual discipline. A disciplined path in life can give you a framework larger than yourself and that gives your personalizing effective boundaries and a firm place to stand. For example, one CEO we worked with is a practicing black belt in karate; he believes this discipline teaches him both restraint and strength in the broader spheres of his life. At their best, professional disciplines do something similar, as does any demanding craft. Scientific study can nurture great passions within objectifying checks and balances. Rigorous spiritual practice can likewise be a potential source of discipline on one's personal reach.

Skeptical inquiry. Science, broadly speaking, tempers personal passions and insightful leaps with skeptical inquiry. Deep personal curiosities and desires drive the imagination beyond boundaries—and then skeptical inquiry double-checks the reach of imagination. Traditional techniques in experimentation—replication and peer review, for example—are ways to brace personalizing with objectivity.

Developing the Competency
of Personalizing

"So many things fail to interest us," says Ortega y Gasset, "simply because they don't find in us enough surfaces on which to live, and what we have to do then is to increase the number of planes in our mind, so that a much larger number of themes can find a place in it at the same time."[19] Craig Wynett of Procter & Gamble calls the place where creative leadership happens *surface area*.[20] This metaphor from the field of chemistry suggests that making sense of complexity is like a chemical reaction: to make new bonds, or new meaning, where there is chaos, people need catalytic surfaces. These surfaces can be the curves and fissures of their own identities and the identities of those around them. Developing the competency of personalizing is really about discovering and extending one's surface area. The following sections look at some ways to do that, beginning with developing individual competence.

Developing Individual Competence

Two effective means for increasing your store of personal experiences and using those experiences in the work environment are storytelling and sabbaticals.

Storytelling. Since the time people first drew the pictographs on the walls of caves, storymaking and storytelling have helped them navigate the challenges of life. The story, in all its forms, is a way to share experiences and ideas with others. Naturally, exploration and storymaking go together.

Peter Orton, a manager at IBM and former Hollywood scriptwriter, explains that stories are a powerful mechanism for teaching and learning because they "enhance attention, create anticipation, and increase retention. Stories use plot and character to generate conflict. They provide a familiar set of hooks that allow us to process the information that we hang on them . . . a protagonist the audience can empathize with, something important at stake, mounting jeopardy, a formidable antagonist."[21]

Stories open the way to connection and reflection. They build a bridge between L-mode (language, temporal sequence) and R-mode (image and pattern, timelessness) attention. Stories express people's most basic wishes and their most basic fears. Good stories are thus rich with catalytic surface area.

Noel Tichy, professor at the University of Michigan Business School, says that leadership stories have three functions.[22] They answer the questions, "Who am I?" "Who are we?" and "Where are we going?" Leadership stories begin with the story of one's identity (Who am I?) and grow outward into more visible stories of group identity and vision. Management stories, in contrast, are passive and look backward. They focus on "What happened?" and "How can we fix it?" and so they create boxes, enclosed in time, space, and possibility.

According to mythologist Joseph Campbell, there is one story form, and it goes something like this:[23]

Home ⟶ Adventure ⟶ Home.

or like this:

Order ⟶ Disorder ⟶ Order.

Even more simply, you could say that stories cover:

Beginning ⟶ Middle ⟶ End.

For example:

Once upon a time ⟶ and then one day, things got interesting ⟶ and they lived happily (or not) ever after.

Stories are more than simply told—they are composed. Although they can be most compelling in their rawest forms, stories are crafted by re-forming and retelling.

Here is a potent technique for composing stories. Remember a situation or event with strong personal meaning that you experienced. Tell the story in the present tense, from the perspective of a character or object other than yourself within the situation. This technique makes compelling stories because it provides different and unusual perspectives on your motivations and values. It gives you the freedom to express these perspectives, because the character is speaking, not you.

A second technique, which complements the first, is *free-writing*.[24] It is a process for writing effortlessly, even in the face of writer's block. It incorporates a pattern of alternating between R-mode and L-mode. You simply put your pen to paper, begin writing, and continue writing without stopping or editing—even if all you write at first is "I can't think . . . I don't know . . . this stinks. . . ." You will be surprised to find gems of ideas amid the gravel. With those gems as starting places, free-write again: more gems, more gravel. Soon you will have a great deal of valuable material that you can edit in a more analytical way.

David Young, a retired brigadier general in the U.S. Air Force, combined these two techniques to tell the following powerful story about what it means to be of service. In telling the story of an event in his life, he opens a window of reflection on the ideas of honor, duty, sacrifice, and personal mission. His story, "The Hand That Held the Flag," describes the military funeral for one of the servicemen killed in the terrorist bombing in Dhahran, Saudi Arabia, in 1996. Young presented the American flag to the serviceman's widow and wrote the following piece "as a reflection of how I felt and what went through my mind." The narrator is not Young but his right hand. The story was published in his local Air Force base newsletter, to great response. Here was a senior leader expressing his emotions and vulnerability. By personalizing in a powerful and integrative way, he touched all who grieved for the loss of a comrade.

The Hand That Held the Flag

Why am I shaking so uncontrollably? I've never let him down like this before. What's going on?

It's getting worse. As I pass his eyes I see the concern, maybe even embarrassment reflected there? What's she thinking? What are his kids thinking? Past the chest to the belt line. I'm totally out of control. This is where the lieutenant said to speed it up, a sharp snap to the boss's side. Man, I'm glad that's over. Still don't know what happened. Like I said, I've never let him down before.

He and I have been through a lot together in this Air Force. I remember the first time: "Do you solemnly swear to uphold the Constitution of the United States, obey the orders of the President of the United States and the orders of the officers appointed over you, according to regulations and the Uniform Code of Military Justice?" "So help me God." I didn't have any problems then.

I remember doing a pretty good job of holding him up as he did his pushups in Basic Training. Did a pretty good job of spit-shining his shoes for him. Thought it was kinda gross, still do.

His first boss told him he did a pretty good job of filing stuff in those big drawers. I really felt a part of this team called the Air Force.

Doing those pushups again at Officer Training School. He graduated; I done good. There I was again, the right side one raised at attention: "Having being appointed a Second Lieutenant in the United States Air Force, do you solemnly swear to uphold the Constitution?" "I take this obligation freely without any mental reservation or purpose of evasion and that I will faithfully discharge the duties of the office which I am about to enter, so help me God." Didn't mess it up then either.

This thing called pilot training; never forget the day his instructor said, "You got pretty good hands, Lieutenant, and you fly a good jet." Man, me and my left-handed buddy were on cloud nine.

How many salutes? I've lost count of the times rendering, returning. Crisp when it was supposed to be, friendly too, sometimes casual. Always with a sense of respect and camaraderie. Always knew I was on the team.

Handshakes: man, this social stuff can get to be a real drag. Met a lot of folks though. Always able to tell the Air Force ones, doesn't matter if they're brown, black, white, greasy, sweaty, small, big, feminine or callused. I can always tell—always a firm grip. I can feel the sense of pride, of belonging, of sharing; always there. Get kinda sore occasionally, though.

Never let him down in Vietnam. Imprinted in my mind is the night over Hanoi as the SAMs crossed in front of us and took down our wingman. I pushed the throttles forward. You see, this was a Press On mission—no turning back.

Then three months later as I wiped the tears from his eyes as we watched our POWs land in the Philippines. Wow, what a handshake when we met up with our buds who'd been locked up in the hellhole of the Hanoi Hilton. Talk about firm; could feel the emotion between them. Wiped the tears away again.

Enlistments, re-enlistments, commissionings, changes of command—I've done it all. Never got shook then.

As we launched his crews and folks to something called Desert Storm, no problem then. Did my shaking and saluting thing. Could sense him reflecting back on when he was on the other end launching to Southeast Asia. I did OK though. We hugged a lot of kids and wives, held their hands, wiped their tears and then the folks came home. Got tired again, slapping them on the back, hugging them, shaking all those other hands.

Starting to figure it out. Think it began just a few minutes ago as me and Leftie held Our Flag so neatly folded in that triangle, as her hands rested on ours, trembling, searching, asking why. I heard the boss say, "On behalf of the President of the United States and a grateful nation, our country's flag is presented as a token of appreciation for many years of faithful and honorable service. May God be with you and your family during your time of bereavement." I've never heard his voice sound like that.

So as I look back to that Teardrop Salute of just a few minutes ago I know why I shook. I could see it in his eyes as I hesitated there for a few seconds. The millions of patriots just like this man lying behind us, Staff Sergeant Kevin Johnson, who'd raised their hands and vowed service before self, who knew that ultimately they may have to give up their lives, who'd been scared but had done their duty, who'd loved and been loved. Who wanted nothing but the best for their country and their families. Who were willing to pay for it with the ultimate payment.

I could feel it in his heart as I moved down his chest. Because you see that's where it really is; always has been, always will be. That's why we in Air Force blue do what we do. It's in our hearts.

Let's return to Noel Tichy's three functions of leadership stories. As a leader, you should frequently consider and compose Who am I? stories for yourself, your intimates, and your closest associates. Those intimates and associates will often be in your stories, as you will be in theirs. Who am I? stories are the implicit foundations for the other kinds of stories you tell, lending them a necessary core of values and beliefs. Who are we? stories are great for group retreats and other times of planned reflection and re-aiming. Without these stories there can be no depth of shared history and shared values. Where are we going? is the obvious payoff. In an organization with creative leadership, these stories get told every day in ways that combine values, vision, and action.

To make and share stories, make sure you are clear about your own starting place. Have you discovered the story of who you are yet? Professor Ray Hedin at Indiana University has a storytelling exercise that helps individuals clarify personal and professional goals. Imagine it is twenty-five years in the future and you have just finished writing your autobiography. Write the dust-jacket blurbs and excerpts from book reviews in the New York Times and elsewhere. What quotations do the reviewers pick out for comment?

Just free-write all this without editing. What surprises you? Share the results of this exercise with a few people who know you. What surprises them?[25] Try doing this same exercise with your work group, but this time focus on a case study someone writes five years from now about the company in which you all work.

We offer six guidelines for effective storytelling in the service of creative leadership. Leadership storytelling requires a comprehensive approach that incorporates each of the six C2 Competencies.

1. *Personalizing.* Whenever you compose or tell a story in service of leadership, your deepest passions should lie at its core. Use the storytelling to learn something about yourself. Novelist Henry Miller tells us: "Whatever effects I may obtain by technical device are never the mere results of technique, but the very accurate registering by my seismographic needle, of the tumultuous, manifold, mysterious and incomprehensible experiences which I have lived through and which in the process of writing are lived through again, differently, perhaps even more tumultuously, more mysteriously, more incomprehensibly."[26]

2. *Paying attention.* Use fresh observations and details instead of stale generalities and stereotypes.

3. *Imaging.* Use metaphors and symbols—things and events that stand for something else, something more.

4. *Serious play.* "Make it strange."[27] Find the surprise, the drama, the intrigue, the unique and new.

5. *Co-inquiry.* Invite others to interpret the story. Remember, once told, the story does not belong only to you—listeners combine with the teller to make the story what it is. Seek impressions without trying to control interpretations.

6. *Crafting.* Practice your story in different settings and from different angles, until it "sings."

Sabbaticals. Taking periodic breaks is an important way to foster your personal strengths, and thus your competence, in personalizing. During these sabbaticals you can explore old and new interests in ways that feed your ability to make sense of new challenges. The English word *sabbatical* comes from the Hebrew *Shabbat,* the holy seventh day of rest, reflection, and reconnection. Sabbaticals can charge your batteries, feed your soul, and foster your flexibility.

One of the biggest issues at fast, young companies is how hard people work. Candice Carpenter, former CEO of iVillage, worried about refreshing her people before they burned out: "I've stood at the elevator with people going on vacation and actually taken the laptop and cell phone out of their hands and said, 'Great, now you can have a vacation.' The only way to be truly creative and inventive again is to be unwired at times in the year and to be in the other part of the world."[28]

Hallmark Cards, Inc., has devised intense sabbaticals of four to six months—what it calls *rotations.*[29] One form of rotation is for creative renewal: you can't expect people to be "all output and no input" and continue to be innovative. Hallmark maintains a facility for the explicit purpose of artistic development. Another form of rotation is for exploring social trends in depth; death and dying in the 1990s was the subject of one. A small team fans out to explore the phenomenon of interest and return with a depth of insight that ultimately gets built into Hallmark products. According to one participant: "Before this rotation, I was always in the passive mode. Now I'm more aggressive. It forced me out of my comfort zone. If we were just told to stay in our cubicles and create all the time, we'd dry up. It's been three years since my rotation and it still keeps me going."

Sabbaticals can take many forms. Renowned physicist Robert Wilson had a radical vision for a life change: moving from being a physicist to being a sculptor. Or perhaps it was not so radical. Wilson had always viewed his passions for art and physics as part of a whole, and now he wanted to test that idea. "Most of my life I've done both sculpture and physics. I don't say, 'Now I'm being a sculptor' and try to be romantic, and then say, 'Now I'm being a physicist' and try to be cold and mean and nasty. I never notice any difference, particularly. I'm an experimentalist. . . . The aesthetics [of physics] have always been important to me and I think they have been important throughout history."

As Wilson was planning a sabbatical to test the waters, the unexpected happened. He was offered the opportunity to spearhead the building of the Fermi National Accelerator Laboratory (Fermilab), the world's premier high-energy physics facility, from the ground up. He accepted and poured his love of sculpting, art, and architecture into this new position. The result changed the course of science: "As a physicist, I had planned to take a sabbatical and see if I couldn't make it as a sculptor. Instead, this other adventure came along. I had that on my mind when accepting. . . . [A]rt and architecture are necessary conditions for building a good laboratory."[30]

Is there a sabbatical in your future? Here are a few ways to think about the possibilities:

• Like Robert Wilson, ask yourself if any part of your profession and your "art" or avocation connect at a deeper level. Take time off to pursue that connection. Start a personal fund for that purpose now, and plan to tap into it in three years.

• Take your team on a two- or three-day excursion around a topic that is beginning to emerge near the edges of your field.

• Award your top performers or your creative risk takers with minisabbaticals in which they are challenged to bring something back for the organization's practices, something from "way out in left field."

• If your company carries out a reduction in force and you are among those RIF'd, consider designing a renewal period before, or in the midst of, looking for your next job. The insights you gain from testing your dream, even briefly, might influence your next move.

Developing Community Competence

As a leader who recognizes the value of unique and diverse experience, you can support community values and infrastructure that encourage competent personalizing. Here are some examples of infrastructural support:

Think of Diversity as Multiple Lenses on Complexity. At the front edge of facing a complex challenge ask people questions like: What about your own experience? When have you handled something like this in a former life or a previous job, or in the country or culture of your origin? What are the phrases or metaphors for this situation in your native language? How do other professions deal with something like this? Competent personalizing on a community basis has at its most basic a two-beat rhythm: first, express divergent perspectives based in wide personal experience; then come together in a well-crafted, collective perspective.

Institutionalize Storytelling. Create opportunities for your team to make and tell the story of the organization, the individual players, and the challenge the organization or the team faces. Make sure the players involved participate in the storymaking and telling process.

Recognize Free Agents. Mobile workers in the new economy, or *free agents*, seek workplaces that legitimize their multiple passions. Recognize that this new work-life style is legitimate; don't force free agents to pretend they are loyal only to their current jobs.

Develop Intranet Personnel Pages. An increasing number of companies have an area for individual home pages in their organization's intranets. In an age of telecommuting and travel, these personalized pages put names, faces, and personalities together with titles. They encourage people to network and develop relationships around all sorts of interests, issues, and personal capabilities. They help "watercooler" conversations and relationships develop among people who might not otherwise meet.

Evolve in Response to the Talents of Individual Members. Nickelodeon, the highly regarded cable network that specializes in children's programming, is a great example of how strong individuality and strong community can feed off each other. One of its leaders says: "You can see [the Nickelodeon environment] at work in the way careers develop here: the company evolves in response to the talents and ideas of individuals, rather than requiring the individual to fit into positions or roles. More than anything, that's how we function inclusively."[31]

Cautions

Investing who you are as a person into the enterprise of leadership entails risk. Many organizations are still hostile to the complexities of the whole person. As you develop your competence at personalizing—and encourage it in others—be aware of the impact this work can have on your identity and sense of self. Opening up brings the richness of your personal expertise to the fore, but part of the bargain is that your work and your colleagues can return the influence, for better or worse. Here are some areas that may need special attention:

Vulnerability. Showing vulnerability is an asset to leaders in times of change—but by definition it leaves you exposed. It is a chink in your metaphorical armor. So you must decide whether and when you need armor in times of complexity. You must decide who if anyone is the enemy (hint: it may not be your close colleagues). Humor can help—so can a certain amount of humility, and so can level-headedness and toughness and courage, all of which ground emotional openness. Emotional vulnerability is a gift you give to those around you. Choose wisely to whom you give it. In return you may be given loyalty, the dedication of others, and the role of leader.

Identity. If who you are is where you work, watch out![32] Although personalizing can be extraordinarily useful for facing complex challenges at work, it can also be a protection from the workplace—an escape hatch. It is in this spirit that a CEO who is a musician and craftsman takes moments away from the hustle and bustle of the finance business he leads: "I use my creativity continually as a balance to my work demands—an escape—a means to get lost in something that provides moments of joy. It is a means to keep me from defining myself by my job. To the extent the job does not define who I am, the freer I am to bring perspective, candor, and acceptance of the new to my leadership style. Then I find that the right-brain experiences I have outside work influence my leadership style naturally and unconsciously."

Self-evolution. Making a personal investment in leadership means that you are willing to grow and change. No longer is it just about "them" changing—now it's about you. After the tornado strikes, facing complex challenges with the whole of who we are requires the equivalent of admitting, "We're not in Kansas anymore, Toto." Taking on a complex challenge means that you have an opportunity to put your stamp on the job, but the job can also put its stamp on you. Is that what you want? If so, be sure you know why. Competent personalizing means sensing which battles to pick and which to walk away from.

Striving for balance. One of the leaders we've worked with characterized her inner creative space as a "secret garden." The garden is a rich resource in all her life including her work. It is full of marvelous things, some of which she is only now discovering. Some of it is fragile; some of it is not—but it all has a wall around it and a gate. The issue for her becomes, "Shall I lower the wall? I want to share [the garden] and make it more accessible, but I am afraid it may be trampled." Surely this wall should not be removed entirely. In her imagination the solution has something to do with the gate.

A few years ago, we had the opportunity to interview a retired senior executive of a large international corporation. We had discovered that he was a gifted sculptor and painter and were curious about how this gift played out in his business life. Early in the interview we asked if he ever consciously brought who he was as an artist into his organizational leadership: "No," he said. "My art was a place for me to reenergize. It was sacrosanct. No colleague could contact me whilst I was doing my art of an evening. They knew where I was but knew not to contact me during that time for any reason. Only my family could do that." Later in the interview we asked him whether he had any regrets on leaving the organization he had led for many years. "Just one," he replied, "that I couldn't help the organization be more creative." His jaw dropped and a look of agonized astonishment flashed across his face as he heard himself say these words. Had he made the connection between his lack of personalizing and the organization's lack of creative capacity? Had his reluctance to let people at work experience him as an artist stymied the development of organizational creativity?

As you make decisions on what to share in the workplace and what to keep private, keep in the forefront of your mind that which makes you strong as well as that part of you that opens new doors.

Chapter Three

Imaging

The world is in the midst of an image revolution. Pictures, stories, metaphors, and visual arts animate the language of the New Economy. The palette of communication options and, more important, of idea making is expanding enormously, transforming the way people think. For today's creative leadership a new kind of literacy is required: a literacy of images.

Straight talk and literal thinking—as valuable as they are—often prove inadequate when addressing complex challenges. Knowledge does not always translate neatly into sentences. Words can fail us by their clumsiness or by what they leave out. The C2 Competency of *imaging* offers a way to go beyond the limits of language.

Imaging is making sense of information, constructing ideas, and communicating effectively through the use of images. Images run the gamut from pictures to poetry; they may be scenarios of the future, for example, or objects that model ideas, sketches by hand, videos, or digital graphics. Novelist James Dickey tells us that the task of imaging is a poetic activity; it is to "pick up all this crippled shrillness of words and throw it with both hands toward the light."

Imaging plays a vital role in collaborative innovation. It makes thought visible as communities create and share images.[1] We believe that creative forms of leadership make imagination shared property by placing images in the middle of conversations, where they can become the clay with which people build creative solutions to complex challenges.

Imaging plays a critical role in people's individual learning processes as well. Master educator Bernice McCarthy warns that people often skip imaging during learning, much to their detriment. According to McCarthy, people process and internalize new information optimally when they employ a specific learning cycle. The same cycle offers an optimal approach to complex challenges. It begins with these four steps: *connect, reflect, image, conceptualize.*[2]

You are *connecting* when you pay attention and personalize. You are *reflecting* when you apply logical analysis to the connection you have just made—a bit of stepping back to organize your raw initial perceptions and experiences. While *imaging*, you express these reflections in terms of rich pictures, as a prelude to *conceptualizing* the complex challenge in formal and precise ways. If you jump directly from reflection to conceptualization (both L-mode processes), you eliminate both imagination and creativity. Imaging, then, is a vital step for gathering R-mode information.

Imaging structured on both sides by analysis is an extremely powerful engine for facing complexity. In this chapter we offer several imaging techniques and approaches that have proven effective in addressing complex challenges:

- Making imagination tangible
- Seeing organizational vision in a new light
- Exploring scenarios
- Making and using metaphors
- Making poetry in the face of complexity

Making Imagination Tangible

"Imagination," says Jacob Bronowski, "is the manipulation of images. . . . Human reason discovers new relations between things not by deduction, but by that unpredictable blend of speculation and insight that scientists call induction, which—like other forms of imagination—cannot be formalized."[3] Imagination is a way of moving things around so they take new shapes, paying attention to the images you construct and constructing with the images you perceive. Making imagination *tangible* allows people to pursue these thoughts in groups and not just in individual solitude. People make imagination tangible by using tools such as pencil and paper, computer graphics, architecture, games, and toys to describe their visions.

Computer software offers many ways to manipulate images for the purpose of turning data into knowledge and wisdom. The recent history of computing chronicles the replacement of pure number crunching with inviting visual interfaces that offer new ways to perceive meaning. Jean Gassée, former European director of Apple Computer, suggests that this was a necessary step in the evolution of computers as scaffolds for the imagination: "*VisiCalc* was quickly supplemented with another program called *Visiplot*. And now we have *Multiplan* and *Chart* and integrated programs such as *Excel* and *Jazz*. Their original feature was to translate arrays of numbers into graphs and pictures with reliefs, colors, and perspectives. These pictures create meaning, they tell a story, they have a power of expression infinitely superior to any table of figures."[4]

But computers by themselves fall short of the full potential of competent imaging. They are simply tools, after all. The key to making them useful is the human innovation and interpretation behind the graphs and grids and pie charts. Let's look at ways to make imaging more friendly to imagination: collage, pictorial language, and star-mapping.

Collage

Collage is a technique invented by artists in the early twentieth century that combines diverse images or artifacts to construct new meanings. It is now widely used to create composite ideas for various media, such as advertising and the Internet. The word *collage* comes from French, where it evokes not only the meaning "collision of ideas" but also "disparate scenes in rapid succession." Collage is an excellent tool for assisting people in crafting new ideas together.

Meena is the director of a medical therapeutic unit struggling with challenges that include HMO conditions, changing demographics, and new treatment models. At first, her staff were dispirited and un-clear about their direction. She helped them find meaning and di-rection by "going visual":

> The people here have the heart for this work. They are able to do it.
> They just didn't know what the vision of the work was. . . . So we
> went visual with the staff. We started creating visuals around the of-
> fice about what we thought the work was, and what the new work
> would look like—and what some people were already actually doing.
> A marketing person started taking pictures of people working with
> clients in different ways, and we [mounted] those pictures all over
> the office. We created a collage in the back, in the staff office. We
> created a whole wall-sized picture about the work. . . . Now they're
> seeing possibilities. There seems to be a spirit.

Collage images can come from a variety of places and build on one another. These colliding images might be externally oriented or reflect a personal perspective. Collage can combine emotional and intuitive information with harder forms of data. Collage can be used as a barometer or a compass. *Ray* is a manager in the software industry who has used collage to take the pulse of his staff as a start-ing point for problem solving:

> My staff and I have had a very busy year, dealing with the usual cor-
> porate issues, such as insufficient resources and a burgeoning workload.
> I sensed much frustration and impatience among my department
> managers. To give voice to some of that and direct them toward pos-
> itive attitudes, I asked my direct reports to bring to a staff meeting a
> couple of pictures illustrating how they currently feel about their
> jobs and another couple of pictures illustrating how they would like
> to feel.
>   Then I asked each person to combine their pictures into a
> larger composition. The results amazed me. Everyone—even the
> no-nonsense, analytical system support manager—put together very
> honest collages. I asked them to interpret their own collages as well

as suggest interpretations for the others in the room. The exercise allowed them a safe way to open to their peers, who were quite supportive. The sharing of frustrations and hopes served as a springboard for a discussion of the realities of our workplace and ways to achieve some of our desired changes.

Pictorial Language

The *Orion Research Center* (ORC) offers a rich, many-layered example of how tangible imagination can be used for collaborative strategic planning. ORC is the central corporate research and development laboratory of *Orion, Inc.*, a $2 billion consumer products company that specializes in advanced office products.

Ten years ago ORC was rigidly hierarchical. Decisions flowed from the top, and *strategy* meant merely the selection of projects. The senior executives gathered annually to determine the work of the division and what would get funded. Then this approach began losing effectiveness. By the early 1990s, there was a crisis: ORC was slipping behind the competition in its ability to develop new products for changing markets. ORC, however, did have a vision:

What the technical world will experience and value: The ultimate high-output, learning-networked community of individuals.

What the business world will see and value: First to commercialize innovative products, processes, and services with measurably higher value for customers throughout the world.

What ORC needed was to foster the creative abilities necessary to implement this vision.

When we met the people in this group, ORC was already going visual as an organization. For example, in addition to expressing its vision in words, ORC had drawings made of this vision and distributed them internally (see Figure 3.1). ORC felt these drawings were necessary because the one hundred or so professionals working in

Figure 3.1. Two Drawings Representing ORC's Vision.

How We See Ourselves

Figure 3.1. Two Drawings Representing ORC's Vision, cont'd.

How Our Competitors See Us

Used with permission.

the center spoke thirty different languages and dialects. English was not everyone's first language and thus not a viable common denominator for conveying ORC's complex ideas. ORC staff warned us, "You won't know the meaning of the whole thing as we show you our picture—but everything in this picture has a significant meaning in the organization." They were onto the powerful idea that pictures can foster dialogue that cuts across ethnic diversity.

Drawn illustrations can be used in a variety of similar ways to cut across blockages in communications, to span distances, and to work out ideas under time pressure. For example, we recall the time *Albert*, an engineering group director we worked with, was on the phone coordinating with several people on his team. Team members were gathering at the airport before rushing off to an emergency meeting in Scotland with their vice president, and they were having much trouble getting their key message in order. Albert said,

"Sit down and make a drawing of your main message and fax it to me." They did, and it cut through the noise and got them all on the same page. The next iteration of the drawing, made on the flight, won the day in Scotland by focusing attention around a shared and compelling image.

Another example arises from the circumstance that as one might expect, ORC handles a lot of patents. When the velocity and complexity of that critical work increased, ORC's patent specialist devised visual methods for tracking and communicating about patent projects. He finds that his robust system has put him light-years ahead of his colleague specialists:

> I used to have a credenza in the back where the patent paperwork was stacked up. I took the credenza out and made my wall a series of charts. We have charts where you're measuring or recording your metrics for cost, quality, and service for patent management. . . . I'm using pencils and things like that and coloring them in. It's basically creating art on the wall, but art that has meaning and value to the corporation. I call that business art. So my whole wall . . . I guess about . . . eleven feet by eight feet wide—is just filled with charts and color. It's very visual. Then we overlay polyacetate over that to aid in removability of the labels, next we cut the surface of the chart itself, and then we apply to that the removable labels, and move the projects around as they progress through the commercialization pathway.
>
> A patent attorney called with a question and after scanning my charts I immediately said, "We have something coming up in three months' time." But his department can't get the information to him very fast. He's got to go through a database and do a search string, and say, "What's due in 2001?" then type *star, search,* and then go through each record.

In some cases it works to use a skilled artist, as ORC did in working up its group vision, but it is imperative that the process be interactive so that it is in fact *you, the person or group with the vision,* that is producing the drawing. All the better if you can sketch it yourself. Immediacy and authenticity win out over gloss. One executive has worked out a series of color drawings about strategy, which he creates from scratch on chart paper each time he does a presentation. He tells us he now achieves a rapport with his audience that he never experienced when using a PowerPoint show. Because the drawings must change somewhat for each audience, this practice also keeps him fresh and present during what has become a repetitive task.

Star-Mapping

We worked specifically with ORC's Strategic Planning Team, led by *Richard,* the director of research. In response to the increasing pace and quality of innovation in its market, ORC began doing strategic planning with a twenty-person team of managers, scientists, and technologists. The purpose was to read the waters of market and technological change more deliberately and to make better decisions. The team members were selected for diverse experience and perspectives and for leadership potential. They had open access to relevant information on internal operations, technology, patents, customers, and competitors.

The team members grew very sophisticated at processing all this data, and by most measures their efforts were increasingly successful— but they ran into a wall. Computer-aided techniques of analysis went far but ultimately proved inadequate. There were simply too much information to take in and too many unknowns to resolve. The team members were frustrated because they thought they could make better use of all these data but were unable to see a way to do it. The team members also knew there was more in the information in front of them than they could articulate or even notice. They felt opportunity escaping because they just couldn't get their arms around everything going on. Something was missing.

One analytical technique the team used was to *spider diagram* each proposed project. Spider diagrams, created from Excel spreadsheets, plot ratings for each project, using criteria for each *leg* radiating out from a center point. The adjacent rating points on the spider legs are then connected with a straight line, and the resultant polygon is cut out with scissors (see the stages of this process in Figure 3.2 and the star-mapping simulation in Appendix D). While examining spider diagrams, team members made a key innovation. They turned the diagrams over so that no numbers or data points were visible—only the overall shapes of the diagrams. They marked the top of each project shape, so the shapes could be compared to each other. The team played with arranging and sorting these shapes and began calling them *star maps*.

The star maps strongly engage visual perception. Team members try to make sense of the patterns they notice. They ask themselves what is missing from an ideal pattern. They exercise their intuition instead of constantly focusing on the numbers. They conduct various exercises in which they collaborate in pushing the shapes into clusters along a variety of dimensions. The language shifts from one focused on numbers, logical analysis, and ranking of criteria to one concerned with shape, form, and appropriateness.

According to one of the group leaders:

> Before, we basically had to memorize or constantly flip through pages and pages of information. There are about sixty different candidate projects, and you had to memorize the same attributes off of a piece of paper. *And people could not remember.* If we had a discussion on a particular area of technology one week, if we had a meeting the next week on the next theory of technology, by the time you tried to synthesize it all together, people could not remember all the information that was conveyed to them without having to flip through pages and pages of information. With this new visualization technique, it was interactive, it was collaborative, it helped facilitate the meeting, and it helped clarify the strengths and weaknesses of the projects.

According to team members, star-mapping has provided the team with several important benefits for its strategic planning:

Figure 3.2. ORC Star-Mapping.

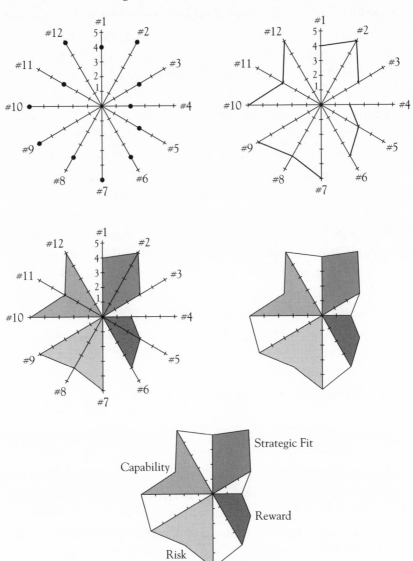

Supplementing formal analysis with pattern finding. ORC had previously identified weakness in attuning to patterns and trends as a main flaw in its planning process. Star-mapping enables team members to better see patterns and make sense of them. "You can stand back and look at the pattern [of all the star maps laid out in a grid]. And you go, 'It doesn't look right.' Then you can take a closer look in and say, 'There's something wrong with that particular star map.' And you take a look at an even closer level at what the attributes are, where the weaknesses are, where the strengths are, and how somebody mischaracterized those strengths and weaknesses. And only then do you take a look at the project name."

Legitimizing intuition. As technologists and scientists, people in ORC clearly have considerable intuitive power; however, the business organization tended to distrust and severely discount intuition. Star-mapping provides a structure that supports intuition but buffers its limitations. Because the star maps emerge from specific data, the process contains inherent checks and balances. "In the past we would just go with what the numbers told us. Now people are more comfortable saying, 'It just doesn't feel right. It doesn't look right. We're missing something.' Maybe our numerical criteria are missing something, and there's this project over here that, even though the numbers don't look right, my gut tells me that we need to be working this area. That [approach] has surfaced a number of projects that probably wouldn't have gotten looked at otherwise."

Fostering open dialogue and teamwork. By temporarily elevating intuition over critical analysis, star-mapping created a more level playing field. Quieter voices—often of those who spoke English as a second language—had more chance to contribute. The team would gather around a big table and look at and handle the star maps. They would make comments like, "This doesn't seem to fit. Where would you put it? What are you seeing that he isn't?" The process of arranging images into larger patterns helped to create dialogue. The team also felt that it "tapped into some natural areas of competency of the quieter people and that brought them out of their shells. 'More visual' is associated with empowerment somehow. The method of looking at and handling shapes has been very empowering because it gives everyone a hands-on approach, and equal footing at the table. There's less hesitation of some of the people lower on the ladder to raise their hand and say, 'This doesn't feel right to me.'"

Bringing negative space into strategic direction. Star-mapping illuminates negative spaces among the projects with respect to overall strategy. ORC members began asking: What do the spaces *between* the projects look like, and what do they imply? What are we not addressing? What's missing from the pattern? "Then we said, 'Is there anything wrong with this picture?' We stood back and looked at it as a group. 'What is different?' 'What is new?' 'What's exciting?' 'What shouldn't be here?' 'What should be there?' 'Where's the gap?'"

Using the hand to train the eye. Kinesthetic attention is a component of the star-mapping process. Not only do people produce the images and look at them but also they move them, push them sideways, and turn them upside-down. People actually hold star maps—they must grasp them in their hands as well as grasp them intellectually—and that helps them grasp the patterns created by the star maps as well. Sometimes members of the ORC team would fight about *how* they were moving the stars around the paper. Literally rubbing shoulders and literally pushing ideas (projects) around seems to facilitate resolution of conflict and promote community building.

An astronomer once told Chuck that he had learned to see more by drawing what he saw through his telescope. The lesson as he summarized it pertains as well to looking at any complex pattern: "The hand trains the eye." When you draw a picture, or build a collage, or put something visible and tangible in the middle as part of mediated dialogue—so that you're actually handling this something in the middle—the hand-eye connection helps you pay attention and image better. Your abilities to pay attention to images, construct them, and reconstruct them are deeply rooted in not just your brain but in your whole body.

Increasing the velocity of innovation. ORC is getting more and better products to market in less time, as measured by the standards of its innovation process, in part because of star-mapping and the wider distribution of strategic leadership among its knowledge workers. Star-mapping has given people the confidence to make decisions quickly that they previously would have agonized over. It has also given them confidence to stretch outside their usual conservatism in search of new projects.

The overall result for ORC in its push to see and respond to patterns more rapidly and collaboratively is impressive: the group's product R&D cycle has been reduced from five years to less than two and a half years. The value of completed projects has increased significantly. Low-value projects are identified and terminated earlier. And ORC's climate for creative work (as measured by the KEYS® to Creativity climate survey) has substantially improved.

Seeing Organizational Vision in a New Light

As more people participate in the process of leadership, it is helpful to realize that there is more than one kind of organizational vision. We find three different types of vision: abstract, direct, and imaginative.

Abstract vision tends to be the most commonplace, employed by managers and usually expressed numerically (often in bullet points): "Next year we will grow by 20 percent," for example, or, "We will be first or second in our market or leave." The concrete appearance of these phrases is largely an illusion, because the numbers describe nothing you can experience directly. Numerical abstractions (important though they can be) can easily fail to capture the passion and imagination of the organization, the vision that answers the questions Why are we here? What are we doing this for in the first place?

Direct vision and *imaginative vision* are most relevant when you face complex challenges and when you share leadership widely within the organization. One meaning of *vision* is simply *eyesight*, and by extension any mode of perceiving what is actually present. Direct vision refers to paying careful attention to what is really in front of you, watching with discernment where you are and where you are going. Organizational learning expert Fred Kofman calls this *the shared horizon*: what people working together see when they look up from their work.[5] Direct vision examines the essence of the organization—its identity and culture, its values and principles. A clear vision of the present includes a picture of where you stand, of velocity and direction, and of the current trajectory of where you are headed. Sometimes we call this *little-v vision*, contrasting it with the *Capital-V Vision* of the organization.

Imaginative vision takes up where direct vision leaves off. It asks, What if? and explores possibilities by creating images of what has not yet happened. Imaginative vision also inspires people toward a common goal. With imagination, you flesh out your inspiration so that it becomes tangible, compelling, and real. In this way, you sustain your passion and reinforce the belief that your inspiration can become reality.

In this pharmacy director's discussion of remodeling his business, for instance, he describes a combination of direct and imaginative vision:

> I had a vision . . . all the time of how I wanted [the pharmacy] to be and how I wanted it to work—but I never put it to paper and I never discussed edges and proportions and relationships. But that's what I had done in trying to frame and move and adjust and create this picture that I always knew existed. . . . I've always been able to do that in other areas. We go to movies and I'd say to my wife, "I enjoyed *that* but I would have done *this*." You know, then, it's just another expression of the artist in me. It's been enlightening to realize that I can be an artist in business.

Most managers crave exactness. For them, control means precise alignment. You could say that freight trains are well aligned; they get where they are going quickly and efficiently. You could also say they have *tunnel vision*. As a leader, you can use tunnel vision when you know precisely where you are going and if you have the engine, the tracks, and the cars to get there. (It also helps a lot if all the signals are working, and if other trains stay off your tracks.) But images and visions in this broader sense naturally have multiple interpretations. That's precisely what makes images helpful in addressing complexity. Images are *polysemous*, that is, they lend themselves to multiple meanings. These layers of meaning depend on unfolding circumstances. Polysemous images are a wonderful antidote to tunnel vision. When two people look at a complex image they most likely see different things—and this most likely doesn't surprise them. As a result, they can talk about the differences and similarities in what they see.

Likewise, events in organizations are polysemous, having many possible meanings. Managers are taught to use language to render gray areas into black and white. Organizations develop jargon, striving for language that is singular in meaning for the workforce. Although managers habitually work to pin meanings down, creative leaders realize that in a complex world meaning is elusive and that the existence of multiple understandings is potentially adaptive. The artistry of creative leadership lies in the differentiating and synthesizing of multiple understandings as part of a larger vision.

When you regard organizational vision as imaging combined with paying careful attention to what is in front of your eyes combined with using the abstract language necessary for business communication, then your creative leadership can bloom. Put images in front of the people in your organization, put images in their hands where they can move them around—and watch how they transform the images and their meanings in adaptive ways.

A masterful description of vision at work can be found in Marjorie Parker's book *Creating Shared Vision*. Parker describes how the CEO of an aluminum company led the workforce to the creation of a vivid pictorial representation of the organization, its major functions, and the work of everybody in it. The picture, and more important the process of creating the picture, enabled the organization to create a work of art that embodied meaning for the whole organization. With Parker's help, the CEO and his senior team envisioned the organization as a country garden—not a typical metaphor for an industrial organization, but one that conveyed the radical nature of the changes envisioned. With the help of a visual artist, the CEO communicated an incomplete image of the garden to the whole of the organization, which through a series of workshops completed the picture so that every employee owned every detail of the picture. Employees were thus passionately engaged in the ongoing mission of the organization.[6]

Exploring Scenarios

Scenarios are possible futures that people deliberately explore. Used by organizations to navigate through complexity toward a preferred future, scenarios are an increasingly common leadership tool.[7] We recommend an imaging technique for exploring future scenarios that we call *movie-making*. The *movie* made is a wall-sized collage of images and words that tells an imaginative story about where an organization might be headed or how certain challenges might worsen or resolve. Movie-making produces searching dialogue in a group faced with a complex challenge.

Typically, when we work with a group, one or several themes in the group's challenge become apparent over the course of the discussions. For a movie-making exercise, we lay out these themes, split the group into sections of four to eight people, and give the people in each section a theme (or have them select a theme) around which to make their movie.

Robin, a VP of software development, explains how movie-making with a large, diverse group of people worked in her company:

I used movie-making to explore a critical issue facing our division. All the attendees at the meeting were leaders of functional groups. Some were my direct reports; the rest were supervisors who report to my direct reports. I created two groups of four each. . . . We covered the walls with big, white rolls of paper. I also provided images from magazines, markers, ribbon, glue sticks, stickers, string, and other craft stuff. I instructed them to work fast and make their movies "as provocative as hell." *And they did!*

Small-Group Instructions for Movie-Making

Goal

A movie is typically fiction with a lot of truth in it. Think of making your movie as *building an imaginary pond with real frogs*. Your movie should explore your theme in a creative way (the imaginary pond), so that the movie can become a basis for a genuine, reality-based dialogue (the real frogs).

Materials

Butcher paper for each group (three meters long)

Scissors

Magazines, trade journals

Pens, pencils, paints

Directions

- Combine words and images on your roll of white paper to create a "movie." Use words and illustrated narrative sequences, moving from left to right.

- The plot for your movie should have these three parts: Once upon a time, there was an organization something like us. ⟶ Then one day something happened, a catastrophe, an invention, a revolution, or . . . ⟶ And so this is how it all turned out, for better or worse.

- Be sure to listen to the "quiet" voices. At some point, have the "big" voices take a turn being quiet.

- Show the movie to the larger group. Use it as a springboard for dialogue exploring your theme.

Tips

- Three meters of paper is twice what you think you will use, but take it; you will need it.

- If you get stuck creating a plot, just start arranging images on the roll of paper. Play with the visual ideas, and explain them later.

- If your group becomes stuck or encounters conflict between two or more members as it wrestles with the content of the movie, invent characters to represent the antagonists, and put them in the movie. Let the characters work out the conflict.

- Encourage your group to be inventive about the catastrophe; choose a "wild card" event (see Chapter 1).

- In the dialogue with the larger group, be sure to carefully explore the middle part of the plot ("and then one day something happened"), so the movie doesn't simply jump from the point of describing the challenge to "and they all lived happily ever after." Ask yourselves, What practical, new processes and events contributed to our progress from being challenged to finding a meaningful outcome?

One group created a movie that went something like this. *Once upon a time* there were four friends who worked at a computer software company which looked like *this. Then one day,* December 31, 1999, to be exact, they committed the perfect crime. They broke into the company directory and payroll system and changed all the employee titles and salaries. *Boss* became *Subordinate,* and all *Subordinates* became *Bosses. This created an interesting series of situations* in which everyone saw issues and problems from a totally different perspective, and they were better able to solve problems because of these new perspectives. The closing frame showed the words "Live the Dream."

This movie stimulated a powerful dialogue for us on these points:

- The need to see issues from more than one perspective

- The importance of acknowledging the perspective of corporate management

- The importance of acknowledging our clients' needs
- The importance of acknowledging our staff's needs and balancing them with what our clients need
- The need to "shield" our clients from our internal problems and issues
- The need to help staff see their clients' perspectives
- The need to improve communication of needs and expectations

Movies need not be about probable events. In fact, we find that the process works best when the group is instructed to build the plot around something "unexpected or even catastrophic." These days it is probable that something unexpected will happen.

Here are a few additional things to keep in mind when you are facilitating the technique of movie-making:

Group hesitancy. Before the process begins people might be concerned that movie-making will be too "touchy-feely." These concerns almost always fade during the dialogue, as real business issues get explored in depth and detail. In fact, increased "touching" and greater "feeling" about complex issues are a key objective of the exercise.

Analytical overdrive. When people start designing movies, their conversation at first is often abstract and analytical. You can facilitate groups' imaging process by encouraging them to "go up to the paper on the wall and start sketching out ideas." Once at the wall, people usually becomes more intuitive, imaginative, and playful.

Valuable metaphors. Metaphors created in these movies usually contain insights about the actual state of the organization, where it is headed, and the means to get there. The group as a whole can take away these metaphors and use them to craft and communicate mission, vision, values, and so forth.

Unpolished drafts. Keep in mind that these movies are more like unpolished drafts than finished scripts. They tend to be nonlinear and less integrated than a traditional story. These qualities are actually helpful to the ensuing dialogue because they invite revision and further what-ifs. Practice in making rough drafts and exploring visions is also good leadership practice.

Making and Using Metaphors

Metaphor is the technique of explaining one thing in terms of another, and it is a superb way of creating new ideas and understandings. Metaphor uses likeness as a gateway to the unknown. The word *metaphor* derives from the ancient Greek word *metapherein*, which means "to carry across." In the city of Athens, Greece, one sees the label ΜΕΤΑΦΟΠΑ *(metaphora)* on handcarts and delivery trucks.[8] Metaphors are the carts and trucks of meaning for the mind at work.

Most people use metaphor casually, neglecting the rich power of this device. But metaphors are a fundamental means through which people make sense of the world. For example, biologists talk of the *grammar* of genetic *code*. Engineers study *fatigue* in metals. Units of measure such as *foot, hand, yard,* and *stone* originated as universal comparisons that all merchants and artisans could gauge. A powerful metaphor was invented when the paper-and-pencil spreadsheet was carried across to become a computer interface on the original Apple Macintosh personal computers. This spreadsheet was a new way for novices to navigate effectively in computing space, and "when this power was extended on the Macintosh, the stage was set for a generalized rethinking of our relationship to information. The use of metaphor was so effective that, at some point, it was no longer clear where metaphor ended and reality began."[9]

Human beings are relentless borrowers of patterns, and the way in which thought, understanding, and action are linked is metaphorical in nature.[10] People are always scanning to see the familiar in new things. When someone spots such a likeness, he or she tends to say, "Ah, now I understand, now I can take action." Creative leadership means making this process more conscious and artful, as well as less automatic and prejudicial. Change expert Gareth Morgan has

observed that beneficial metaphors can be identified and propa-
gated. His ideas about organizational change are the basis for the
following model:[11]

Metaphoric ⟶ New   ⟶ Creative
thinking   understanding   action.

Morgan calls metaphor the genetic code of an organization: a
compelling image of "who and what we are" will replicate widely,
inspire people to act upon it or achieve it, and thus become self-
fulfilling. Hewlett Packard has directly embraced the metaphor of genetic code, recently summarizing the company's core principles and
disseminating them internally under the moniker "our HP DNA."

Metaphors as Invitations

Metaphors themselves aren't solutions to problems; rather, they are
invitations to explore new situations with fresh perceptions.[12] Because they are often ambiguous, they enable each person who in-
teracts with them to create her own images. Metaphors drawn from
sports, for example, are often effective because many people can relate to them from personal experience. But leadership often calls for
an image like orchestration—a less widely experienced metaphor.
We have recently spent time with Roger Nierenberg, conductor
emeritus of the Jacksonville Symphony. Roger helps organizations
develop a compelling metaphor of an orchestra to describe and reconcile organizational complexities. He sits the management team
amid a live orchestra—with musicians who have never worked before with Roger—and plays out various functional and dysfunc-
tional situations described by the business executives. Everyone
participates by listening, responding, or taking a turn at conducting. The situations come alive through music at its most beautiful
and its most cacophonous. All those involved readily carry both the
metaphor and its lessons back into the organization.[13]

To develop competency with metaphor, be aware that what you are building is a scaffolding of interpretation. A historical reason for some people's suspicion of metaphor is what psychologist Miller Mair calls the "tyranny of metaphors"—when the scaffolding is mistaken for literal truth.[14] For example, the useful metaphor of the machine has unfortunately led many to believe that many things literally *are* machines, including organizations, nature, and the human mind.

Metaphors for culture have cycles of influence. Some rise as others fade in meaningfulness. In one organization David belonged to, the vice president of marketing turned up for a presentation to his staff dressed to kill, literally. In his Rambo costume, with machine gun and belts of ammunition crossing his chest, he declared, "This is war." David recalls thinking: "That's not why I come to work. This has no meaning for me. He's more likely to shoot one of us than any of the competition." The sports and war metaphors that have dominated Western business and defined its culture in the past are now wearing thin. In recent years, businesses' cultural metaphors have been more likely to invoke webs (the Internet), ecologies (Amazon.com), or play spaces (Nickelodeon, Sony).

Ask yourself, ask your people, and inquire of your context: What is the next metaphor? What new invitation will help us explore the next steps in facing our complex challenges? What metaphors have worn thin?

Metaphors in Practice

Metaphors can be used internally and externally. Internally, leaders can employ metaphors to disseminate ideas, inspire passion and creativity, solve problems, and invite collaboration. Externally, metaphors can be used to disseminate brand identity, sell products, and build relationships with customers.

Donna used a metaphor to help her cross-functional team think about the problems *Chemstar* faced. To overcome quality problems, the company's R&D lab had been focused on inventing new chemicals. This strategy sprang from the company's founding pattern of inventing radically new technology. But the lab team had a breakthrough with this insight: "In our culture we keep wanting to invent something new as a way out of our problems. That often has been successful. But that approach leaves us with too many new formulations with their own problems. We need to learn how to tend what we already have experience with—our garden."

Donna and the team came to view their work as a garden in which they grew many useful plants—a metaphor for what they manufactured. If a gardener has a problem in his garden, he doesn't replace the plants with all new ones. Rather, he looks long and hard at what already is growing and goes from there. Through this metaphor, the Chemstar team members reconsidered their plan to invent a new line as a way out of their problem. This decision, in turn, legitimized the people on the team who had wanted to leverage existing technology rather than invent something new. Yet another breakthrough came when team members overhauled the product cycle, again bypassing the lure of the classic "let's invent something new" fix. The garden metaphor offered a way for the team to think about a dimension of the problem and to make that dimension perceptible.

Richard Zaltman of the Harvard Business School has developed a novel use of metaphor for marketing professionals to use, which he calls the Zaltman Metaphor Elicitation Technique (ZMET).[15] Zaltman makes the point that thoughts travel as images. The ZMET technique employs images to get at consumers' underlying relationships with products. Product marketers help consumers describe their experiences with a product by having them cut pictures out of magazines that represent their intuitions, thoughts, and feelings about the product. Groups of subjects are invited to the lab to speak about the product by using the images. The conversations are highly metaphorical and deeply revealing, illuminating associations that lie far beneath the surface.

The sanitized language people use in business masks the richness of their deeper knowledge. Human reasoning about something always mingles with emotions and hands-on experience. Thus it is no surprise that words often fail people. Treating metaphor as if it were merely a decoration for language is a mistake. In the next section, we look at poetry in this same functional way—not as lines on a page but as a vehicle for metaphorical thought.

Making Poetry in the Face of Complexity

When we speak of poetry, we mean it in a broader sense than literary verse. A poetic frame of mind is invoked whenever individuals consciously use metaphors to make sense of experience. Poetry, said author Harry Emerson Fosdick, is "a profound matter briefly stated." Poet David Whyte asserts: "Poetry is not about the experience, it *is* the experience."[16] As Whyte suggests, there is a profound difference between an *event*, which can be described in literal terms, and an *experience*, a kind of drama for which literal thinking is never fully adequate. Wall Street investment banker and published poet John Barr believes that both "business and poetry are organizing activities that are carried out by the self in response to a chaotic world."[17]

The Intersection of Poetry and Creative Leadership

As an element of creative leadership, poetry lies at the juncture of language and the C2 Competencies. Leaders today are expected to be brief yet inspiring, profound, and precise in their public speech. Poetry can provide both the precision and profundity that leaders today seek. Poetry offers a kind of communication that speaks to people's heads, hearts, and imaginations.

President John F. Kennedy's poetic sensibility made him an able critic of the words and images put forth by others. Speaking at the dedication of the Robert Frost Library at Amherst College, he described the value of poetry, offering a reminder that poetic sensibility guides strong, effective, and just leaders. "When power leads man towards arrogance, poetry reminds him of his limitations. When power narrows the areas of man's concern, poetry reminds him of the richness and diversity of his existence. When power corrupts, poetry cleanses. For art establishes the basic human truth which must serve as the touchstone of our judgment."[18]

Val, a former VP of marketing in the computer industry and now a strategy consultant, has found an area of competence for herself at the intersection of strategic planning and poetry. Val has connected her vocation (business) with her avocation (literary poetry), to become a creative leader:

> I now call myself a poet. But first it was a hobby, then I made it an interest, and then I said, "No. I know that the essence of who I am is a poet." I've started to realize how being a poet makes me a stronger business person. Before, I used to separate them. I believe the reason I am so strong at making connections, particularly between disparate things, is because I'm a poet. When approaching a business problem, in general I'm not going to see it vertically or linearly, I'm going to see it much more horizontally and holistically; I'm going to connect the dots more quickly. Being a poet means that I play. I play with ideas. I play with words. I juxtapose things. That's what we do when thinking strategy. You have to bring people with you—and to do that you have to paint them a picture.

Using Poetry as a Tool

Poetry has developed a unique home and performs an unusual role at the *Johns River Station*, a coal-fired power plant. The engineering managers learned about a Japanese form of poetry, haiku, from us, and they shared it with others at the station. Traditional haiku is a three-line poem with five syllables in the first line, seven in the second, and five in the last. Haiku caught on quickly at Johns River Station, especially during the highly stressful outages, when the plant shuts down for round-the-clock maintenance and troubleshooting.

An unplanned outage can happen anytime. But one is planned for maintenance every year at about this time. There's a lot of work to be done and we are stretched very thin. When you're doing technical work you have to keep a logbook going. You record events to help people because the next shift's got to take it over from there. If you're in the plant and there's been some weird thing happening you've got to pass the log on to somebody so they can continue the work. Now we [also] keep a book of haiku where each of us shares our struggles during these high stress situations.

Workers write the haiku for themselves and for each other. They capture the essence when "there's been some weird thing happening" and pass on this essence to the next shift. At a calmer moment we witnessed the team using this haiku collection to recall stories of past events from which they had individually or collectively learned. As they sat around a lunch table, workers read their poetry and laughed, remembering the experiences in minute detail, with obvious affection for each other and the memories—and acknowledgment of the pain they had all suffered.

The engineers at the plant grapple with titanic problems. The work can be life threatening. The competency of *serious play*, discussed in more detail in the next chapter, is reflected in their use of poetry. Outages are so stressful that levity is required to balance them. This poetry has depth; it provides a way to play with strong emotions and explore the challenges individuals face. Some poems discuss heroism. Others invoke worry, relief, and wisdom. Each holds a story or a mystery (see page 98).

Developing the Competency of Imaging

Imaging is a part of what author Eric Booth calls "the everyday work of art"—but it takes practice and awareness.[19] Here are some ways to further develop your imaging competency at both the personal and community levels.

Johns River Station Haiku

The Outage

The outage is coming,
The outage is coming.
One if by MD&A,
Two if by FW/Zack,
Three if by GE;
Aspirin
Aspirin
Aspirin!!!

Blast Gates

Worn, leaking badly
Fly ash here, there, everywhere
New gates, new life, great.

The Higher Haiku

Thin like margarine
All my footsteps are guided.
We've got it covered!

The Spot

Docks, drains, separators, ponds;
Sheens, smells, spills, and leaks.
Ever moving,
Never found.

Shelley's Haiku

Normal day
Concerns arise.
Stress, tears, prayer
Good report, rejoice!

Developing Individual Competence

Employing a journal and searching for your own root metaphors are two excellent ways to increase your personal competency in imaging.

Visual Verbal Journals. Practically all scientists, artists, and inventors keep some form of what we call a *visual verbal journal* (VVJ), a journal of both words and illustrations, for tracking their observations and ideas. VVJs are an effective way to develop your competence in imaging. First, they are typically private, so they provide a place to try out ideas before taking them public. Second, a working journal integrates the technical and the personal and provides a risk-free place to develop your personal voice and style. Lastly, keeping up a VVJ blurs the lines between R- and L-modes—words and pictures, analysis and synthesis, thought and emotions, focus and tangent—and thus is ideal practice for creative leadership.

The technologists at ORC often explored new angles in their journals. Says one manager: "When an event occurs, I make a picture about it in my journal. Later, looking at the picture, I notice so many things. In the middle of the discussion or meeting, you miss so many details. By remembering it with the picture I can see important details that went unnoticed. Many times that's the solution."

Another emerging leader told us:

> Journaling is a regular thing for me now. I am not artistically inclined, but I have done some drawing in it. I'm an engineer, so I'm going to diagram things; I'm going to flowchart things. If I want to do just a special piece of correspondence, I go to that VVJ and work it out there before I do it in final form. I had a situation with a peer where he and I disagreed. I rarely am raised to the level of anger—I pride myself on control—but this time was difficult. I used the VVJ to work it out and then addressed it with the peer. Without the VVJ it would have been much longer, and more collateral damage would have been done.

If you don't currently keep a visual verbal journal, start one. If you are already in the habit of keeping a VVJ, make sure you use it for observation and analysis as well as aesthetics. Use it to craft new ideas and play with old ones. For artists and creative professionals a VVJ tends to be mainly aesthetic but with a great deal of analysis and even science: What works? How do we know? What's the formula?

Here are some tips for keeping a VVJ:

- Keep it in a notebook separate from other papers. Plan on a series of such journals, with nice bindings. Embellish the cover with symbols of your personal identity. Keep it in a private, protected place.

- Cultivate an artistic style in your journal sketches and illustrations. Acquire a fine set of colored pens strictly for the journal. Some people like to use a high-quality fountain pen for entries.

- Cultivate a scientific style in the way you gather and weigh evidence, and create new hypotheses.

- Pick a theme for the journal and stick to it. Don't let the VVJ become a catchall. Consider keeping more than one journal, each with its own focus. A theme might be personal—your career development, for example, or important life lessons. It might be scientific—some key question you want to crack. Or it might be one particular complex challenge.

- Some people prefer to keep their journals on the computer. Keep a special file, intended for permanency and regularly backed up. Date the entries. Paste in items from other sources.

- Return regularly to past VVJs in order to reflect on ideas and gain insight into your development. One of our colleagues spends a day around every tenth birthday—at age thirty, age forty, and so on—dusting off and reflecting on the entries of the past decade.

Root Metaphors. Deep within individuals exist metaphors that guide the way they are, the lives they live, the things for which they

feel passion, the work they desire, and the work they do that sustains them or takes them to the next step in their leadership journey. These root metaphors are the images you return to when
describing yourself and making sense of your life. They are touchstones and beacons that guide you. They are lighthouses that keep
you from foundering on unseen rocks, or distant stars that exert a
pull on you that maintains your orbit or trajectory.

Organizations and individuals alike have metaphors woven into
the fiber of who they are and how they act. Yet people are often unconscious of these metaphors. Part of your leadership journey has to
do with discovering these metaphors by paying attention to your
own life and tracing consistent themes and patterns that play out
over your life.

Root metaphors in their detail are as unique as DNA. One person
is a rock. Another identifies with an eagle. One executive we worked
with thinks of himself as a farmer. His metaphor helps him notice the
emergence of a new idea or opportunity, weed out unworkable experiments, and patiently nurture an idea into a ripe application. As a
manager of other scientists, he finds that the farming metaphor guides
him in creating an environment in which the work of others flour-
ishes. It provides him with a source of compelling language for envi-
sioning the growth of his department and the people in it.

For example, when David Horth was a child of nine, his father
told him the family members were direct descendents of the great
explorer Ferdinand Magellan, the first to circumnavigate the world.
David was over forty before he realized just how well the Magellan
metaphor has guided his life. For David, exploration into uncharted
territory, whether out in the world or inside himself, has been a constant theme. Fascinated with the process of innovation he has been
an R&D engineer in the computer business. Passionate about music
he has also been an itinerant folksinger. He has worked and lived in
several countries, beginning these peregrinations at a very early age.
As a leader, he has sought to navigate new areas of endeavor without the aid of well-documented maps.

Metaphorical storytelling is a powerful device for developing
skills in using vivid imagery and imagination. It is also a method for

discovering the metaphors that punctuate your individual leadership journey.

What are your root metaphors? Have they come from family, teachers, fables or nursery rhymes, catalytic events, geography, history, literature? How do they play out in your life and your leadership work? How might they guide you through intricate challenges? How do they illuminate your strengths and development challenges? Take the time to think about your root metaphors and then write your thoughts down or diagram them in your visual verbal journal. Keep these metaphors in mind when you find yourself stumped or run into roadblocks—you just may find a new perspective there.

A root metaphor is a deep connection between personalizing and imaging. It is a source of images as you develop as a leader. The metaphors that enlighten you about who you are are the same ones that will help you navigate through turbulent waters. Your root metaphors are a powerful connection to your passion. They will evolve as you evolve.

Developing Community Competence

Old-style imaging is a top-down affair in which visions and symbols are used to control behaviors. New-style imaging is a participatory affair that leaders and communities can encourage in a number of ways.

Develop Physical Space. Physical workspaces can either enhance or limit people's ability to share their imaging. Create workspaces that incorporate reusable wall space for building collages, sketching, movie-making, and similar activities. Repurpose traditional spaces such as bulletin boards, whiteboards, hallways, windows, and external cubical walls. ORC created a *war room* dedicated to ongoing strategy development and competitive analysis. The latest iteration of the star maps could usually be found on one wall, comparative activities of competitors on another.

Develop Virtual Space. Make an accessible studio and gallery in virtual space for shared imagery. Shared digital whiteboards allow people to sketch ideas as they talk or mark up documents. Digital cameras are now cheap and easy to use and let people post pictures of what they are discussing on line. The Motley Fool is an on-line personal finance resource that uses vivid storytelling as a way to personalize otherwise abstract topics (as discussed in Chapter Seven).

Legitimize Visual Analysis. Communities legitimize the kinds of *languages* people can use to communicate. If town meetings are conducted entirely in business-speak and bullet points, that sends out a message about the ground rules for participation in the community. The Orion Research Center greatly enhanced leadership participation by people in various cultural and functional groups when management legitimized storytelling, metaphors, and the use of image-based processes such as star-mapping.

Increase Shared Imagery. Too often corporate images are imposed from the top down and are officially hands off. Shared meaning making requires that people be able to get their hands on the images in circulation, morph them as a way of sense making and communication, and receive feedback from others on the impact of the evolving images. When you establish a norm of handcrafted imagery, you encourage and support others' participation in leadership. Try banning PowerPoint for just one meeting, and use only paper and colored markers instead. Ask directors to create public displays or posters for their quarterly reports instead of packets of numbers that few others ever look at. *Steve*, a regional sales manager, had his team create a twenty-minute video of a breakthrough project with a key client. The video became a point of pride and was circulated to other sales regions.

Continue to Develop Trust. For inspired collaboration, groups need to be open and honest. Community members must be able to comment on the functions and aesthetics of organizational imagery without fear of censure. How you encourage collaborative imaging— and how you respond to the results of collaboration—sends the strongest message.

Cautions

Like any of the other C2 Competencies, imaging comes with risks as well as advantages. Competence in imaging comes from practice and from watching others who are good at it. Images tend to be more slippery and open to interpretation than words—although language is saturated with metaphor, and in practice the control it offers is often illusory.

Cultural considerations. General Motor's Nova brand-name— evoking "bright star" in English—hit a bump in Mexico, where in Spanish *no va* means "won't go"! The Hewlett Packard icon of the original Palo Alto garage in which Dave Hewlett and Bill Packard began the business is intended to stand proudly for the idea of invention. But German consumers tend to have a very different interpretation of the garage icon; they see it as a decrepit old shack—the antithesis of high-technology cutting-edge products that the image intends.

Threats to established order. Imaging invites participation, which can sometimes threaten established order. When ambiguity and uncertainty are explored through images, people at all levels may experience anxiety over losing the known comforts of authoritative leadership. When you use images to help people discover their own path through the complexity, you practice a new order of leadership. Imagery provides a new source of participative meaning making; however, organizations are just beginning to understand what Sally Helgesen calls *webs of inclusion.*[20]

Manipulating images. The scientist Richard Dawkins writes, "A brain that is good at simulating models in imagination is also, almost inevitably, in danger of self-delusion."[21] Images are not free

from misuse. They can be employed for enchantment and deception.[22] They have been used to impose tyranny. Hitler used the new
media quite powerfully to construct a nightmarish vision and project it onto the senses of the population.

Visual capture is what psychologists call the tendency of compelling visual input to invade and hold our attention. Television,
advertising, and architecture, for example, take advantage of the
power of the image to seize the imagination. James Joyce called this
"the ineluctable modality of the visual." The danger is that misin-
formation and stereotypes can be forced on us through aggressive
imaging techniques.

Maintaining checks and balances. Every metaphor both illuminates and hides. The latter trap is sprung when individuals come to
believe that their particular *image* of reality is reality itself. Several of
our colleagues at ORC see danger in unbalanced reliance on images
and pattern perception: "Biases in some cases were built into the visual images [star maps]. Yes, I do see patterns. I see patterns a lot.
Sometimes I see that as a hindrance. I try to struggle not to fall into
a certain thinking pattern or behavior pattern. Because once you've
fallen into the pattern, then you probably lose the creativity."

The role of the leader-poet is often to "make it strange," providing eye-popping perspectives, shaking people out of their ruts.
The trouble is, that which shakes us up can dig the new rut: "We
may thus be caught and fossilized by the very power available to us
in particular metaphors . . . [if] we take a similarity as evidence of an
identity, if we come to believe that our particular metaphoric view
of reality is in very truth reality itself."[23]

Yes, there is danger in creating new images—and there is danger in
not creating them. In times of complexity, soliciting wider participation in creative leadership becomes vital. Literacy in imaging,
then, is a necessary complement to verbal literacy for empowered
consumers, employees, and leaders.

How often do we effectively make and remake our visual world
rather than passively succumb to its enchantments and deceptions?

How can we create the metaphors that allow positive growth and change? These are important questions for creative leaders to answer in their own realms of influence. The curriculum for a twenty-first century literacy of imagery is still largely unwritten, but it can be discovered in the context of the other C2 Competencies—paying attention, personalizing, serious play, co-inquiry, and crafting. The cultivation of your own critical poetic sensibilities, in the broadest sense, is a good base from which to competently create images, discern their meanings, and guard against their excesses.

Chapter Four

Serious Play

In the new workplace the lines between work and play are blurred. Organizational learning expert Peter Vaill explains why. In the face of complexity and chaos the most strategic competency one has is "the capacity to shelve one's competence in favor of an openness to the new."[1] This concept is not new but perhaps rediscovered. A Chinese proverb, for example, instructs, "To learn something, give up something." If individuals are to practice fruitful unlearning, shelving their competence and opening up to the new, they must loosen the tight grip of control and take on the mind of the beginner. What do beginners do? Good beginners play.

Play introduces a light touch of curiosity and a selective relaxation of constraints that can transform serious work. We call this type of play *serious play*. It is the generation of knowledge through free exploration, improvisation, experimentation, levity, and sport.

The term *serious play* has recently entered social sciences vocabulary from several directions, even as we have noticed its qualities in our leadership research. Social psychologist Kenneth Gergen uses the term to describe a way in which people can communicate in spite of entrenched differences. Serious play, according to Gergen, is a style of communicating that explores similarities and differences, not by deconstructing the other's point of view (an all-too-frequent response), but by playfully exploring new combinations of perspectives for something fresh and useful.[2] Serious play in this view is a matter of learning to hold your deepest beliefs lightly for a moment, rather than squeezing more tightly when they are challenged.

Michael Schrage, researcher at the MIT Media Lab and author of *Serious Play: How the World's Best Companies Simulate to Innovate*, describes innovation through the use of models, simulations, and prototypes as *serious play*. Schrage believes that "you can't be a serious innovator unless you are willing and able to play."[3] Managers have a bad habit of using only abstractions for thinking about innovation. Serious play is a matter of building a *toy* in the best sense of that word—a model or a prototype—and then batting it around with others exuberantly and creatively; often it breaks. Innovation is often more visceral than cerebral.

The qualities of play—curiosity, exuberance, spontaneity, improvisation, uninhibited movement and thought, a feeling of being outside of time—have unfortunately been largely purged from people's increasingly efficient organizational lives or confined to the few "creatives" that organizations hire to play for them. Psychologist Carl Jung once said, "The creative mind plays with the object it loves." We observe that the inverse is often true as well: through play the mind becomes creative and falls in love with the object of play. In this chapter and throughout this book we will return to the idea that putting something in the middle of one's community and playing with it is a way to make shared sense of a complex challenge.

Serious play develops energy. It fires up new commitment from you and your colleagues and spurs you on. Serious play takes you on excursions, which may at times appear to slow your forward progress. But true progress in times of complex challenges is best measured, not by output or progress against a schedule (a characteristic of *technical* challenges), but by the new sense you are making of the situation.

In this chapter we examine how people learn from serious play and how they can incorporate the qualities of play into the service of work. Three central attributes of play are what make serious play so important:

- Play enhances learning amid turbulence.
- Play is a community activity.
- Play is the heart of science and technology.

Play Enhances Learning amid Turbulence

Children play as a way of learning how the world works. Too often adults neglect the gift of play, not realizing that its mature forms are effective tools for learning in the midst of an ever-changing world. According to organizational learning experts Fred Kofman and Peter Senge, "Learning often occurs best through play—through interactions in a transitional medium where it is safe to experiment and reflect."[4]

In *Managing as a Performing Art*, Peter Vaill introduces an intriguing metaphor for the change and uncertainty that now characterize organizational life: *permanent whitewater*.

> Most managers are taught to think of themselves as paddling their canoes on calm, still lakes. . . . They're led to believe that they should be pretty much able to go where they want, when they want, using means that are under their control. Sure there will be temporary disruptions during changes of various sorts—periods when they'll have to shoot the rapids in their canoes—but the disruptions will be temporary, and when things settle back down, they'll be back in the calm, still lake mode. But it has been my experience . . . that you never get out of the rapids. . . . The feeling is one of continuous upset and chaos.[5]

The ways that people develop efficacy in the turbulence of whitewater are suggestive of the ways people can develop efficacy in the turbulence of organizations. Let's explore Vaill's metaphor in more depth, keeping in mind that we are connecting and applying three C2 Competencies: imaging, personalizing, and serious play.[6]

The metaphor of permanent whitewater speaks strongly to us as authors, both as professionals who have spent considerable time studying individuals and organizations in the midst of change and as experienced whitewater river runners. During the past twenty years Chuck Palus has kayaked many expert-class eastern U.S. rivers, including the Upper Youghiogheny River, the upper Gauley

River, and the Chatooga River. David Horth is an advanced novice who, in a raft, has tasted the joy and fear of Class 5, the most difficult level.

One of the first lessons of whitewater comes from *reading the river*. A novice river runner typically sees what appears to be a random froth of rocks and water. Properly speaking, however, whitewater is not random; it's chaotic. Chaos has random elements, but it also contains exquisite patterns. The chaotic patterns of rivers are related to the natural patterns in cloud formations, leaves, and so forth. The study of chaos in complex, dynamic systems continues to emerge as an exciting field.[7]

In rivers the patterns of a current tend to be quite stable, so that a snapshot of any single area at one moment looks the same as a snapshot at another moment, even though the area is occupied by different water molecules at each moment. Reading the river is a matter of recognizing the patterns within currents and learning the effects of those patterns on boats. The most important element in a whitewater pattern is water that moves upstream. Yes, *upstream*. Certain features in the underlying riverbed offer resistance to the fast-moving water, creating eddies and waves of localized, upstream currents. You might think of the overall pattern as one of great masses of water moving more or less straight downstream but embellished at the edges by circular swirls, or *turbulence*. These swirls make all the difference. A skillful boater can, with little effort, place his or her boat on even a small eddy and use its action to slow down, turn, stop, or even move upstream.

How does one learn to read a river? First, from instruction in the types of river patterns and the rules for navigating these patterns and, second, through play. Skillful play is a hallmark of the expert boater. This play consists of stopping at some point in the current and exploring a single pattern or a series of patterns. For example, a boater might play by *surfing a wave*, moving back and forth across a stationary river wave rather than moving downstream with the current. This play involves discovering rules and testing them, breaking rules and inventing new ones. It requires relative safety, so that the consequences of breaking rules will be minimal—for instance, the boater plays above a large, still pool rather than above a dangerous waterfall.

A popular metaphor describes *shooting* a whitewater rapid, but that is a clumsy notion. It implies riding the mass of water as a kind of projectile, with the swirls functioning as impediments. (Don't we all tend to think of turbulence in any realm as an impediment?) Shooting a rapid is the act of someone with an undeveloped reading of the water. A more useful metaphor describes *playing* a rapid. "She played the rapid with ease" indicates confident, skillful negotiation. Serious play is a spirited way of deeply but safely exploring patterns that have significant longer-term implications. For example, part of the boater's reason for playing on this wave today is that tomorrow she may need to surf a wave to avoid a dangerous waterfall. All whitewater play is a little bit serious.

The lessons to be learned from the whitewater metaphor are many. The chaos of whitewater requires innovation at crucial moments, just as chaos in professional settings does. As Peter Drucker says, "The greatest danger in times of turbulence is not the turbulence; it is to act with yesterday's logic."[8]

Chaos in organizations is not random. Organizational turbulence is full of patterns. Developing competence in reading your organizational river is not a frill. Enfolded within chaos are initially unimaginable layers of order. The nature of this order can be surprising and is sometimes invisible to conventional wisdom. Turbulence can be an aid, rather than an impediment, to prediction and control. This seems counterintuitive, but the leverage is this: patterns repeat, in time and across dimensional scales. Here are some ways individuals learn the patterns:

- Constantly ask the questions, What am I seeing now? and, What is *this?* as a way to ensure fresh observation and to avoid seeing only the analysis or pattern you wish to see. After a while, with your patience and attention, the new patterns will present themselves, sometimes snapping into focus in a moment of epiphany.

- Love or learn to love the patterns for their own sake before trying to exploit them. If you spend the enormous amount of time it takes to read turbulence and you don't have some love (or at least deep respect) for the materials that form the turbulence, the chaos can literally make you sick.

- Deliberately introduce a small, temporary amount of turbulence and observe how the old patterns shift and new ones form. Creativity scholar Stan Gryskiewicz recommends inviting a guest speaker from outside your field into your organization and looking for transference of ideas and clarifying metaphors.[9]

Play develops your eye for patterns within chaos. Play is essential for finding the patterns with chaos that lead to action and innovation, and serious play is a vital supplement to traditional learning. Being consistently rule-bound is crippling when the situation you face is beyond the rules. Organizational play develops your eye for patterns, but it requires safe places in which you and others can break rules, make mistakes, and recover—and then try it again. Discover play processes for your organization. Find higher-order rules that will govern breaking rules with relative safety.

Fundamental innovation comes from serious play on the fringes of the organization. Groups of mavericks busy violating common sense aren't all that bad. It is all too easy to dismiss the playful passion of those "surfing upstream." Creative leadership will act to ensure that making sense of chaos or turbulence is ultimately a community venture that includes both those engaging in analysis at the center and those playing at the fringe. Make sure that speculative projects at the edges of the community (called *skunkworks,* says Tom Peters, perhaps because of their different scent) are not in exile from the community. Keep an eye out for what Clayton Christensen has identified as the *innovator's dilemma:* new technology often contra-dicts established mind-sets and comes from players at the periphery.[10]

Speaking of Play

Some innovative whitewater kayaks barely float. Maverick white-water enthusiasts have invented a kayak shaped like a potato chip. It has a very thin profile, slightly concave on top, with bubbles built in for the kayaker's legs. Because it contains only a small volume of air, this kayak almost doesn't float in calm water.

Does it sound unworkable? That is what common sense suggests—but here common sense is wrong. In whitewater, all or part of such a *squirt* boat can be made to dive beneath the swirls and into the masses of water beneath, which contain their own distinct patterns. These patterns are inaccessible to kayaks that travel only on top of the water. They afford means of river running and play that were previously unimaginable. This new design performs like a wing in the laminar flow of the deeper currents: it "flies" underwater.

The most recent kayak designs selectively incorporate both surface properties and squirt properties, so they can take advantage of every possible passageway. Some of these—short, sleek, and maneuverable—can be run on unusually steep and tortuous creeks. Extreme athletes now run waterfalls up to one hundred feet high; during this feat the critical variables include how well one's stubby boat performs as an object in free fall.

Sadly, the death rate among kayakers has soared in the last few years. The new designs have made it possible for less experienced people to play in more dangerous places. The paddling community is in the middle of a dialogue about the morality of risking self-destruction in pursuit of happiness. They have raised some powerful questions for any profession or avocation: What does it mean to play responsibly? When does serious play shade into folly? How do people make that call for themselves or others?

Improvisation amid action is a basis of effective leadership. Improvisation means thinking on your feet, and inventing the best moves out of your individual and collective repertoire. Often the best way to navigate a complex challenge, to go down an unknown river, is to form a good enough team, get packed, and go. A bias toward action goes a long way when you are dealing with complexity. Reflection requires that something tangible be in motion to reflect upon.

Play Is a Community Activity

Having the capacity for individuals to play together competently is a cornerstone for successful communities. Play is an inviting front porch activity, which then draws people inside to participate in deeper matters. Serious play is both a stimulant and a glue for meaningful community. One senior executive told us he was looking for managers who "play well with others." People who play well only by themselves often find that their results are either marginalized or co-opted as a bright veneer to disguise otherwise gray and dull products.

We have worked with a company called Play, which designs marketing campaigns and media events for companies such as American Express, PricewaterhouseCoopers, and Disney. Serious play is its core value; it is the way people at the company do their work. Says cofounder Andy Stefanovich, "Creativity is not a solitary occurrence. It's very much a collaborative effort. One person is as creative as the next. That creativity just needs to be discovered within each person. What we're doing is building a creative community—not mystifying creativity as a special talent of a chosen few."[11] Indeed Play's corporate climate for creativity pegged at the high end when we measured it with the Center for Creative Leadership's KEYS to Creativity survey.

What does community play look like at Play? First of all, everyone is on the creative team. Nobody is in a support role. The client's people are always pulled out of their stuffed shirts and into the spirit of play. "Play's willingness to push us was critical to the success of [our] project," says John Aman, brand officer for Nationwide. When any Play employee red-flags his or her project as a potential crisis needing group attention, no one goes home until the crisis is resolved. Employees hang out together, blurring the distinction between work and personal life ("I get to act like me," one explained). They take *radical sabbaticals* to explore unfamiliar territories, with a key purpose of bringing fresh *mojo*, or collective magic, back to the group. A posting on the *Fast Company* magazine article describing Play sums up the company climate: "Absolutely inspiring. Please hire me!"

Improvisation

Improvisation is a fresh and artfully rendered response to the unique complexity of a new moment, based in the depth of one's experience. In *The Web of Inclusion*, Sally Helgesen points out that improvisation is crucial to maintaining the weblike organizational structures that characterize the new economy. Sensitive to changing conditions, these webs constantly adjust and repair themselves. Information gathering and execution are often coordinated at the periphery of the web, which is in touch with but not tightly bound to the center of the web—an achievement requiring mutual improvisation rather than strict control.[12]

The Trucking Company (TC) is exemplary in using improvisation to leverage knowledge from the periphery of a weblike structure. Dispatchers at TC assign hauling jobs to a fleet of interstate trucks. The old method called for the dispatcher to refer to an optimized decision tree that considered such variables as driver seniority, client priority, cargo type, and so on. The new method mixes a powerful application of imaging with serious play. Everyone in the company is trained to recognize three modes of operation and to select the currently appropriate mode in relation to the level of turbulence in operating conditions. TC has named these modes *classical*, *jazz*, and *jamming*—seeing them as metaphorically parallel to these styles of music.

In classical mode, which is predictable and highly structured, the dispatchers follow a traditional set of optimization rules. When conditions are busier, dispatchers turn to jazz mode, which recognizes the increasing need for improvisation. Jamming is used during chaotic conditions, such as severe weather. During jazz and jamming, the structures for formal decision making are present but as *under-tones*. TC describes this process as "the strategic art of employing and deploying resources for the customer and the company." At TC, improvisation based on experience and conditions is not only permitted, it is expected and taught. TC employees play together—as a virtual team of drivers, dispatchers, and even customers—within the constraints of novel situations as they arise. Jamming is an ensemble performance: the dispatcher directs the band and the players share the lead. Dispatching in the jamming mode is highly regarded as effective grassroots leadership. The drivers, ever sensitive to fairness in work assignments, appreciate the individualized attention this system offers.

Trust

Serious play goes hand-in-hand with trust. People at play need to take risks together. If you create an environment where serious play is the norm, eventually trust also becomes the norm. One leader we worked with explains that he created this environment of trust through demonstration: "One of my department managers said to me, 'You know, my folks have told me they really appreciate that you go out on a limb for them.' That was interesting to me because I think that's another metaphor for risk taking. . . . [A]llowing myself to drop some of my natural reserve and be more flamboyant or demonstrate a bit of flare or certain [other] things that I've done, the way I've conducted meetings, have been helpful in letting people know that I'm willing to take personal risks."

A manager at the *Orion Research Center* describes how a coworker has thrived in ORC's seriously playful environment: "One of the wonderful things that V. did was bring a three-piece ensemble to play during the lunch hour—once a month or maybe once every two months. She actually brought in a mime one time to a business meeting. It was an environment where she could do that.

Yes, some people said, 'Oh, this is a waste of time.' But even if you didn't like it, it was a point that you could talk about and discuss . . . share your views, and communicate with your colleagues."

The motto at Hewlett Packard has long been "invent." A powerful moment at HP was the time Bill Hewlett found the door to the supply room locked. That would never have happened in the old garage where the company started, where trust and tinkering were the order of the day. Hewlett ripped the lock off with a bolt cutter and left a note that said, "Don't ever lock this door again."

Providing some structure for serious play helps manage issues of risk and trust around improvisation. Like jamming at The Trucking Company, serious play when structured takes on aspects of a (serious) game. A *game* can be defined as competition within constraints. The star-mapping process at ORC (described in Chapter Three) is an example of structuring serious play into a kind of game. The rules of the game might emerge in the playing. During one iteration of star-mapping, for example, *Richard,* director of the ORC Strategic Planning Team, invented straw voting with chocolate: "I said to the group, 'Well, here's the way you're going to vote today: we've got mint patties, ten for each of you, and you're going to actually load mint patties on the star map of what you think is the most appropriate project.' It brought the quieter people out of their shells and led to some frank dialogue. And quite a few laughs."

Play Is the Heart of Science and Technology

At the best, people come to technology from a heartfelt place. Yale computer scientist David Gelernter expresses this sentiment wonderfully: "Transformed childhood joy: That's why we do technology. . . . It's all emotion. When you think of technology, that's what you ought to think of—the kid riding his bike, or sledding downhill, or charging over a grass field trying to get his kite to fly, just because it feels great, it's the human thing to do."[13]

The spirit of scientific and technological innovation is the spirit of the playground: curiosity, experimentation, a thirst for knowledge.[14] When you combine this kind of passion with the C2 Competencies, the results can be astounding. Entrepreneur and theater artist Eric Booth only half-jokingly speaks of everyday artistry as "endless intercourse with attractive objects." (We explore Booth's observations about everyday artistry in Chapter Six.)

Such is the world of digital technology for many people, businessmen included. In his book *The New Thing*, Michael Lewis describes the restless, playful energy of Jim Clark, computer scientist and founder of Silicon Graphics, Netscape, and Healtheon. Clark changed the game of investment by taking Netscape public in 1996, before it was even close to making a profit. Lewis describes Clark's version of serious play: "He left himself open to accident. This was as true of his work as of his leisure; indeed, it was hard to say where the work stopped and the leisure began." Lewis reports, "I never once heard him refer to his ability to see the future. He couldn't see it—that's why he had to grope for it."[15]

An Eye for the Awry

Play has sparked many of the discoveries and innovations that have shaped modern society. It's a trade secret among scientists that discovery hinges on play. Scientists have an "eye for the awry" and are adept at capitalizing on experiments gone wrong. Writes scholar William Beveridge of the discovery of penicillin: "[Alexander] Fleming told me that he was just 'playing about' when he discovered penicillin, by which he meant he was not working on a planned research program. Nowadays . . . [there] is a strong disincentive to 'playing about.'"[16] It was also play that in the nineteenth century led Gustav Kirchhoff and Robert Bunsen (of Bunsen burner fame) to an understanding of the composition of the sun:

> One night, while working together in their laboratory in Heidelberg, they observed a fire raging in the port of Mannheim, ten miles away. Playfully they turned their spectroscope [newly invented, and previously used only on heated gases in the laboratory] in the direction of the fire and were amazed to observe the telltale lines of barium and

strontium. . . . [Kirchhoff] wondered out loud if it would be possible to focus their spectroscope upon the *sun* and learn that distant body's composition. Bunsen said, "People would think we were mad to dream of such a thing." Kirchhoff, undaunted, immediately set to work on this problem.[17]

Technology as a Playground

Many people today have learned to use a personal computer, and a fair proportion of these people first learned in the old days of the MS-DOS operating system (OS) and its arcane rules of operation. Learning DOS was difficult for many because playing with it was difficult—any mistakes made were usually costly. When the Macintosh OS came on the scene with its *desktop* metaphor, it introduced a radically different paradigm. Now people could learn complex ways of computing by playful experimentation, easily pushing the system's metaphors and secure in the knowledge that most mistakes would be reversible. We have found that people who don't play with their computers and learn only by the book or in classes tend to learn and innovate more slowly than people who do play.

What does technology mean to you? Is it a booby-trapped hazard or a serious toy that is fun to pick up, hard to put down, and filled with possibility? Many find surfing the Internet like playing with an enormous toy—and no doubt it has revolutionized the way just about everyone approaches communications, business, technology, and community.

Experimentation

A passion for *experimentation* is a major bridge from a dry technical mentality to creative leadership competency. *Donna* at *Chemstar* has a Ph.D. degree in chemical engineering. A breakthrough in her leadership came, in her opinion, when she began to apply the spirit of experimentation to her leadership role. "You know what engineers do?" she said to us. "Engineers experiment. They build experiments and try them out and see what happens. If I think about some of the human resource issues we've got here—some of the emotional issues, and so on—[I might ask:] Is there some experiment I can set up to cause something to happen? Is there some way I can apply who I am as an engineer to the new domain of human resource development?" Observed one engineering manager who worked for Donna: "We gained a willingness to try things that had typically been out of bounds. Not that there's more ideas but there's more willingness to *try* those ideas. For example we're doing a lot of things around shorting the pipeline that we never even considered. There's a new degree of freedom and a willingness to try new things."

An accomplished scientist on the Chemstar team described to us different styles of inventing polymers. As in whitewater kayaking, a rigid and formal style is not usually effective. Rather, a playful kind of tinkering with the complex materials at hand, rooted in R-mode but flanked by analysis and refinement, creates success. "People want to apply very rigid experimental design and statistics to these polymers. It doesn't work. The reason is there are at least twenty variables you have to control. You need a lot [of] analytical information on it but that's not enough. It's a lot of mixing things and looking, touching, feeling, observing, and chemical intuition. I think you can actually visualize what's happening to the molecules of the material and form a visual picture of the mechanism."

But don't make the mistake of thinking that only sexy new technology relies on serious play. Take a look at *Johns River Station,* the thirty-year-old, coal-fired power plant. *Pam,* the plant manager of JRS, told us how she now views the plant operators with a greater appreciation for their R-mode abilities: "We have good operators, people that operate the plant. I think that good operators function from the R-mode. Go into the control room, and if we have a problem you can see them working that way. They are not verbal. I think they are doing it from feeling, sensing, experimenting, and trying. They are in a zone." Once when an operator in the power plant had successfully restored full load, Pam had asked him to write down the sequence of things he had adjusted to resolve the problem: "It doesn't work like that," said the operator. "One day I might do the same thing and it doesn't solve the problem. I have to get a feel for it and I just have to play with it—you know what I mean?" We both observed this virtuosity on a visit to the plant. The lead operators found a problem and moved to correct it. It was like watching a master musician improvising at a keyboard.

Listening to Pam took David back to his days as a novice engineer in the computer business. One day in the fairly early days of large mainframe computers he watched in awe as a senior engineer played with the keys on the engineer's control panel while paying careful attention to the tones emerging from a speaker on the panel. He was tracking down, isolating, and finally, fixing an electronic fault a quarter of a mile from where he stood. "I'd like to be able to do that one day," thought David, "what fun!" Yet it was serious too. The fault had been costing the customer millions of dollars while the computer was down.

Developing the Competency of Serious Play

"Play subverts boundaries and opens us, sometimes painfully and against our will, to a wider field of experience and phenomena."[18]

Developing Individual Competence

To develop personal competence in serious play we recommend that you dig up your natural ability to play from wherever it has been buried. Take on the attitude of *irreverent student*. And suspend any demanding agendas or schedules you have long enough to let something new happen.

Realize You Already Know How to Play. Everyone is born with this competency. All right, yours may be a little rusty. You may have deliberately suppressed the urge to play when you joined a profession. If you want to participate in leadership, now's the time to get it back. A good place to start is in whatever avocation, hobby, or sport you enjoy—start doing it for joy rather than competition or compulsion. Then transfer some of that attitude to work, specifically those challenges that don't yield to command and control.

One manager told us: "Corporate life can be kind of dulling. You hear me yawn? Sometimes you need a stimulus to kind of wake up your latent characteristics and bring them to the fore and say, 'Who's going to fire me if I play music while my staff come into the staff meeting? Who's going to say that this doesn't work if I get the result I need?'"

Become a Student Who Questions Conventional Wisdom. Mathematician Jacob Bronowski once observed, "It is important that students bring a certain . . . barefoot irreverence to their studies; they are not here to worship what is known, but to question it."[19] Don't confront established wisdom head on but rather as a good learner, with a beginner's mind.

It helps to smile occasionally. During our research into the characteristics of a coachable manager, this strong criterion emerged: *does not take herself or himself too seriously*. Many managers are too serious, too perfectionist, too irritable, too unapproachable, too stiff, and too rigid. Although this attitude may work for command-and-control situations, it does not work for many challenging situations in this age of complexity. One group director we worked with reported: "I am becoming comfortable exploring. For example, I added cartoon graphics to a corporate presentation knowing it was a risk, but it paid off as many people at the meeting commented on the freshness and effectiveness." As a wise person once said, "The secret of life is finding out just how far to go too far."

Temporarily Suspend Your Formal Agenda or Schedule. If you're always walking a tightrope, you don't have any slack. Create time and space for something unexpected to happen; be alert for it when it does; and finally, play within that unexpected moment in order to understand and appreciate it.

St. Louis community leader Jim McDonald talks about the lesson he learned of "floating in an energized way." Between jobs, he was afraid of merely drifting. He coined the term *floating* to describe a more purposeful and more alert state. For McDonald, floating is a form of risk taking that counters the safety of filling up your time with what everybody expects you to do.[20] A union-management facilitator observes: "I'm feeling less at risk now in putting something playful in a serious content piece that I'm doing. The first time that we tried to conduct a labor dialogue here, I had this overwhelming sense of, 'Let's just play, let's roam. Let your mind go where it wants to go. It's outrageous but you can say it. That's okay.'"

Developing Community Competence

The enormously successful "Intel Inside" campaign is an example of how a manufacturer used playful techniques to make sense of its markets and improvise a strategy. When Intel's original 386 chip flopped in the marketplace, a small, pickup group of engineers and marketers was sent off to explore a fresh idea about reaching out to end-users rather than traditional OEM customers. Intel's culture encouraged constant, organic reorganization around what works. As a result this pickup team, with support and cover from top management, was able to organize as a flexible web rather than a hierarchy.

Team members pursued a daring idea, unheard of for Intel: touting the esoteric virtues of 386 technology directly to consumers. The basic components of this marketing idea were enacted faithfully on a small scale, in the city of Denver. The idea seemed to work. So they expanded the approach to twelve new markets, *taking a slightly different approach in each* to see what would happen. They introduced key innovations at this stage, such as starting advisory boards with Fortune 500 management information system directors and personal computer dealers. Slowly, Intel nurtured a network of PC end-users. The company realized a key refinement when manufacturers of 386 clones started muscling in on newly created consumer awareness. With the new clout of a recognized name, Intel branded the outside of every machine with "Intel In-side" labels.

Executive staff member Carlene Ellis observes that Intel "plays by sandlot rules," people work together, learn, and improvise as if some new kind of pickup game were being invented in a vacant sandlot.[21] How can you, as a leader, encourage sandlot play within your organization? How can you build community competence in serious play?

Networking Thrives on Improvised Relationships. All of us have noticed that the most valuable part of business conferences can be the unstructured time where we exchange ideas with others. Con-sider how you can cut across hierarchy or functional boundaries to create work-social networks. What forums can you adapt or create?

Invite Others to Play. Community play starts with this explicit or implicit invitation: "Who wants to join this effort? What can you bring? Relax and take a shot at this challenge with us." If the invi-tation comes from a boss, it is a form of permission. Loosen up for-mal communications so that they invite a seriously playful response. Invite rather than command.

Take an Excursion into Adventure Learning. Serious play can re-quire adrenaline and guts. You engage in this kind of play viscerally (that is, through your internal organs). This is the "old brain" feed-ing stuff into intuition, up into our consciousness, and back again. *Adventure learning,* play-oriented, team-building activities such as ropes courses and outdoor challenges, gives teams opportunities to practice working at the edge—with a net, both literally and meta-phorically.

Create physical spaces that invite play. Such an area might be a corner of your workspace, around the watercooler, or anyplace peo-ple meet and network in a more informal way than they do else-where in the company. The CEO of a bank with whom we have worked has adapted the boardroom to make a playful space where serious work is done. The room features high-quality art, hi-fi music and acoustics, and a waterfall. Traditional tools such as a projection screen are also available although normally hidden from view. The room is available to all employees for individual reflection or team meetings. The CEO's own meetings are typically framed by agendas that feature some level of personalizing or play to promote creativity in the collective work being done.

Play with Models, Simulations, and Prototypes. Playing with models, simulations, and prototypes is what Michael Schrage advises in *Serious Play.* These elements can become "toys" in the best sense. Prototypes let you try new things safely. They can give large numbers of people a common basis of experience for going forward. They let you put something in the middle of a practical dialogue. And if you break your new toy, you have probably learned something and had great fun in the process.

Harvest the Learnings from Play. Conclude play activities with time for reflection and dialogue. Ask your team, no matter the result of an activity: What have we learned from our improvisations and experiments? What powerful questions should we retain from this? Where do we go from here? How has this added to or challenged our knowledge base?

Cautions

There is a fine line between play and serious play. Play becomes serious only when you apply it. But as with any playful activity, serious play has its risks. Play can get out of control, accidents can happen, and players can get injured.

Here is a cautionary story from one of the professionals we've worked with: "I think becoming more playful has helped my sanity a bit, my perspective a lot, and my friendships. But it does create some difficulties. It's often seen as not being serious, and if I take a serious issue and make a joke, and I propose an outlandish thing, just for the moment—then there are inferences that involve my seriousness. I have to watch that I don't become agitating or turn others off by contrasting their seriousness with my playfulness."

A familiar way to screw up while playing is to take what is sometimes called a pratfall: taking a risk only to trip and become a spectacle. But organizational scholars Karl Weick and Karlene Roberts suggest that even pratfalls can be *artful* for those experienced at play. *Artful tripping* is above all *heedful*, these authors say, the kind of stumble that suggests not blind clumsiness but rather such cultivated qualities as, according to G. Ryle, "noticing, taking care, attending, applying one's mind, concentrating, putting one's heart into something, thinking what one is doing, alertness, interest, intentness, studying, and trying."[22] At play you are vulnerable; in tripping you may reveal your deeper self.

Here are tips for safe play in support of creative leadership:

Start small. If you are not naturally playful, start with little experiments in places where you are well supported. Make sure you can cover your losses.

Practice before jumping in. Play requires some skill, sometimes quite a lot. Watch someone else, then try and try again in a place that tolerates your potential pratfalls.

Make mistakes. Master photographer Dewitt Jones of *National Geographic* reminds us that "fear of mistakes is the single greatest enemy of the creative spirit."[23] Perfect sterility is the great danger of perfectionism. Try, fall down, get up, and try again. You will eventually learn to do this sequence artfully, even in public.

Don't play frivolously. Serious play is for serious challenges, not for comic diversion. Don't denigrate play by making it merely an "icebreaker." Childish play—unlike childlike play—is a step backward. Work toward serious goals, and make sure others understand the point of the play.

Play kindly. Check whether people are playing along. If they are not, desist, and find out why. When people around you get the idea that the play is all about your game and your way, then they don't want to play. Also be careful not to make other people the butt of the play, either intentionally or unintentionally.

Get lots of feedback. Play depends on timely feedback—accurate data about process and outcomes. Playing in the same rut all the time is incompetent. Remember, play is about learning.

Know where the exits are. Play can go unexpectedly wrong. Plan on getting out gracefully if there's a problem. Have a backup plan, but don't apologize for having tried to play.

Creative leadership makes shared sense of complexity and chaos. Much of the time this means throwing yourself into the teeth of it, getting spit out, reflecting a bit, and then going back in. Creative leadership needs people, lots of people (not just a few leaders), who are agile of mind, light on their feet, and have a sense of humor. Be sure to play with complexity because, surely, complexity is coming to play with you.

Chapter Five

Co-Inquiry

Complex challenges have a great urgency for action, but because they resist formulaic approaches, their solutions require deep and sustained reflection. The paradox inherent in confronting chaos— the paradox of urgency coupled with reflection—can be bridged by the C2 Competencies. Co-inquiry, the fifth competency, is a kind of social container that allows these competencies to work together in concert among diverse people and roles.

Collaborative inquiry, or *co-inquiry*, is dialogue within and across community boundaries. It involves cycles of action and reflective attention. Co-inquiry invites loyal skepticism, challenging questions, and a plurality of perspectives. Working with these elements, groups synthesize shared meaning. In particular, co-inquiry sustains a discerning community, one that critically tests the intuitions and tentative insights that arise during paying attention, personalizing, imaging, and serious play.[1]

Station manager *Pam*, for example, told us the *Johns River Station* had had "a horrific year of problems." Nevertheless, she could also report that people at the plant "have become a team of great problem-solvers. During our ten-week outage one company was causing an extension to the outage. We creatively used relationships, contacting people we would never have contacted. We don't just accept, we ask questions. We went far by being bold and not settling for people's first responses."

An important form of co-inquiry is *appreciative inquiry*, which focuses on asking, What are we really good at? Instead of focusing on finding problems, appreciative inquiry senses where the deepest strengths lie in the organization, identifies them, and then fully embraces those strengths.[2] For Pam, appreciative inquiry led to a breakthrough: "I stopped looking at what we don't do well, and I focused on what we do well. I started to observe the little opportunities rather than only the problems. And that's when things started to happen for me."

Co-inquiry is adventurous and illuminating—and often risky because it can take you and your colleagues into uncharted waters. In this chapter we talk about what is required to practice collaborative inquiry successfully while addressing complex leadership challenges. We examine five key ideas:

- Building creative leadership communities
- Creating spaces for group work
- Conducting dialogue
- Putting something in the middle
- Crossing boundaries

Building Creative Leadership Communities

Creative leadership has often been thought of as coming from a highly talented individual standing in front of a group of followers. This is at best a half-truth. Creative leadership arises from communities of people pursuing shared interests and passions. Increasingly, it is the people rather than the formal leaders who are carrying out essential parts of the leading.

No person is creative by himself or herself. Somebody else is always involved in making that creativity happen. You might be sitting there pouring forth an idea, but other people will have inspired you, directly or indirectly. New ideas and products evolve within networks. Great inventions always involve a confluence of ideas; they bring these existing ideas together to make something new and valuable.

The invention of Post-it Notes is an example of a truly collaborative effort that grew in the fertile soil of passion and loyal skepticism. Different people asked powerful questions all along the way. First, 3M research scientist Spence Silver discovered a glue that sticks to itself better than it does to anything else. For five years Spence gave seminars and buttonholed people about this unusual glue. Along the way he picked up a champion in new products manager Geoff Nicholson, and they both caught the attention of Art Fry. Fry was a researcher who sang in a church choir and found that his scrap-paper bookmarks kept falling out of his hymnal. During a boring sermon he imagined that a half-sticky piece of paper could really grow up and be something in the world. Fry solicited engineers who, after first pointing out how difficult this weird glue was to process, responded to Fry's plea: "If it were easy, then anyone could do it. If it really is as tough as you say, then 3M is the company that can do it." And there was VP Joe Ramey, who despite his initial reservations kept this suspicious little project from being killed. He cold-called on businesses up and down the streets of Richmond, Virginia, to see if they could sell the product. People couldn't keep their hands off the new notes, and the rest, as they say, is history.[3]

Co-creativity is what it's all about.

The quintessential image of the Wright Brothers envisions them on a windy beach at Kitty Hawk, alone with their machines. But a more revealing image of the brothers would depict them in Dayton, Ohio, living and working among an extended community of inventors—teachers, artists, and other citizens. According to scholar Patricia Gray, the members of this community helped each other create cash registers, washing machines, refrigerators, starters for gasoline engines, no-knock gasoline, and oh yes, airplane wings with a design that allowed engine-powered flight.

> [The Wrights] were nurtured by a community culture which revered
> self-discipline, education, and teachers, believed that the status quo

could and should be improved upon, and generally had a "can do" view of life.

It built and vigorously supported significant libraries, museums, performing arts organizations and spaces, public parks, and the community's infrastructure. It is this legacy that deserves understanding.[4]

Fostering co-inquiry within your organization means setting up both an environment that feeds creative exchange and an infrastructure for collaborative questioning. Wallenius-Wilhelmsen Lines, a global ocean-shipping company, uses what it calls *coaching groups* to organize around the work that needs to be done.[5] These groups meet at least three times a year to give each other feedback, coach each other, and ask powerful questions about their shared work. The coaching groups are typically made up of a superior and his or her direct reports. (Which means that each superior participates in *two* groups, one as boss and one as direct report.)

When people at Wallenius-Wilhelmsen Lines meet for the purpose of coaching, they operate under a set of dialogical ground rules: openness and honesty, mutual feedback, and an attitude of learning rather than defensiveness. Feedback in this forum starts with a focus on each person—"What am I doing well, and not so well?"—and shifts to a group focus—"What are we doing well, and not so well?" Other coaching groups cross functional lines. Members of these groups entertain what-if scenarios around difficult issues. The culmination of all this activity is that each group can make sense of its business at the level of service delivery to the customer and also now feed its evolving knowledge throughout the organization.

As you might expect, development of the coaching process at Wallenius-Wilhelmsen Lines was not without difficulty. Management first implemented coaching as part of a sweeping effort to modernize a traditional maritime company. The company was rigidly hierarchical and its culture was based in authoritarianism derived from the naval backgrounds of its many sea captains. A few of these captains did indeed dominate the coaching process and attempted to hide their own shortcomings. Such old-style authoritarianism was rather quickly and widely perceived as inconsistent with the new direction. As the culture shifted to a flatter and more leader-full one, those who would not accept coaching from peers, superiors, and subordinates were the ones to leave. Many employees saw coaching as a radically open door for evolution into something quite new.

Creating Spaces for Group Work

Having a dedicated, shared space is important for encouraging creativity in groups. Many offices today *hotel* their space and thus their employees. But work is not just something carried in people's brains, briefcases, and databases. Creative groups make workspaces their own. They put their personal and collective stamp on them. Less creative groups have members who personalize their spaces individually—hanging pictures in their cubicles, for example—but not as a team.[6]

People who work together effectively inevitably find ways to express the meaning of their work onto their shared space. A shared workspace functions as a sort of canvas, a place to think with the help of group objects, images, symbols, tools, and so on. "Innovation actually thrives on exchange. It's very social, and you want an environment that speaks to that," says Pfizer's George M. Milne Jr., executive vice president of global R&D and president of worldwide strategic management and operations.

Milne talks about designing spaces in Pfizer's new drug discovery building. There, work groups are organized into sets of seven called *families*, and ten families make a *tribe*. Each family and tribe has a gathering area. Traffic funnels through common areas designed to create what Milne calls *front-porch interactions*, serendipitous conversations among colleagues. Such interactions between scientists from different fields have led to significant discoveries. Pfizer itself was founded when a chemist and a confectioner collaborated on a pill to kill intestinal parasites. Milne believes intelligent building design can be an attractor for recruiting the best employees. Job candidates "can tell winners," he says, "and part of that has to do with the architecture."[7]

The best group workspaces we have seen incorporate some of the following features:

Low-tech and high-tech media. Corkboard walls can be used for butcher-paper maps, collages, and charts. Colored paper, scissors, glue, and similar construction materials encourage imaging and creative presentations. Digital collaboration is fostered by tools for Internet access, audio and video teleconferencing, and videotaping and by other interactive technology.

Various art and lots of it. Interesting objects, artifacts from diverse cultures, and artifacts of the trade stimulate idea sessions, exploration, and lateral thinking. A jukebox stocked with bring-your-own CDs can literally affect the tenor of a work group. Music as a regular feature at the beginning of meetings sets a tone. Changing displays of art from artists in the surrounding community, with opening receptions for the artists and the public, can also enhance the environment. Similar displays of art made by employees can be arranged.

Customizable arrangement and embellishment. Spaces that can be rearranged and decorated invite personalization and allow people to refresh their surroundings. The latest cubicle systems allow employees to make just-in-time rearrangements, by hand, without tools. For example, John Vernon, president of e-business consulting company Approach Inc., wanted to create "an idea factory" made up of quick and creative teams. Once employees were allowed to create their own space arrangement, says Vernon, "people wheeled tables around, they plugged in their computers in new places, they put them up against the walls, and they formed different groups." "You can create a new work area just by sliding the hanging partitions," says the company's architect. "Our space now is open, and our organization is open," says Vernon.[8]

Leave-it-for-later surfaces. These areas are for displaying short- and long-term projects, group member profiles, and competitor and partner profiles. They can also function as virtual team homerooms. Some groups set up *war rooms* equipped with everything they need to support a high-priority campaign. When the U.S. Army Future Group started pursuing a project, someone would say, "Let's put it on the wall," which meant gathering all the artifacts of what people were working on and pasting them up on a white space, connecting related points with string, and arranging everything as a flow.[9]

Coves and caves. A balanced interaction between private and public space fosters collaboration. Some arrangements have *caves*, private spaces for individual or one-on-one work, convenient to *coves*, large, open spaces for large-group interaction. Caves ideally will have space for a chairs-in-a-circle dialogue among as many as twenty-four people.

"Shoes of our customers" features. These features should be constantly evolving. Avery Dennison, Xerox, and Hewlett Packard all provide work teams with their versions of the "world's coolest" or "state of the future" work and home environments so that team members can play with and actually experience and live with new ideas.

Attractors. Attractors might be conversation nooks, toys, or coffee bars, things that promote front-porch interactions. Avoid designs that funnel employees from different office spaces away from each other. Create *collision areas* where people from different workspaces are compelled to share pathways. The renowned Aspen Center for Physics was designed so that people from otherwise disparate fields of physics would mingle. Founder George Stranahan says of this plan, "I really found you talk physics." He takes credit for too few bathrooms in the initial facility: introverted physicists would have to stand in line—and talk. Germinal conversation, according to the center's recent brochure, "takes place on the benches under the trees, in the halls between the offices, on the trails behind the campus or hiking in the surrounding mountains. . . . Frequently, a casual, spontaneous discussion gives rise to a new collaboration."[10]

Corporate DNA. Reminders of core values and vision and historical and founder memorabilia are among the carriers of corporate DNA. Willenius-Wilhelmsen Lines (mentioned earlier as innovators in coaching groups) is the world's largest ocean-shipping company. Its award-winning headquarters in Oslo, Norway, is shaped like a sailing ship, the architecture reminding one of decks, crow's nests, and wind in sails. It sits a few meters from the edge of a fjord dotted by sails. The inviting reception areas doubles as the corporate cultural museum. Throughout massive corporate change, the ancient values of seafaring have remained a visible inspiration.

Conducting Dialogue

Conversation is conducted atop layers of meaning. What you mean when you communicate, and what you think you understand of others, is both enriched and confounded by unspoken assumptions and the private textures of prior experiences. The less standard and the more complex a topic is, the more confusion between participants is likely. When different people view the same situation, they may start with different assumptions, pay attention to different things, and form different interpretations. *Dialogue* occurs when people temporarily suspend their certainties, exploring basic assumptions with each other and asking questions for which they don't already know the answers.[11]

For example, people discussing financial trends must share basic understandings about economics and the marketplace for the discussion to go anywhere. Usually, their shared understanding is adequate for the purpose of conversation. But say the topic is retirement and the conversation is between a financial adviser and her client— then dialogue needs to take place. Both parties must deliberately and consciously dig into the layers of meaning that underlie *retirement*. They examine things like personal values, income data, and assumptions about the future. It is likely that meanings will be clarified and that something new might be created as a result, such as more practical career goals. Even though the technical knowledge of the financial adviser will help guide the conversation, holding a true dialogue is important. Without that dialogue, the adviser may act on fundamental misunderstandings about the client, and the client may entertain too few options for retirement.

Dialogue is a form of skilled, searching, critical, supportive, open, and honest conversation that is sustained over time. It is not uncommon among members of high-performing groups such as scientific research teams or championship athletic teams. However, we have observed that it is rare in business organizations, even though dialogue is increasingly important in times of growing chaos and complexity and when exploring new territories.

What you know as good conversation already contains the seeds of dialogue. Let's look at how leaders deepen dialogue and sustain it under rocky circumstances over periods of time.

Sally Helgesen describes how the *Miami Herald* successfully implemented a campaign of intense dialogue in 1991. At that time, bitter divisiveness threatened to strangle the news organization. An old-boy network ran the company. Woman and minorities were effectively shut out of important roles. Seasoned publisher David Lawrence was brought in to lead the company out of the spreading morass. To study the situation, he commissioned a Task Force on Fairness in the Workplace, which tapped twenty-three employees from all levels and factions. What made this program work was the commitment from the top to explore the issues at stake and not just apply a veneer of shallow initiatives.

Task force cochair Sue Reisinger tells of an initial period of disarray: "I wondered how we'd ever get anything done, especially because people came from all over the company, were very different, often barely knew one another, and had no experience working in this unstructured way." The group improvised its way forward, however, discovering the key principles of good dialogue as it went: openness of information, respect for foreign-sounding points of view, speaking with passion, listening with both head and heart, and commitment to change in oneself as well as in the organization. Says Reisinger, "We, all of us, began to find ourselves in these intense conversations with all kinds of people, about where they worked, how their workplace functioned, and how they felt about it. We started thinking in very big, imaginative ways."

One payoff from this new dialogical thinking came on and after August 23, 1992, when Hurricane Andrew swept in and crippled Dade County. The *Herald* staff realized they were a lifeline of information, and they self-organized to solve thousands of logistical problems. Helgesen observes that because of the organization's prior learning in overcoming rigid divisions, it was uniquely able to respond to the disaster with "speed, grace, and total involvement. . . . People were accustomed to being in things together, to thinking in terms of the long run."[12]

Fertile imagination requires the counterpoint of disciplined doubt. Dialogue is not brainstorming. It is also not the time to stress alignment of thinking around a single point of view, even the corporate vision. Here are ways we have found to promote dialogue to help groups make sense of the challenges they face. They draw directly on the C2 Competencies of paying attention, personalizing, imaging, and serious play. They also pave the way for people to engage in the final competency, crafting.

Designate a time. Opportune times for dialogue are group retreats or when a team faces a new challenge. Make explicit your intention to have a different kind of conversation. Set a start time and an end time (when you and your team will return to conversation as usual).

Create a space. Rearrange the space to rearrange behavior. When people sit in the same chairs around the same table in the same room as they always have, they have the same conversation as they always have. Sit in a circle without a table, so you and your team members can make eye contact without having to move and no one is in a position of hierarchy. Eliminating the table decreases the distance between individuals and allows them to perceive each other's body language.

Agree to norms. Keep these norms simple. Post them. Agree on the kinds of information arising from the dialogue that can be shared outside the room. If a norm is broken during the dialogue or after, call it.

Consider using an outside facilitator. The first few times a group tries to talk in these new ways, an experienced facilitator can be especially helpful. Dialogue can at first feel uncomfortable; a facilitator can keep people from simply reverting to old, comfortable habits. A skilled facilitator can also help people avoid spirals of conflict.

Discourage interruptions, talking over others, and side conversations. Make sure each speaker has space to finish a thought without being rushed. Some groups like the device of the *talking stick*—the stick holder talks, the others listen, and then the stick is passed to another speaker. Organizational change expert Robert Goldberg playfully introduces a small stuffed giraffe into dialogues. The person temporarily holding the giraffe is seen as "sticking his neck out" and thus deserves the respect of being listened to. Dialogue, which has the potential to become slow and somber, benefits from such serious play.

Respect silences. Pauses in the talk, even long ones, can be constructive. At the same time, long-quiet voices should be respected and given the chance to speak. *In and out chairs* is a technique we find works well: the dominant voices ("you know who you are") move their chairs one step back for ten or fifteen minutes as the quiet voices ("and you know who *you* are") have their say.

Remember your intent. State the purpose of the dialogue at the beginning of the session. Remind the group of this purpose if members stray. Check at the end: Was the intent realized? If not, why?

Call the impasse. A facilitator can help the group identify impasses at first, but group members should learn to do this. If the group faces an impasse, have group members reflect silently on the purpose for a moment, then resume the dialogue.

Balance advocacy and inquiry. Advocate for particular positions, but be sure to respectfully inquire about the assumptions and data behind those positions.

Affirm others' personal competence when disagreeing with their ideas. Disagree with ideas, not people. Create an environment in which people feel secure speaking unpopular thoughts.

Practice loyal skepticism. All points of view are hypotheses open to testing. Cynicism is poisonous, but doubt combined with commitment is healthy. At the same time, skepticism should not be used to undermine the inquiry. One manager we worked with expressed healthy skepticism with the simple statement, "Not proven, but carry on."

Legitimize intuition and emotion. Hunches are valid. So are what-if excursions of thought. Passion for the issues is positive. Interpersonal conflict over issues should be acknowledged but taken off-line for the duration of the dialogue.

Express chains of reasoning. Make sure individuals explain the explicit reasoning that got them from the data to their conclusion.

Build shared meaning. As the dialogue continues, try to integrate the various points of view into meaningful wholes. Often it is someone who stands apart from two opposing points of view who is able to glimpse the synthesis. Sometimes the integration appears first as an image or metaphor or a vision of how things could look in the future.

Use multiple modes of paying attention. Dialogue involves shifting gears in paying attention and is an important time for engaging low-gear attention.

Provide positive turbulence. Invite the occasional guest in to stir the pot—a customer, partner, or someone with a radical point of view. During these visits, maintain the ground rules you have established for dialogue.

Voice the perspectives of others. No one person owns any point of view, and it is helpful to "try on" others' perspectives.

Consider collaborative knowledge-making software tools. Introduce these tools after establishing a basic process of dialogue within the group. Consider tools such as Mind Manager, Inspiration, Quest Map, or Compendium.

Put something in the middle. Place a literal or theoretical object in the middle of the dialogue. This is the biggest suggestion we have for using dialogue for creative leadership, and we discuss it further in the next section.

Debrief the dialogue. Spend five minutes or so reflecting on how well the norms were kept, whether the process needs changing, and so forth.

Continue the dialogue over time. Reconvene on a regular basis. Improve the process. Assess the dialogue for progress on shared understanding of the challenges at hand. Supplement face-to-face dialogue with electronic forums such as e-mail, listservs, and intranet discussion rooms.

Dialogue can be risky if people aren't prepared for it. For example, lack of mutual trust can result in heightened cynicism or abuse of openly shared feelings instead of true dialogue. Some favorable conditions should be established before conducting dialogue. The team members should have

- *Prior team-building experience that has made them more aware of themselves and of others*. Ensure that team members have leadership development experiences as individuals and as a group, and cultivate well-founded trust among them.
- A *voiced challenge*. Articulate to the team a shared and compelling challenge and the sense that this challenge may be complex or chaotic.
- *Analytical knowledge*. Immerse team members in high-quality data appropriate to the challenge.
- *Requisite maturity*. If the group on the whole is emotionally young, make sure that it includes at least several members who are mature and confident enough to serve as role models and anchor points.

After the dialogue it is beneficial to

- *Come to explicit closure*. If closure on the issues is not possible, be explicit about how you will continue to address these issues within or outside the dialogue process.

- *Record insights for revisiting and reusing.* Appoint a group reporter beforehand to take public notes and write them up.
  First, make sure the group agrees to this activity; individuals
  must have veto power over dissemination of their comments.

- *Take action based on the meaning the group creates.* At the *Miami
  Herald*, for example, after several months of often-difficult dialogue, the task force recommended nineteen specific actions,
  all of which were implemented and monitored. If the entire
  process ends with no tangible outcomes, your group may feel
  cynical about the dialogue—even when it is clearly beneficial
  to defer action until the issues have been thoroughly explored.

- *Communicate salient parts of the dialogue to constituencies beyond
  your group.* Beware of appearing to the rest of the organization
  like an elite group meeting secretly. Conversely, don't violate
  the trust of the group by going public with information and
  opinions expressed under assumptions of confidentiality.

The potential rewards of dialogue are great: a vastly deeper and
wider exploration of the challenges faced, robust shared understanding, a stronger team—all leading to effective action.

Putting Something in the Middle

Putting something in the middle is a powerful way to learn to hold a dialogue and increase its effectiveness. The technique is simple: you
place a tangible object in the middle of your group and focus dialogue on it. The object may stand for an idea but is something you
can actually look at and touch. Objects we have seen used include
a video of a visit to a customer site, star maps, personal photos selected because "they say something important about our leadership
values," a product prototype, a Web site page projected on a large
screen, and a competitor's product.

Why use an object? Objects focus attention in a positive way.
People are typically less polarized and argumentative when they are

describing their observations of an object rather than their thoughts about an abstraction. Objects also help people make personal connections. They suggest images and invite metaphors and stories. They can be appreciated, played with, recrafted. The object in the middle becomes a symbolic vessel that holds the truths spoken by the group and transforms them into a collective meaning. The object in the middle often spurs serious play, and like Goldberg's stuffed giraffe, keeps the dialogue from becoming merely serious.[13]

The star-mapping process at the *Orion Research Center* (described in Chapter Three) is an example of putting something in the middle. The star maps help people surface, display, examine, and reconstruct the underlying meaning of things so that the team can take confident action. Says one ORC team member: "Individuals would take one star map and lay it down next to others. Another individual has put one down previously and says, 'Oh, no, the position is in the wrong order.' And they'll flip [the star maps] around, and then someone else might say, 'No, we think it's the other way.' And it creates a dialogue."

At the Center for Creative Leadership we have developed a general purpose tool called *Visual Explorer* (VE) for facilitating dialogue. VE is a set of over two hundred diverse color images (photographs and art reproductions) selected for their potential for rich literal and metaphorical connections to professional challenges. *Visual Explorer* is available as a commercial product. Alternatively, you can make your own set of images from postcards, magazine clippings, and the like.

One wintry weekend, we met with the senior management team of Angstrom Inc., a telecommunications company, as the team members worked to craft strategy in the face of significant change, fast-paced competition, and lots of ambiguity. First, a number of industry experts gave presentations. Then we used *Visual Explorer* to assist team members in holding a dialogue about what they had just heard and what it meant to them. This process took about one hour.

The *Visual Explorer* Exercise

Goal

This exercise helps people process information from speakers, data, previous discussions, or other sources of information. They can surface and examine the salient points for the group and the challenges it faces. Steps 1 to 4 are done individually, before group discussion.

Materials

Visual Explorer images, spread out on a table

Journal or notepads for all the participants

Process

1. Think about one topic or detail from the information presented (for instance, competitive analysis or state of the industry) that really stands out for you in its importance or possible implications.

2. Write down your thoughts about the information that stands out for you. What you write in your journal will be private unless you choose otherwise. (3–5 minutes)

3. Browse the images and find one that evokes your topic. The connection between topic and image may be intuitive, emotional, or literal. The image may "speak to you" in ways that are hard to verbalize. Browse without talking, take your time, and look over all the images. When you have selected an image, return to your table. (5–10 minutes)

4. Write down what you see in the image, and then write a few thoughts about the connection to your topic. (3–5 minutes)

5. Break out into groups of three or four. Share and discuss the images, each person in turn going through the following steps:

- Describe your image to the group, paying attention to the details and to the image as a whole. What is it? What's going on? Why were you drawn to that image? What do you wonder about in the image? (2–3 minutes)

- Say what the image means to you with respect to the topic. How is the image connected to the topic? What does it mean to you in that connection? Does it bring out anything that you hadn't thought of before? (2–3 minutes)

- Have others in the group describe what they see in the image, and the connections they make to it. People should speak to the group as a whole rather than to the individual who selected the image. They should use language such as, "What I see in this image . . ." or, "If this were my image . . ." (3 minutes per person)

- Have a "last word" about the image, possible meanings, and connections to the topic. Thank the group members for their observations. (1 minute)

6. Take a moment to reflect on the group discussions and write your thoughts in your journal.

7. Save the selected images for the next rounds of mediated dialogue.

Tips

- A journal is a good companion to dialogue. Occasional brief periods in which participants organize and write down private thoughts are a valuable complement to the public verbal exchanges.

- Playing music during the image selection process supports R-mode attention, as does a rule of no talking during image selection.

- It is important that people spend time reflecting on their chosen image before going on to describe its connection to their topic.

> Otherwise, they have a tendency to speak abstractly about it,
> ignoring its details; however, it is the image that makes this
> process different from standard conversations.
>
> • Dialogue works best in multiple sessions that deepen the explo-
>   ration and culminate in decision making.

For example, one Angstrom executive, *John*, selected a photograph
of a person fishing through a hole in ice (see Figure 5.1). He then
described the simplicity and the demands of hunting fish and related his thoughts to Angstrom. Angstrom is a high-tech business,
yet for John the work came down to certain similar basics: patience,
focus, and a bit of suffering. John's group noticed some additional
points. One was that the fisher in the picture was alone, and they
wondered what to make of that. *Mary*, another Angstrom executive, selected a picture of a rock climber (see Figure 5.2) and talked
about the exhilaration as well as the fear she experienced at
Angstrom. When someone noticed that Mary was holding the
image upside-down, the conversation shifted to perspective: What
would happen if one were to invert certain key assumptions Angstrom had made?

Visual Explorer puts something in the middle that is dynamically
interactive. It invites play. When people put their images together
in an implied or actual collage, their shared construction brings
with it the opportunity for uniquely new meanings. *Collage*, as we
noted, is related to *collision*.

Images mediate dialogue in six ways:

Images are tangible. Improvised sentences in conversation evap-
orate, whereas a printed image stays. A well-told story or a poem
also tends to linger in memory. These media maintain a space
where interpretations can play. Images serve to return a discussion
to its original meaningful intention, even as the conversation roams
far and wide. Participants can at least agree that they are looking at
the same physical detail even as all other points of agreement slip

Figure 5.1. The Image John Selected.

and slide. Images can then be recycled for use in subsequent conversations or presentations.

Images lend themselves to multiple perspectives and meanings. Most participants accept the reaction of "you see *that* in the image, but I see *this*" as a natural situation. Such natural differences become a scaffold for acts of inquiry, appreciation, and taking perspective. Seeking clarification of meaning is frequently awkward in verbal discussions but is more natural when images are used as mediating agents. *Perspective*, after all, is a vision-based metaphor.

Images invite projections of hard-to-articulate meanings. Images can convey nuances of intuitions and emotions. Because images are obviously artifacts, people apply and withdraw their projections without becoming overly attached to the images themselves. People easily handle images as suggestive, rather than literal, displays of fact. The images become temporary shared screens on which are displayed deeper meanings, hunches, and feelings.

Figure 5.2. The Image Mary Selected.

Images invite transformation. Images can be building blocks for creating larger ideas. In the movie-making we described in Chapter Three, for example, images can be cut up and recombined in ways that produce something more than the sum of the parts. During the *Visual Explorer* exercise, people often select more than one image to emphasize the compound angles of a larger idea. Even single images can morph during prolonged scrutiny. For example, the telltale fin of a shark may transform into a drama what was first perceived to be a placid fishing scene.

Images provide aesthetic distance from wicked challenges. Aesthetic *distance* is a term from the arts for a circumscribed place within which people temporarily suspend disbelief and participate by acting or observing. The aesthetic distance created by mediated dialogue gives people perspective on objectified meanings and then allows them to reclaim (or recast) those meanings subjectively at the close of the dialogue—much as one does after a compelling theater experience.

Images provide a method for handling language. Words by themselves often fail people, particularly individuals whose strengths lie in nonverbal fields. Mediated dialogue provides handles for words; it offers images, metaphors, and stories through which you can grasp a situation, sometimes actually in your hands.

Crossing Boundaries

Boundaries are places where two or more cultures, disciplines, systems, or perspectives meet. What were once lines of demarcation in the Old Economy are now highly trafficked thoroughfares: biology and engineering, computing and graphic design, hip-hop fashions and basketball, submarines and archeology. The list continues to multiply. As a result, new forms of dialogue are being invented that cross these boundaries and build useful knowledge.

Only a short time ago Johns River Station was highly regulated; its internal and external boundaries were routine and simple. Rapid deregulation has meant that every boundary JRS has—with its labor force, with customers, with the surrounding community, and so on—is alive with new problems and potentials. Coal-fired power plants, once regarded as aging relics, are now center stage in global economic and environmental concerns, with all the attendant requirements for creative leadership.

Orion Research Center is intent on planning strategy within a highly open system with wide participation. It has opened up participation in its team's conversation on strategy to include customers, corporate divisions, bench-level scientists, and even competitors. Notable results of this approach include cutting the time from idea inception to commercialization from five to two and a half years.

Co-inquiry in the new economy often takes the form of networks of diverse people who share some common interest. Novartis AG, for example, fosters what it calls *knowledge networking,* an approach meant to be less rigid and hierarchical than knowledge management. Knowledge scouts from each business unit scour the globe for new ideas and lead on-line discussion groups. Four times a year the company holds knowledge marketplaces to bring everyone in the networks together for face-to-face exchanges. One project to spring from this process is a collaboration between Novartis's nutrition and pharmaceutical businesses to explore ways of adapting the composition of normal foods to prevent age-related bone weakening.[14]

Bridging the Customer Gap

Co-inquiry, now more than ever, includes the customer or client. The intent of co-inquiry goes far beyond the intent of focus groups and customer feedback. According to John Seeley Brown, director of Xerox PARC, "The ultimate innovation partner is the customer." PARC aims not just to make and sell products but also to collaborate with all kinds of people to understand how their work practices are changing and then to work with them to define new solutions.[15]

Early adopters are the first people who use your product or service. Often they know more about your product—and why it is valuable—than you do. The trick is to cross the boundary into their world to start with and then to sustain a dialogue. Says Jim Taylor, senior vice president of global marketing at computer-maker Gateway, Inc.: "When we launch a new product, we identify a collection of early adopters and christen them 'pioneers.' . . . As we discover bugs [with the pioneers' help] and fix them in subsequent revisions, we go back to our pioneers and upgrade their machines for free. The effect is a sustained dialogue that benefits both sides."[16]

Patagonia, an outdoor apparel and equipment company based in Ventura, California, makes it a point to hire its customers (affectionately called *dirtbags* because of their obsession with wilderness adventuring), give them gear, and send them out into the wilderness. They come back filled with stories, which are funneled straight into R&D. Founder and chief dirtbag Yvon Chouinard spends at least six months a year doing what he loves, mountaineering and whitewater boating, while testing and developing his company's products. Customer stories are the backbone of the Patagonia catalogue, giving the enterprise the feel of a close-knit yet welcoming community.[17]

How do *you* bridge the customer boundary at your own organization? Consider the following questions as challenges: Where do you share stories with customers—the real stories, not the polite, superficial ones? Where and when do you seriously play with customers? What are the images customers have of your products and services—the honest images, not the clichés fed to you in a survey? When was the last time you invited any customer to a retreat or strategy summit, not just for a sanitized speech but also for some form of dialogue?

Bridging the Language Gap

Language may become a peril when you are communicating across boundaries. People from different disciplines or cultures do speak in "tongues"—different jargons, dialects, and languages. When cultures meet and cobble together a practical, working language, it is called *pidgin*. Pidgin languages use a simplified vocabulary and syntax. The name *pidgin* probably arose from a Chinese pronunciation of the English word *business*. What so many of us know as *business-speak* is in effect a pidgin that cuts across many cultures. It tends to be financial in its grammar and content,[18] and when speaking it, people pay attention primarily in L-mode. A creative alternative to using business-speak is to construct a pidgin for your group that articulates both L- and R-modes, as the employees at ORC have done. Explains an ORC Chinese expatriate: "We use metaphors and things like that to explain things. One of the Chinese, a senior scientist, . . . often uses metaphors. He often quotes something from the Chinese literature, and he'll translate it [into] English. It is a good way to do it—to convey my message to someone using some metaphor. To convey my feeling, my thinking, more clearly, I give the picture to somebody. The picture is a little bit more powerful than the words."

Chinese-based and other cultural metaphors have thus entered the business-speak of ORC to create a more user-friendly language, drawing out what some at ORC refer to as "the quiet voices."

People who work in different areas of technology often have trouble speaking with one another because of gaps in experience and language. In his book *Image and Logic*, Peter Galison argues that there are two cultures among specialists in subatomic physics: imagers and logicians. Imagers produce elaborate visuals in their experiments, and logicians use devices that precisely record events for statistical analysis. The two cultures speak to each other in pidgins or creoles that allow them to swap information in local "trading zones." They develop "trading languages that bind the diverse subcultures of physics into a larger . . . and more resilient whole."[19]

What are the languages and pidgins spoken across your organization, professional community, and customer base? Where are the quiet voices in your organization; what is their cultural base? How might you construct language that includes them?

Developing the Competency of Co-Inquiry

Successful dialogue changes people. Once you have taken the perspective of someone else—and thus enlarged your capacity for thought and feeling—you can't *untake* it. In a surprisingly similar fashion, you harbor within yourself a variety of voices, corresponding to various mentors and other key influences. The practice of group dialogue helps you learn to sort out your own internal dialogue in a constructive way.

Developing Individual Competence

Vic Bubnow was the vice president for finance at the *Miami Herald* and cochair with Sue Reisenger of the *Herald's* Task Force on Fairness in the Workplace. Vic was comfortable in the world of finance and to him the task force at first seemed "alien, not a real part of business." Looking back now, he believes it was "the most meaningful thing I've ever done in my work life. It just simply changed how I approach people. The reason it worked was that it wasn't just this dry intellectual experience. It was this soulful, emotional process that took place at the level of your guts. It changed me. Now I'm actually comfortable talking about this stuff. I know how to listen. I'm now a different sort of person."[20]

Pam, the JRS plant manager, had long known that she was a highly intuitive person. Her growth came from creating an environment that acknowledged intuition and used it for dialogue. Often when Pam went into an intuitive space, she couldn't quite articulate things, stumbling for words and using phrases that didn't make much sense. With dialogue, Pam got used to people looking at her curiously whenever she went into this space. She adopted co-inquiry to put her stumbling words out there for people, saying, "Well, what do you think? Can you help me talk this through?"

Donna at *Chemstar* sees her leadership development in terms of working with top management and consultants:

We have a lot of bosses around here who say, "This is it." Because they've already gone off and they put together what they think the vision is. Their protocol is to give [their vision] to the people. During our recent troubles, I counterproposed that we take a half a day where we provide an environment for the individuals to develop their vision of Chemstar as a fast cycle time company. To have a mechanism of sharing that [set of ideas related to fast cycle time] and then seeing where the common ground is. Put the vision that the consultants have into the conversation and see where the differences are. And then have our leadership put out the expectation that we will hold some creative tension in the organization around some of these differences.

The experience of co-inquiry gives people more options for expressing themselves, thus drawing others into participating. One manager told us, "I have a greater appreciation of the language you use in the inquiry mode. I tend to be a black-and-white, bottom-line kind of person, and it doesn't serve me well. I've come to realize the value of using language in a way that draws people out."

And a manager at ORC learning to foster co-inquiry said: "I'm making more of an effort to reach out and work with people that I've never worked with. Working with people who are perceived to be difficult to work with. I've been successful in the last three to four months at doing that. We need to work together, and some of these people are very bright people—loners, but very bright people—who could really help us out. I'm making a very conscious effort to go out and tap into their expertise and see if we can work together somehow."

Here are some ways to develop individual competence in co-inquiry:

Ask More Open-Ended Questions. Ask, "What do you think?" without necessarily immediately saying what you yourself think. Think of yourself in your questioning role as a coach or reporter rather than as an inquisitor.

Seek Out and Read Opinions You Disagree With. Intentionally expose yourself to other points of view. For example, read op-ed pieces written from a political stance different from yours. Ask yourself what life circumstances and influences might cause someone to adopt these different points of view.

Practice Identifying the Quiet Voices. During conversations, practice drawing the quieter individuals out with encouraging questions. Build space for these voices into your process, so that engaging them becomes second nature.

Sum Up Others' Views. Summarize the points of view already on the table before offering your own. Revise the summary if necessary, until the proponents of those views agree that your summary versions are correct. Notice whether your careful summary of others' views encourages others to listen more carefully to your point of view.

Developing Community Competence

As communities provide time and space for sustained dialogue, as they find multiple ways to cross boundaries, competence in co-inquiry becomes part of their culture. Gradually, creative leaders can build the capacity of the organization to conduct co-inquiry and reap the benefits. As you embark on co-inquiry with your group, keep the following in mind.

Establish Places for Co-Inquiry. Start by arranging defined places for co-inquiry. Special events like retreats or leadership meetings are a good place to start collaborative inquiry. Invite people from different functions; later expand participation and include people from outside the company, such as suppliers and customers. Frame the effort as an experiment in ways to begin to address the leadership challenges the group faces. Later, solicit feedback about what worked and did not work in the experiment.

Identify Who Is Responsible. Be clear about who the sponsoring authority for the inquiry is. Who will "take the heat" if controversial issues arise? Who retains the authority to make unilateral decisions affecting the collaborations? Who is in charge of following through on issues that arise? Who will protect and support those who voice unpopular opinions?

Maintain the Process. Keep the process going over time. Reconvene the participants in co-inquiry, the *collaborators*, with some regularity. Co-inquiry is not an event; it is a process and a sustained attitude. Check in frequently with formal and informal collaborators. Keep track of action items and make sure they are completed. Publicize co-inquiry activities and progress.

Take the Time to Work on Trust. Slow down for issues of trust. Misunderstanding across boundaries is common, and when unaddressed, leads to loss of trust. Deal with trust issues in the group as soon as they arise; do it with honesty and humility. Spend lots of *face time* just getting to know one another, sharing stories, and looking for cultural similarities and differences.

Explore Strongly Held Opinions. Welcome intense points of view. These are assets to be brought into the middle and explored. Surface and explore the ends of the spectrum of opinions and conflicting needs. As you do so, a middle ground or a synthesis of seeming opposites will gradually become apparent.

Cautions

Co-inquiry encourages open exploration and the discovery of new territory, accompanied by a transformation of established territory. It is not without risk. You may reach the place described by philosopher Friedrich Nietzsche, in *Thus Spake Zarathustra:* "A rope over an abyss: A dangerous crossing, a dangerous wayfaring, a dangerous looking-back, a dangerous trembling and halting." It is for this reason that the discussion in this chapter applies mainly to what we have been calling complex challenges—those without easy answers—rather than to technical challenges, for which a formulaic solution may exist. Save co-inquiry for what really matters but seems unobtainable through the same old routines. As you engage in co-inquiry, be particularly alert to the risks in these issues:

Confronting authority. Co-inquiry, although collaborative in spirit and goal, is most safely initiated by those with the authority to do so. Those without authority who initiate dialogue on contentious issues risk becoming a lightning rod in a confrontation with authority.[21] For those without authority, a safer way to achieve the benefits of co-inquiry is networking, building a web of personal relationships based on information sharing. Recognize also that co-inquiry is long term and exploratory, especially if you lack authority. Be patient, learn the territory, choose moments for expanding the dialogue, and then evaluate the lessons of those moments once they are realized. Make sure you assess what is to be gained and lost, keeping in mind that risk avoidance is also the risk of lost opportunity.

What lies beneath. Co-inquiry is a way of seeing more deeply into what is unclear, unfinished, conflicted, or confused. One manager in our studies spoke of leadership as "reminding people what they have lost or forgotten." But beware; some of what you uncover may be unpleasant or worse. Be prepared to deal with such findings. Co-inquiry runs the risk of censorship. In some organizations the act of seeing what is hidden may be punished—and those in authority are not at all exempt from punishments imposed by a constituency intent on maintaining the status quo. Don't be surprised if others act to sweep the results of co-inquiry back under the rug. The best preparation for facing what lies beneath may be a grounding in the classic human values of patience, humility, courage, compassion, and optimism.

Co-inquiry invites strong emotions, but when handled well, they can be used to motivate. Donna and the Chemstar team uncovered great fear—fear that a comprehensive solution to their

problems would eliminate their jobs. It turned out that the organization as a community was better able to face these fears than were
isolated individuals. The ongoing dialogue people established together proved a good way to surface the harsh realities of their situation and begin to do something about it.

Group needs. Co-inquiry can appear indecisive to people who
expect leaders to provide answers, easy or otherwise. Creative leadership thus needs to walk the edge between sponsoring inquiry and
imposing good-enough solutions.

Cynicism and posturing. There is a big difference between loyal
skepticism and cynicism. Loyal skeptics ask powerful questions to
balance and steer an inquiry without blowing it up. Cynics tend to
be saboteurs. Encourage skeptics and cynics to make their full contribution, including their full measure of criticism—and then to become part of a solution. A group up to the task of co-inquiry will be
willing to confront members who at this point remain saboteurs.

In some organizations in which we have worked, attempted dialogue defaults to competition between intelligent but stressed individuals trying to look smart in the eyes of their colleagues. The
best antidote to such posturing is to "turn up" the elements of personal relationship and mutual support and "turn down" the emphasis on solving technical aspects of the challenges at hand.

Co-inquiry was an imperative for our own work when we first began
the research described in this book. We had been commissioned to
develop new interventions and programs for the Center for Creative Leadership. But we soon realized that the world was far too
complex for us to be able to develop these products and services
without the full engagement of our clients and all parts of our organization from the earliest possible moment. We had to understand
the nature of the complexity of our clients' worlds, all the while creating ways to help them develop robust solutions that were up to
the same level of complexity. No one person could be "the expert"
or could be seen as such. We were in this together, working on a

confluence of agendas. In creating interventions and programs with our clients, we realized that co-inquiry had to be integrated into both our delivery and our applications. We have both witnessed and experienced co-inquiry as a best practice within the community of leaders with which we work.

However, you may have noticed something still missing in this discussion of co-inquiry. Highly effective communities of inquiry hold common methods and principles for achieving and recognizing what the community considers *beautiful work*. They acquire these methods and principles through tradition and collaboration. These communities and their members, in other words, are competent at *crafting*, a subject to which we now turn.

Chapter Six

Crafting

After years of studying how organizations actually form strategy, Henry Mintzberg finds the notions of *planning* and *control* inadequate. Strategy making, Mintzberg argues, is a matter of *crafting:* "Managers are craftsmen and strategy is their clay. . . . [T]hey bring to their work an equally intimate knowledge of the materials at hand."[1] Crafting is essential to well-executed creative work of any kind: science, art, architecture, engineering, and so on. This is no less true for creative leadership and the handling of complex challenges.

The C2 Competency of *crafting* is the ability to synthesize the materials at hand—issues, objects, events, and actions—into integrated, meaningful, and beautiful wholes. Inevitably, these wholes are larger than the sum of their parts. Crafting can be thought of as a gestalt, the integrated totality of the other five competencies. Crafting includes skillfully selecting and applying the C2 Competencies, and the ability to envision, to stand back from the whole new concept or product, much as painters might select and mix from their palettes.

Although paying attention is the master competency for creative leadership, always primary and central to the rest, crafting is the integrative competency. Crafting orchestrates the other competencies, resulting in well-wrought outcomes of various kinds: products, processes, architectures, relationships, decisions, strategies, and so on. The best practices of crafting reside in the accumulated experience of disciplined communities. However, craft can be invented by resourceful individuals, standing on the shoulders of giants who have come before, and through collaborative inquiry.

In this book we have drawn lessons about our central theme—making shared and useful sense of complex challenges—from creative work in many fields. In this chapter we focus on creative leadership as the practice of a unique form of art joined with the discernment of science. As we explore the competency of crafting, we address the following key concepts:

- Thinking in wholes
- Crafting decisions
- Building scaffolds for learning
- Developing leadership as science and as art
- Learning from artists

Thinking in Wholes

Much of organized work is analytical: reducing things to parts and then building through formulas. But we all know that the whole is greater than the sum of the parts. Crafting complements *analysis* (the act of breaking things into component parts) with *synthesis* (the act of building with parts to create a nontrivial and often beautiful whole). Crafting is about developing elegant solutions to complex challenges by knowing and feeling that the solution is right and by using but transcending analysis.

Consider a maritime architect charged with designing a luxury liner. She breaks the task down into parts: *this* much stress to this beam; *these* qualities of a certain steel; *this* much buoyancy for this much cargo; the balance point must be *here*. She does this according to formulas and standards of practice. But unless the design is entirely formulaic, analysis is only half her job. She also faces choices that are not decided strictly by analysis. They require a vision of the future use of the ship and a nose for what is right.

Analysis has an air of certainty about it. With a good set of rules an architect can design a technically functional ship. Synthesis is a fuzzier matter. The bigger picture is almost always greater than you can grasp at first. Who might own the ship in ten years? How might standards of service shift? What does *luxury* really mean, and what could it mean if the intent were to gain an advantage over competitors? Using shipbuilding as a metaphor, the dean of an engineering school said, "We know how to teach people how to build ships but not how to figure out which ships to build."[2] Analytical certainty is seductive, but it conceals pitfalls.

In fact, every profession faces challenges like these—complex, future-oriented challenges that require judgments beyond the reach of formulas. In their book *Whatever It Takes*, Morgan McCall and Robert Kaplan quote an executive who describes the challenge of his work as a kind of *fabrication*: "[Information] comes at you in very unique ways, ways you never expect. You hear one thing here, one thing there, and you've got to put the story together in your mind. Now a lot of times the thing you fabricate is wrong, but by the very act of trying to put it together, you get more data."[3]

The scientists and engineers we work with among our clients and collaborators tend to be analytical in the way they approach their work. For many of them, synthesis is what we described earlier as black-market knowledge, important to their work but not officially recognized in the workplace. In the process of their creative leadership development, they recognized how they synthesize and began doing it more deliberately. Says one: "I tend, in my mind, to make a list. It's listing; it's analytical. Now, I realized that there's another way to look at this. To be able to step back and visualize more what it is you're trying to do. Visualize it from even a broader perspective, a higher plane—like I do building a cabinet in my shop at home. What's that cabinet for? What is its end purpose? I'm not pounding a nail into a piece of wood. My objective is to build a cabinet. What's that cabinet for?"

Similarly, a manager at *Orion Research Center* describes how he helped design a new business based on the scale-up of a laboratory process into a full-scale chemical engineering operation:

When I designed this new venture, it was much more holistic as opposed to task oriented. The idea was to see [it] as a whole as opposed
to seeing it as a series of sequential or even parallel steps. Whereas
everybody on the project at the time was so busy making incremen-
tal steps through it. People just tried to say, "Take A plus B plus C
and hit the target." I tried to take [the project] away from that
strictly technical approach. We did a lot of different things on a lot
of different fronts and linked them all as we went, and that was quite
different for that organization. [We asked] What's the breadth of
what we're making here? Can we be a business? It was bringing [peo-
ple] back to what the whole picture in front of them looked like.

Crafting requires thinking in wholes. Consider the lesson in the
story of the man who meets two people carrying bricks from the
bottom of a hill to the top. He asks the first one, "What are you
doing?" The person responds, "Can't you see? I'm carrying bricks up
the hill." He asks the same question of the second person, who
replies, "I'm building a cathedral."[4]

Crafting Decisions

Decisions in organizations flow from the top down, right? The truth
is, most organizations have seen a dramatic change in this traditional pattern in recent years, with a diversity of thought from
across the organization becoming much more important.[5]

Increasingly, decisions are being pushed closer to the customer,
closer to the market, closer to the frontline work. Although this can
be very effective, in many cases we have seen it lead to *paralysis by
analysis*, a situation in which people delay making a decision as they
collect more and more data or search for the perfect formula. Some
of this activity is purely defensive—people are covering their backs.
In such cases the problem can be solved by trusting people and letting them make a few mistakes. More often, paralysis by analysis
stems from a misunderstanding about how to make decisions, especially when the situation is complex and requires an original or cre-

ative move. In such cases the decision maker must shift the emphasis from rational analysis to a more subjective, experienced-based craft. We call this latter process *crafting a decision*.

Let's pick up Mintzberg's metaphor again. Crafting a decision is like making a pot. One aspect is analytical—measuring dimensions, compounding the clay, using proper chemistry, and so on. The other aspect is synthetic—feeling the components as they take form and respond. When creating a pot, the potter wordlessly brings a lifetime of experience into that moment of creation. She might reject mistakes but she might also work with them to uncover a new and better shape. The final pot fits the potter's formal specifications for size, strength, and function, but it also fits her criteria for beauty, quality, and creativity. Crafted decisions exhibit such qualities too.

The Analytic Sandwich

The Center for Creative Leadership has been sponsoring research on how to make the best decisions when selecting candidates for senior management positions. Rick Guzzo and Shannon Palmer conducted two studies using the Center for Creative Leadership's Peak Selection Simulation, in which participants collaborate to select the best candidate for an executive position. They are given a description of the position, a slate of candidates, and a computer database. Guzzo and Palmer originally predicted that the more fact based the group's deliberation, the better its decision would be. (An expert-determined "best" solution was embedded in the design of the simulation.) But that's not what happened. Participants made better decisions when their intuition and personal preferences dominated the *beginning* of the deliberation and their more careful analysis *followed*.[6] These particular studies didn't reveal why that was true. However, we suspect what happened is that the intelligent people doing the selection quickly made a variety of well-informed stabs at the correct answer. These stabs represented the full range of possible hypotheses, which were then tested against the data.

Crafting a good decision often starts with perceptions, feelings, and hunches. Analysis alone might be all right under static conditions, but it can be a kind of blindness in unusual conditions. It can't account for the full complexity of the situation. For example, sociologist Dianne Vaughan after nine years of analyzing the space shuttle *Challenger* disaster concludes:

> The story of the *Challenger* is a story of how people developed patterns that blinded them. . . . Complex organizations and technical systems will inevitably fail some of the time because their parts will interact in ways that cannot be planned for and because of environmental conditions that cannot be foreseen. . . . The traditional insistence on proving arguments with data got in the way of good decision making. An engineer's argument based on intuition and observation should have been enough to stop or delay the launch, but that's not the way things were done at NASA, and no one thought or dared to proceed differently.[7]

Gary Klein is an expert on experts. He and his colleagues have spent years studying how experts make decisions under field conditions of high stakes and ambiguity.[8] Firefighters, pilots, intensive care nurses, manufacturing engineers, airport baggage screeners, and military commanders, for example, tend to use what we call the *analytic sandwich* to craft decisions. Their decisions are analytically supported but surrounded by a thick layer of experientially tuned perceptions, intuitions, and imagination. People using the analytic sandwich tell stories. They run through mental simulations. They have a ready bag of analogies to apply to new situations. Because of the way they tune their perception, they see what other people overlook. As a result, they often imagine their way to a solution, which they can then double-check in the light of cold, hard facts.

When faced with a situation you suspect is complex and might require the crafting of a decision, consider the following differentiating factors. A situation calls for straightforward decision making or problem solving when

- People are *ignorant;* there is uncertainty and too little information.
- There is a clear problem with definite boundaries.
- People can figure out what they don't know and what they need to know.

Deliberate crafting is in order when

- People are *ambivalent* or *confused;* multiple, equivocal, or con-flicting interpretations exist.
- The meaning of the situation and the nature of the problem are unclear.
- People don't know what they don't know, and don't know what they need to know.[9]

Heifetz and Sinder call situations that require crafting *Type III Problems*[10] (see Table 6.1). Many times people act as if their problem is clear and, as a result, set out to solve the wrong problem. They find themselves behaving like the drunk who lost his wallet and was searching for it under the lamppost. Asked where he had lost it, he said, "In the alley."

"Then why are you looking here?"

"Because the light is better."

Table 6.1. Type III Problems.

	Problem Definition	Solution	Response	Primary Locus of Work
Type I	Clear	Clear	Decision making	Leader
Type II	Clear	Unclear	Problem solving	Leader and members
Type III	Unclear	Unclear	Crafting	Members

Source: Adapted from R. A. Heifetz and R. Sinder, "Political Leadership: Managing the Public's Problem Solving," in R. Reich (ed.), *The Power of Public Ideas* (New York: Ballinger, 1988), p. 186.

People tend to frame problems where "the light is better"—that is, in terms of the familiar and the solutions they have in hand. In our experience, groups do better when they spend more of their time making sense of the situations they face—really paying attention and connecting with all the issues—before going on to solve the perceived problem, which may now differ from what at first appeared to be the problem.

Decision-Making Guidelines

Here are our guidelines for crafting good decisions related to complex challenges in your organization. This approach balances subjectivity and objectivity in tightly knit, diverse, open, and honest teams.

Craft good decisions by cycling through all the C2 Competencies. As a general rule of thumb, pay attention, connect with personal experience, create new perspectives by exploring evocative images, and experiment and play, all in the broader context of collaborative inquiry. Craft decisions by integrating all this work with the best of your analytical skills.

Legitimize intuition. Many scientists and technologists have told us that their organizations' managers become hyperrational in pursuit of business goals, squeezing out the intuitive side—and squeezing out creativity in the process. Instead, practice the kind of listening that encourages people to air their hunches without fear. Ask people to intuit the whole of which the present challenges are merely a part.

Use the analytic sandwich. Critical analysis is a check on the looseness and potential excesses of intuition. Intuition and feelings are a release from paralysis by analysis. Deliberately intersperse intuitive and analytical tools. Use them to inform and enliven each other.

Tap into experience, wherever you find it. Experience is what allows analysis and intuition to mesh into good decisions.[11] Don't fall into the trap of sitting behind your desk and letting subordinates get all the hands-on experience. In times of complexity, leave the door open to people with diverse experiences, even those only peripherally related to the topics at hand, and listen as people argue, imagine, and trade stories. And get out there and try it yourself.

Honor and replicate the whole craft of your experts. According to Gary Klein, experts have various "sources of power" through which they turn years of experience into nuanced decisions.[12] Don't just abstract their (or your) knowledge into formulas. Expertise includes stories, analogies, imagination, and hard-to-articulate experiences. It also includes aesthetic judgment about what constitutes an elegant, well-shaped, wise, and complete set of choices. (This last item points to the importance of artistry in crafting, a topic we explore later in this chapter.)

Building Scaffolds for Learning

People are builders. You don't learn by accumulating data in a pile. You learn by assembling. You arrange your experiences, knowledge, and emotions within frameworks. For your larger or more inventive buildings, or learnings, you need to assemble the frameworks too, even as you build your learning within those frameworks.

We call this framework for learning *scaffolding*; it is analogous to the physical scaffolding used to construct a building or paint a mural on a wall.[13] Let's explore this metaphor. Scaffolds are usually temporary, not a part of the final construction. Scaffolds are not of the same materials as the building. Scaffolds don't have the same appearance as the construction. Instead, scaffolds provide a place to stand and work close to the building. During the construction phase, the scaffold is sturdier than the building. Scaffolds provide a safe place from which to apply leverage and gain perspective. Scaffolds are a reliable way for the builders, the inspectors, and the owners to climb up and down as the thing under construction is being made.

One of the most exciting demonstrations of learning in modern times used a scaffold. James Clerk Maxwell was a nineteenth-century scientific giant who anticipated Einstein in his methods and ideas. Maxwell wrote the famous equations that unify the phenomena of light, electricity, and magnetism. According to historian Arthur Koestler, Maxwell was "a super-visualizer." He played within an imagined world to facilitate his learning. His was a hydraulic world of plumbing and flowing, of tubes, vortices, and eddies within a fluid called *ether*. The skill of this builder became clear when, having worked out his historic mathematical formulation of electromagnetism, *he then discarded the hydraulic model.* As Koestler puts it, "Maxwell kicked away the scaffolding from under himself . . . and remained freely suspended."[14]

Another kind of scaffold is used in the Suzuki method for nurturing the ability to master the violin among young children. According to developmental psychologist Howard Gardner: "One of thirty students beginning at age two or three will be able to play a Vivaldi concerto at six . . . and even the average student will have reached this competence but a few years later." Suzuki students love to practice. Musical training, although obviously necessary, is not sufficient to produce these results. In this method the attainment of musical ability rests on the child's relationship to his mother. The mother begins to learn the violin first, and the curious toddler watches without even being permitted to try. Then he and Mother hold and examine the instrument together. Formal lessons are at first based on the mother and child learning as a pair. The maternal relationship is used in service of the violin at every turn. Eventually, musical learning is weaned away from dependence on the scaffold of the maternal relationship. Gardner sums up the formula for the success of Suzuki this way: "Strong *interpersonal* knowledge is used as a means to negotiate a complex *musical* pathway, in the context of great cultural support for such an undertaking."[15] This summation can be used as a general formula for constructing learning scaffolds if one substitutes other domains of learning for the words *interpersonal* and *musical*.

How might scaffolds be used to craft organizational learning? One organization Chuck has worked with has used outdoor adventure exercises—*high ropes*—to build teamwork. In one exercise each person walks across a balance beam fifty feet in the air, as two other team members anchor the beam walker's safety rope. In this case the whole outdoor arena is a scaffold for building team skills. The outdoors provides a place apart from the workplace, but with close parallels to the workplace, for individuals to try out ways of working with others. It supports directly confronting issues of fear, risk, and trust—difficult issues to work on without a safe, artificial, temporary framework. When the learning is done, this scaffold can be completely removed.[16]

The lessons for using scaffolding in the service of creative leadership include the following:

The scaffold should be brought very close to the work. Connections between the scaffold experience and the work should be drawn in fine detail. For example, it is not sufficient simply to provide an outdoor adventure experience: participants must actively explore the connections between this scaffold and their lives at work. In looking at these connections, push beyond the easy and general relationships (for example, "we need to trust each other"). Surprising and creative discoveries often lie in the detailed, difficult connections made between seemingly disparate realms (for example, "trust can happen when I feel your steady, responsive pulling on my lifeline. At work this might mean . . .").

Scaffolds may eventually need to be removed. Maxwell showed his genius by removing the unnecessary metaphors from his finished work. A Suzuki student's musical practice is gradually weaned from dependence on the mother. A difficult but potentially creative act is defining the boundary between work and scaffold and then eventually removing the scaffold.

Scaffolds may be wrong yet still useful. Cardboard versions of the history of science are hard on those who posited a universal fluid called *ether*. Yet Maxwell climbed high on this wrong idea. The lesson may be that we all should be respectful of ideas and practices that we think may be in error but that temporarily give us a place to stand. The corollary is to be able to discard ideas and practices that have outlived their use as scaffolding. For example, *quality circles* were a temporary scaffold in many organizations for learning more about effective means of production.

Scaffolds can come from outside the business world. One manager we talked to loves theater and has spent a lot of time volunteering backstage. She says this helps her with orchestrating meetings at work, creating ambiance, and sensing the rise and fall of tensions in the room. Another manager, a woman who has to make things happen in a blue-collar environment, loves and understands professional sports. She feels strongly that her effectiveness at work is greatly enhanced by her ability to "talk sports." This kind of scaffolding can be especially valuable in helping people invest their work with personal energy, ideas, passion, and novel connections.

Creativity can come from the intersection of very different kinds of learning, knowledge, interest, or ability. It is well known that innovation often occurs at the intersection of different fields of knowledge or practice. Learning scaffolds can be part of such intersections also. Hobbies can provide unusual frames for work. As we described in the previous chapter, the person who invented 3M's Post-it Notes was trying to find a temporary way to mark pages in his church choir songbook.

Developing Leadership as Science and as Art

David Gelernter has written about the important role of aesthetic appeal in the development of machines of all sorts and particularly in his field of software. He claims that "the best computer scientists are . . . technologists who crave beauty."[17] And so it is with leadership: leadership is both an art and a science.[18] But what does it mean to say this? Science and art are often portrayed as opposites. They tend to be disconnected in today's educational systems, workplaces, and communities. Many scientists warn that science is under attack from those who regard it as a set of opinions rather than a source of objective truth. So how can science and art be so readily mixed in the practice of creative leadership? If one values the objectivity of science, is it a good idea to blend in the biases of artistic construction?

We have been studying how people successfully understand and resolve complex challenges—those that do not yield to unambiguous technical solutions—in their shared endeavors. We have worked with a wide variety of people, including those who are leaders as well as scientists and artists. As we watch them explore challenges in their work, we are struck by the relatedness of science and art—not in the specific products, which indeed tend to be very different, but in the underlying processes. Perhaps science and art are not so different. If leaders knew more about the ways science and art are alike, they could better apply this combined power to leadership situations.

We define *science* as careful observation in the course of forming and testing ideas, subject to a questioning community. *Art* we define as the modification of things by human skill to achieve form, function, and meaning. (This includes much more than the fine arts.) Although specialization often requires high levels of expertise, these general definitions can embrace all sorts of people in organizations, including leaders.

Connections Between Science and Art

The underlying ways in which science and art are related are many, and they vary by specialty. Here we offer four fairly general traits: science and art are sensory rich, personalized, based in inquiry, and experimental. According to prevailing cultural stereotypes, the first two traits are strongly associated with art and the latter two with science. But here we look not at the differences but at the *connections* and consider what they mean to individuals as leaders. Remember, these traits describe underlying processes—how to do the work—rather than the final products.

Science and art are sensory rich. Because its origins lie in primitive astronomy and agriculture, the practice of empirical science has called for heightened sensory and perceptual awareness. It is true the physical senses—sight, touch, taste, hearing, and smell—can be unreliable. But ever-improving methods and instruments have enhanced rather than diminished people's use of their senses. Geneticist Barbara McClintock spent a lifetime observing heritable features on ears of corn that she raised herself; the patterns she saw led to a Nobel Prize in medicine for her discoveries about genetics. McClintock's knowledge was based in ceaseless and skillful looking, in intimacy with the corn itself and not just abstracted data. Her biographer defines McClintock's distinctive talent as *eyesight*—"the continuity between mind and eye."[19]

What are the equivalents of eyesight in the domain of leadership?

Science and art are personalized. To be considered valid, scientific knowledge must stand independent. Scientists, however, invest enormous personal passion in their work. Novelist and expert lepidopterist Vladimir Nabokov often insisted on "the precision of poetry and the passion of science," taking pleasure in the reversal of the stereotype.[20] Scientific work often takes on the character of a quest, replete with all manner of "unscientific" beliefs, tastes, and biases. Successes from such personal pursuits are well documented. Isaac Newton articulated the laws of motion and calculus while pursuing alchemy and magic. The voyage of the HMS *Beagle* defined the person of the young Darwin, who in turn defined the study of evolution. Personal bias in science is corrected not by eliminating personalization but by peer review, further research, and the practice of critical self-awareness.

How can you both encourage and correct for personalization in leadership situations?

Science and art are based in inquiry. These days everyone is bombarded by art intended to shock or manipulate, but most art (as we have defined it) is part of a question-rich conversation, an inquiry between the artist and the viewers of the art. Consider the invention of point perspective during the Renaissance. For many centuries, artists drew and painted their subjects with little attention to the way the human eye actually perceives the relationships among objects situated at different distances and angles. Then Giotto and his colleagues introduced the startling technique of representing the world from a single, geometrically precise point of view, thus obtaining a unique perspective. This technique embodied a fruitful question: What happens if one looks at the larger world in this new way? This inquiry quickly spread to cartography, navigation, architecture, and engineering. As a result of the practical demand for this new skill, some Renaissance children were educated to become professional *perspectivists*. Point perspective eventually becomes a scaffold for Newton's physics.[21]

How can leadership sustain fruitful inquiry into complex challenges?

Science and art are experimental. Although art is often viewed as mainly an expressive outlet, in most cases rational experimentation plays a central role in the ongoing process of creating good art. Potters, for example, are kin to chefs and chemists: they develop recipes for clays and glazes, keeping detailed records of their tests and forming guiding hypotheses. Very few artists are aloof from the opinions of their audience or customers and at least implicitly experiment in making their work more desirable or effective. Surgeons are often viewed as artists, operating creatively within tight constraints as they encounter novel situations. Effective surgery is based in experiments by the field and, more informally, in the findings of individual surgeons as they analyze their experiences. The term *operator* as applied to surgeons originally had negative connotations of sleight of hand; rational experimentation was the element that elevated surgery from quackery to a robust and respectable art form.[22]

What is the role of leadership in promoting experimentation?

Our research suggests that these crossing points between science and art can also enhance leadership for groups addressing complex challenges. But two cautions are in order. First, an adequate level of competency is required in these processes. For example, it helps considerably to be aware of your own personalizing and to be able to *depersonalize* when necessary. Experimentation requires discipline, practice, and group support. Second, these four processes are ideally mutually correcting and should be used together in concert. Inquiry and experimentation help you recognize sensory and personal biases, and vice versa.

Successful Artistry

Human intelligence is perhaps not so radically different across its various endeavors as it may appear. Consider how two very different communities, one at Fermi National Accelerator Laboratory (Fermilab) and one at Apple Computer, found leadership at the intersection of art and science. Robert Wilson was the founding director of Fermilab, the high-energy particle accelerator facility long at the forefront of modern physics. Wilson, a leading physicist and an accomplished sculptor, designed Fermilab to embody the aesthetics of science, with the belief that "the way science describes nature is based on aesthetic decisions." He modeled the administration building on the proportions of Beauvais Cathedral in France (once referred to as the Parthenon of French architecture). Wilson admired the community of medieval cathedral builders and compared it to the community of accelerator builders: "Both were daring innovators, both were fiercely competitive along national lines, but yet were basically internationalists. . . . I am sure that both the designers of cathedrals and the designers of accelerators proceeded almost entirely on educated intuition guided by aesthetics. . . . [The cathedral builders also] recognized themselves as technically oriented; one of their slogans was 'Ars sine scientia nihil est!'—*Art without science is nothing.*"[23]

From inside to outside, Macintosh computers are beautiful because the people who build them consider themselves artists. Apple cofounder Steve Jobs explains: "When you're a carpenter making a

beautiful chest of drawers, you're not going to use a piece of ply-
wood on the back, even though it faces the wall and nobody will
ever see it. You'll know it's there, so you're going to use a beautiful
piece of wood on the back. For you to sleep well at night, the aesthetic, the quality, has to be carried all the way through."[24]

As a company, Apple has been built with aesthetics, from code
to design to brand name and identity. Jobs composed his vision for
the fledgling company in vivid detail. The signatures of the designers were deliberately placed *inside* the case of the original Mac,
where they would be viewed by historians rather than consumers.
The famous *1984* television commercial (portraying Apple as the
liberator from Big Brother IBM) was run just once, in the belief that
artistic uniqueness was superior to numbing frequency. The company's icon was chosen for its bold and appealing symbolism. The
original apple, as the story goes, was the forbidden fruit of the Tree
of Knowledge in the Garden of Eden, the first taste of which
launched all of human history. Another apple is supposed to have
led Isaac Newton to the discovery of gravity and the beginning of
modern science. Thus Apple has positioned itself to be remembered
centuries from now as the third great apple in human history.[25]

In January 1983, when the Macintosh project was months over-
due, Jobs scrawled three words on an easel: "REAL ARTISTS SHIP."
Successful art doesn't exist until it leaves the artist's hands. Aesthetic sensitivities mean nothing without delivery of the goods.
The craft lives in the finished product.[26]

Learning from Artists

David Bayles and Ted Orland comment that "to make art is to sing
with the human voice. To do this you must first learn that the only
voice you need is the voice you already have."[27] The competencies
that we understand to underlie art are also the foundation of leadership. Thus, when you take an excursion from your work life and
explore how you think about, appreciate, and create art, you will

discover strengths that can be brought into work to address leadership challenges more productively.

Bayles and Orland are artists who have written with great insight about the perils and rewards of making art. They believe that most art is part of the fabric of everyday life and made by ordinary people. Here are four powerful ideas they offer to foster artistry, no matter what the domain:[28]

"Becoming an artist consists of learning to accept yourself, which makes your work personal, and following your own voice, which makes your work distinctive." Artistry emanates from the deepest human qualities—values, spirit, strengths, and failings. It is your personal voice that guides your journey as an artist and leader. Your voice is the sound to which others will listen and respond. Finding your voice—personalizing—is essential.

"Making art provides uncomfortably accurate feedback about the gap that inevitably exists between what you intended to do and what you did." Style or intent by itself counts for nothing. Real artists ship. So, take it, put it out into the world, and pay attention to what comes back. *Bounce* is what Eric Booth calls the momentum one gets from finishing a piece of work, taking the lessons from it, and moving on to the next.[29]

"The function of the overwhelming majority of your artwork is to teach you how to make the small fraction of your artwork that soars." Artists work every day, even on hard days. Their studios fill with oddities and experiments. Their pattern of failures offers them as much knowledge as their triumphs. And even the triumphs change color in the light of a new day.

"Making art and viewing art are different at their cores." The finished product usually hides the process that produced the product. The painter's scaffold is removed and hidden when the completed work goes on display. Sometimes your signature goes on the inside where nobody can see it. Watching others perform will not usually reveal what is needed to achieve such a performance. Artists make it look easy, but it's not—so don't worry when it isn't.

Everyday Art

Everyone is an artist. What *kind* of artist is the question—there is bad art and good art, superficial and resonant art, art imbued with value and art that is valueless. Fine art is just one narrow category. What Eric Booth calls *everyday art* is everywhere.[30] It springs from the craft we apply (in our better moments) to work, play, and relationships. Anthropologist Mary Catherine Bateson calls this "composing a life."[31] A manager we spoke with calls it "business art," and a chemist we know calls it "polymer art."

According to Booth, there are three basic actions in making everyday, or *nongenius*, art:[32]

1. *Making things with meaning.* Art that is only about appearance, even beauty, is ultimately shallow. This of course applies to leadership. Resonant art has meaning—not always known at first—to the artist and the viewer. Conversation between the viewer and the artist-leader is critical because it amplifies and multiplies the meanings of the artwork. Within the individual leader's vision there is space for others to co-inquire and construct personal meaning.

2. *Exploring the things others have made.* Artists have other artists as a core constituency, and similarly, leaders have other leaders. Pay attention to how other leaders perform their craft. Real artists may openly copy or mimic other artists, giving credit where it is due, knowing that their own voice will transform the act into something fresh.

3. *Encountering daily life with the work-of-art attitude.* Artists keep their artist's eye awake at every moment: asking, attending, and making connections. Creative leadership improvises to the tune of the moment with an eye on the big picture, what Booth calls *life jazz*. Opportunities for art and leadership slip in under the cloak of the mundane; everything is grist for the artist's mill. R-mode attention transforms "*I* know that" to "What is *that*?" or simply "Hmmm." Booth calls this *reading*,

much as a whitewater kayaker reads the water for the complex patterns that indicate where to run and where to play.

The Transportable Laws of Artistry

In our own research and practice we have spent considerable time with artists, professionals, technologists, managers at all levels, and leaders. These dedicated people share our passion for finding valuable lessons at the intersection of art and leadership. Here are additional rules—full of omissions, exceptions, contradictions, and paradoxes—that we have gleaned from these diverse "artists" through dialogue and observation. We have christened them the *transportable laws of artistry*.

Creative potential increases with knowledge of a medium. Master a medium even if it is one uniquely your own. Know your materials; know how they respond. It is true that novices can sometimes step in and make a contribution. When that happens, typically these novices have imported their own practiced artistry and applied their familiar knowledge to the new field.

Creative potential increases when borders are crossed. Mark Ptashne was one of the first to explore the border between genetics and biochemistry. In his explorations as a self-proclaimed amateur in this new area, he discovered the long-sought repressor molecule (Chapter Two). Borders are often chaotic. Many artists thrive near the edge of chaos. Others make their way by exploring niches in familiar territory. Artists and leaders make fresh connections.

Art is social, "that solitary work we can only do together."[33] Most artists work in a context of intense connections to others, even if some phases of the work are silent and solitary. Like leadership, art is a shared process of making sense and meaning; it is not what one person does all alone. Cultivate your artists' network, and don't be afraid to cross traditional professional boundaries.

Artists are hot-wired to their passions. Call it your core, genius, Muse, inspiration, yearning, Spirit, live wire, or uncensored source.

Artists and leaders are connected to deeper wells, which they sel-
dom can describe. Beware of uprooting your passion and replacing
it with someone else's—to paraphrase the poet David Whyte, beware of sleepwalking your way into someone else's life and mistaking it for your own.[34] Learn to listen to your Muse, lest she leave you
for more attentive ears.

Artists move in the direction of discomfort. Bateson describes "the
double rhythm of pattern violation and pattern creation in the arts
that must characterize any society undergoing change."[35] Artists and
leaders engage in creative destruction, both within themselves and
in their communities. Pattern violation can be incredibly disrup-
tive; sugarcoating the dislocations of change is a shallow form of art.

Artists practice the aesthetics of imperfection. Jazz musicians are adept
at taking a mistake and building something interesting out of it. Scientists have an eye for the awry and capitalize on experiments gone
wrong. Rich Gold, director of the Xerox PARC Artist-in-Residence
program, says, "Artists make art from the mud of the river bank that
flows by their village." Perfectionism is often sterile; practice being
a competent *imperfectionist.*[36]

Art can take you far, fast. We have discussed creative leadership
as often being a matter of slowing down, using R-mode attention,
and avoiding shortcuts. But this misses something essential: art is
hot. Art can strike quickly. Imagination flies. The practiced artist or
group can work at a white heat and maintain a high level of aesthetic competence. In the words of Vincent van Gogh to his
brother Theo van Gogh:

> It is in life as in drawing, one must sometimes act quickly and with
> decision, attack a thing with energy, trace the outlines as quickly as
> lightning. This is not the moment for hesitation or doubt, the hand
> may not tremble, nor may the eye wander, but must remain fixed on
> what is before one. And one must be so absorbed in it that in a short
> time something is produced on the paper or the canvas that was not
> there before, so that afterwards one hardly knows how it got knocked
> into being. The time of discussing and thinking must precede the

decided action. In the action itself there is little space for reflection or argument. To act quickly is the function of a man, and one has to go through a great deal before one is able to do so. The pilot sometimes succeeds in making use of a storm to make headway, instead of being wrecked by it.[37]

Artists see with new eyes and help others do the same. A function of art and leadership is to help yourself and others break habits of seeing in order to see something as if it were new. A corollary is that artists and leaders help people sustain new habits of perception, consistently seeing what has before been subtle or invisible. Look for the familiar in the unfamiliar, and the unfamiliar in the familiar.

Seeing with New Eyes

As an experiment in "seeing with new eyes," we have been teaching leaders of all kinds to draw.[38] In about three hours, using principles developed by educator and artist Betty Edwards, almost anybody can be taught to draw his or her hand (see Figure 6.1).

The first of these drawings was made before training. The second was done the next day by the same person, after immersion in techniques for seeing differently. What's the difference? The first is soaked in the preconceptions and shortcuts of L-mode attention. It is the *stereotype* of a hand. The second was made using R-mode attention. It reproduces the detail and texture of a hand.

Figure 6.1. Hand Drawings Made Before and After Paying Attention.

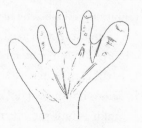 

Many of the leaders are stunned that they can draw like this after the briefest of lessons. They say, for example: "I thought I had zero talent in this department. If I can do this, then what else can I do?" Most people learn just how readily accessible R-mode is given the right conditions; R-mode helps them to see *more* and to see *differently*.

One software development team leader made this link to his work: "In my group we work with clients to write specs for software applications that we then develop. It can be very frustrating because what the clients offer us is like the L-mode hand. Every client gives us the same kind of specs. Likewise, everybody knows this is a hand—it has a palm and five fingers—but all the really unique and important detail is left out."

Another leader said: "When I first tried to draw my hand it looked awful. It doesn't look like a hand. When I learned the concept of negative space, and I quit trying to make my hand look like a hand, then it looked like a hand. The same with many issues at work. Looking directly at the issue, there are no solutions. Look at what's between the issues, and the real issue appears."

The most commonly asked question that emerges from these training interventions is: "What does drawing my hand have to do with leadership?" Think of the hand as a complex challenge, requiring new perceptual skills to represent it accurately. The preinstruction drawing is typically a symbol of a hand. It could be any hand. It is recognizable as a hand because it appears to have something like a palm and digits with some symbolic representation of knuckles and so forth. Similarly, every organization has some ability to make sense of new challenges. All people have symbolic language that they use to make sense in order to take action. However, when people are confronted with higher levels of complexity, symbolic language is not enough. Words fail them. They have to make sense of *this* particular issue, a situation analogous to needing to see *this* particular hand. Just as they need to slow down their looking at the hand in order to draw it in accurate detail (and it is a wonderful paradox that slowing down to look at what one is drawing speeds up enormously

> the larger process of learning to draw), they need to slow down their looking at the complex challenge in order to represent it accurately. From *this* transformed and subtle set of perceptions, they can then craft a response that fits.

Developing the Competency of Crafting

Developing competence in crafting is trickier than becoming competent in the other areas we have explored because it is the orchestration of all those competencies. Craft is typically embedded in communities and spans generations. It often feels larger than oneself, a calling, a journey. Some describe the feeling of crafting as a spiritual commitment. The development of crafting is a lifelong process.

Developing Individual Competence

A few powerful questions are a good starting place for developing the competence of crafting. Ask yourself, *What is my art?* Ask others around you, *What is your art?* When we pose this question to businesspeople,[39] the answer comes back in two parts, both valid and important. The first part is literal: "I am a woodworker"; "I paint in my spare time"; "I like to restore old cars"; "I am a gardener"; "I build things"; "I write"; "I used to be a dancer." The second part speaks to their artistry in the world of leadership:

> The portion of it I like to think of as being an artist is what I think I'm good at: working with people, leading organizations, communicating. That in its own right can become an art form.

> One of the things I've always thought of myself being very good at is making connections between very disparate, unrelated things and making them useful. I always thought that was my art.

I tend to look at things from all different angles; I like to open up the box completely and look at as many alternatives as possible and then start to home in. I also want to follow multiple strategies simultaneously. I like to work on things for the short term at the same time I'm putting energy into the long term.

Often someone responds with the equivalent of, "Oh! You mean this old rag of talent that I have nurtured in the dusty corner of my being actually counts for something?" Yes, it does. We all have an underlying capacity for crafting. Training is a matter of bringing it to the surface, out from rust and neglect.

We often use the Visual Explorer (described in Chapter Five) to unearth these talents. Each team member is instructed to browse the set of images and chooses one that speaks to the question, How am I an artist? or, Where is the place in my life where I am most creative? These are usually good areas for a team to explore together and linger over. Another approach is to ask each person to bring a memento, artifact, picture, or treasured object that helps him speak to these questions. After exploring individual images, ask the group: Which of these talents are valuable for our shared work? What needs to be invited into the organization? Which of these spirited pursuits needs protection from the demands of work, needs to be nurtured so the source of our own craft won't die? These last few questions are ones people often have a hard time answering for themselves. Noticing the gifts of others and acting through them is what draws teams closer together.

Recognize Your Creative Competencies. Use the Creative Leadership Competencies Worksheet (in the following box) to identify the passions and experiences from which you derive your individual artistry. Your own sense of crafting originates from the places and times in which you experience more than one of the C2 Competencies. Building bridges between these places and your current work and life is well worth the effort.

Revitalize Your Art.   Make space in your life for that artful pursuit you've neglected since—when? As a guide in this endeavor, many of the alumni of the Leading Creatively program have used the books *The Artist's Way* and *The Artist's Way at Work*, which lay out a solid process for revitalizing your art and bringing it into your professional life—and confronting the obstacles to doing so—one day at a time.[40]

Associate Yourself with the Masters.   Find out who the artists are in your professional field. Seek them out for conversation, feedback, and perhaps collaboration. Get a mentor. Be a mentor to up-and-coming masters. Become a connoisseur of crafting in the fields that adjoin your own. Learn where the artistry comes from and import its underlying attributes into your own work and life.

Creative Leadership Competencies Worksheet

Your goal in this exercise is to identify areas in your life in which crafting has already developed, so that you can further develop competency in those areas or transfer the competency to other areas of your life and work.

This exercise can be done in as little as twenty minutes. Record your answers in a journal for further reflection later. You can also use this exercise as part of a group discussion, and it works well as a prelude to a Visual Explorer session exploring these questions: What is my art? How am I creative? Where is the place of these competencies in my work life?

Process

For each of the following items, briefly describe in writing an activity, a project, an experience, or a moment in any part of your life, now or in the past, that matches the item.

1. You are a clear-eyed observer. You see (or sense) freshly, deeply, accurately. You pay attention and notice things that others might not. This is *paying attention*.

2. A hobby, an avocation, an art form, or a personal quest or passion contributes something significant to your work. This is *personalizing*.

3. You create a story, a metaphor, or a visual image to communicate something complex. This is *imaging*.

4. Work feels like play, an engaging puzzle, a sport, or a game worth playing. This is *serious play*.

5. A group you are in maintains a high-quality, creative dialogue over a period of time, asking searching questions and exercising critical thinking without always expecting immediate answers. This is *collaborative inquiry*.

6. Something you've made is well crafted: the parts fit into an original whole, and it is complete, well put together, and beautiful in its own way. This is *crafting*.

Developing Community Competence

Healthy communities of craft have cultures that nurture and exalt sublime work. Culture has often been called "the giant in the room." When this description came up during our collaboration with ORC, someone commented, "Yeah, and our giant is an artist!" ORC's R&D culture has a strong subtext of aesthetics and artistic appeal, which people there have been able to surface and legitimate with positive results. Creative leadership is largely a process of developing the undercurrents of craft that already exist in a community.

Develop Widespread Leadership in Addition to Good Management. We have observed many organizations that have a dearth of leadership but hyperactive management, usually in a frenzy to meet performance objectives. Such organizations develop a *craft of management* that works in a machinelike way—a good thing if you really do need a machine—but that is brittle in the face of complex challenges. Instead, nurture the kind of leadership that encourages people at all levels to invent new best practices and bring these practices into the middle of a dialogue about which ones to adopt.

Do a Craft Inventory. Survey your group members to learn all their areas of expertise, however tangential or rusty such areas may at first appear. (A common reaction to statements of expertise beyond the immediate work is, "You do *that?* I had no idea.") Then have the group members brainstorm possible connections between these areas and the complex challenges they face. Rethink your challenge and response in terms of what the craft inventory reveals. Your group will be less likely to perform as a specialized cog in a management machine and more likely to perform as a self-creating unit that adapts to new situations with comprehensive and proactive responses.

Apprentice Beginners to Seasoned Experts. Consciously develop formal structures and informal relationships so that people learn the whole craft and not just techniques. Instead of always sending people away for training, tap into your native expertise, and have people in your group offer training sessions, including topics such as "insider's wisdom on how to get things done" and other black-market knowledge.

Bring About Creative Marriages. Xerox PARC's Artist-in-Residence program attempts to make *marriages* between technologists and visiting artists, based on complementary patterns of interests. Director Rich Gold points out that both art and technology in the San Francisco Bay Area are electrified and digital: "We had no trouble finding artists that were already using dialects familiar to scientists who were fishing in the same waters."[41] Here are some of the marriages:

Embedded data visual artist—Embedded data scientist

Real-time communication artist—Interface designer

High-tech photographer—High-resolution LCD inventor

Documentary filmmaker—Cultural anthropologist

Electronic performer—Video recognition scientist

Cross boundaries by inviting in artists in residence, not for their decorative value but for their ability to translate their gifts into new domains. Seek out creative marriages to add to or foster depth and breadth of craft within your workplace.

Cautions

Those who would develop their craft may at times face scorn from those who would have them tone it down, making it conform to standard recipes. Bayles and Orland remind us that "making art can feel dangerous and revealing. Making art *is* dangerous and revealing."[42] Creative leaders shake things up. Not only must you develop your ability, you also have to maneuver in a world that is afraid, often justly, of revelations and transformations. Western society has a love-hate relationship with art and artists. Modern and postmodern art is by turns intimidating, opaque, slick, and provocative. Society places some art on a pedestal but views the rest with suspicion and sometimes even rancor. Why is this?

Responsible Artistry

One reason the reputation of art has suffered is its connection to facade, trickery, and sleight of hand. Artists play with reality and appearances, sometimes irresponsibly. Artists revel in spinning illusions, and frequent ill effects of such spinning are not hard to spot. *Vision* and *delusion* are cousins in the imagination family, as are *intuition* and *wishful thinking*. According to historian Barbara Stafford, L-mode attention seized the upper hand in the seventeenth century, in direct response to excesses of R-mode thinking: "Schematic logic, judged capable of determining truth or falsehood, was erected as a bastion impervious to the blandishments of sensory misrepresentation. The regulatory role of writing, method, and mind thus came to govern scientific and aesthetic practices since the seventeenth century, especially those prone to less predictable optical, gestural, and emotional forms of communication. Any fine art that purported to demonstrate something . . . and any scientific experiment sustained by machinery . . . was liable to the accusation of *trompe l'oeil* and pandering to spectatorial desire."[43]

Organizations are operations. An operation may be perceived variously as an action, a performance, an act of management, a speculative move, or a manipulation. Adept operations may employ clever acts of hiding and revealing. Running a good operation is based partly in appearance and aesthetics—allowing much of what is underneath the surface to be hidden if and when the operator so desires.[44]

Fabricating is a term for "making things" and also, disparagingly, for "making things up." Yet "making things up" is a literal way to describe the creative process of induction. Just as you might weave threads into a *fabric* to keep yourself warm, you might weave ideas or facts into a fabric for some purpose. The origin of the word *fact* is Latin *facere*, meaning "to make." Facts are made. Factories are one place where facts get fabricated. "Facts on the ground" become real by virtue of their physical presence. The downfall for an artist is in abusing the fabrication (or fact-building) process, fabricating without evolving toward truth. Questions about the ethics of fabrication have haunted us since Plato first denounced artists as those who simply made things up.

We make our devices today in an awesome rush. Questions about the propriety and the fruits of knowledge are swept aside. Artists steal fire from the gods. But it is not unwise to be suspicious of art. In this era we stole fire at Los Alamos and may yet burn down the house. Skepticism without cynicism is a healthy stance, providing requisite checks and balances.

Constructive and Reconstructive Art

Creative leaders have a responsibility to weave shared meaning in ways that, in co-inquiry with others, lead all involved to fuller truths and constructive ends. Art originated as a communal activity to represent and make sense of experience. The principal evolutionary context for the arts is activities of perennial importance: birth, puberty, marriage, death, spiritual connection, finding food, securing abundance, going to war, and resolving conflict.[45] Too much emphasis today is given to deconstructive art that pulls things apart, tears down, and shakes up. Tradition and its associated values lie in shreds. What we need now is a reconstructive art that is capable of restoring and reinventing in positive ways.

Most of the tactics used in the artful construction of things and making meaning of things lie below the surface. Therefore informed critics and loyal skeptics are valuable. Science is that part of human artistry that ceaselessly looks, checks, and corrects. The best contribution critics and skeptics can make is to get beneath the surface, using forms of collaborative inquiry.

In making sense of our research data, this final competency, *crafting*, was the hardest for us to recognize. It was definitely there, but we had no words to articulate it. We have noticed that as we lead an experience with our co-inquiry partners, the number of people in the room always feels like $n + 1$. In addition to the people in the room, there is an additional, unseen body of wisdom and experience—what one might call "the giant in the room." This body of wisdom and experience tends to have an artistic bent, a way of making sense out of complexity and chaos. We encourage you, as a creative leader, to feed this giant: it represents collective leadership for making sense, making new things, and making things happen. As groups become skillful at co-inquiry, they observe the complexity of organizational challenges, then select from the palette of C2 Competencies to craft beautiful, new organizational fabric.

Chapter Seven

Creative Leadership in Action

Now that we have examined each C2 Competency in detail, let's consider how to use the competencies in concert—not as six separate skills but as six different perspectives on making useful, shared sense of complexity and chaos, as symbolized in Figure 7.1.

This chapter looks at how real leaders have used the C2 Competencies, individually and communally, for internal development, for customer development, and for product development. Six case studies examine real-life complex challenges and show how managers have creatively used combinations of sense-making activities to face them. As before, people and organizations whose information is not of public record have been given pseudonyms (shown in italics on the first use) to protect their privacy.

Compare the behaviors and activities in these case studies to your own experience, and adapt what's useful to your own understandings. In this book we have demonstrated how the six sense-making

Figure 7.1. The Sense-Making Loop.

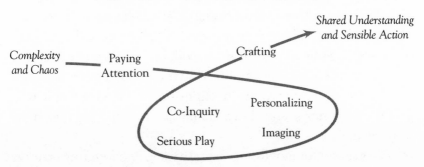

activities lie at the heart of creative leadership. These activities flow well in the order in which we have discussed them—but remember, improvisation and combination are the rule.

The six case studies in this chapter concern

- Task force collaboration, using a digital shared display
- New media and personal investment leadership: The Motley Fool
- Individual leadership coaching and development
- Creative product innovation
- Executive interdependence in a changing marketplace
- Inventing a new manufacturing paradigm: Xerox Lakes project

Case Study 1: Task Force Collaboration

Steve heads up a task force at XYZ, an international telecommunications company. Steve's task force has been commissioned to establish a protocol for installing a new broadband switching system called D4, a daunting task. The days when providing a reliable dial tone was a telephone company's main job are long gone. Now, phone systems are constantly changing and more complex than ever. New digital technologies mingle with legacy platforms. On top of everything else, XYZ is being pressured to provide a "total digital experience"—whatever that means—for its customers.

Steve sits down in the conference room, catching his breath before the first meeting of this task force. He closes his eyes and runs over the issues one more time: operational excellence; customer service; the chaos resulting from mergers; the explosion of broadband; the multiple groups doing the same work but unaware of each other and the multiple authorities directing them. Steve counts at least five *Web heads* coming to the meeting—a new breed of techie who lives for the Internet and always champions it over aging telephone technologies.

As one tool for mobilizing the task force and fostering creative leadership, Steve has chosen to use Compendium, a proprietary meeting-facilitation technology. Originally designed as a platform for business process redesign teams, Compendium provides a shared display, projected from a laptop, for capturing, structuring, and restructuring comments made in a meeting. Compendium is an example of what organizational scholars Karl Weick and Dave Meader call a *sensemaking support system.*[1]

A trained Compendium facilitator helps Steve run the meeting by keeping people's attention on the shared display. The facilitator types in comments, paraphrasing them. He keeps track of what is a question, what is an answer, and what decisions are made. He notes gaps in knowledge and tags them for future reference. The group members argue about the structure as it appears on the display, making changes and additions. They correct misperceptions in the paraphrasing. They link tangents to central issues in a kind of collective *mind map*.

At the end of the meeting the items labeled as decisions are printed out in tabular form. Unresolved issues are highlighted on another printout. A record of decisions is posted on the task force Web site for future reference by members of this and other teams. Steve reports the initial findings to his boss, the vice president of the Integrated Systems Group, and is told the task force will become a team focused on the burning issue of companywide systems integration.

Let's pause to look at this situation in terms of creative leadership. What might at first be seen as a technical set of problems is actually a complex challenge: the issue of establishing protocol for the broadband system spills over into a much larger landscape of changes going on in the company. The team used its C2 Competencies in the following ways, aided at many points by Compendium as a tool set for collaborative knowledge management.[2]

Paying Attention

Compendium helped people to focus their attention on the questions at hand and also to place new questions "on the radar." The verbiage flying around the meeting was made to "stay put" for closer examination on the shared display. The facilitator drew attention to the points being made: "Did I capture the gist of what you said?" "Show me where this idea fits into the rest of our discussion." In this way the facilitator helped the group slow down and really look at the challenges. The facilitator also tagged key items for future attention.

Personalizing

The people at the first task force meeting did not know one another. When Steve learned that the mission of the task force was expanding, he realized that team building was in order. In a special off-site session the group members introduced themselves to each other, revealing their backgrounds and their unique perspectives on the new assignment. Steve had a picture of each member posted on the team's Web site, with links to each person's background data in Compendium. As a result, people learned more about why their teammates took the perspectives they did, and new team members could catch up by browsing the photo gallery.

Imaging

The complex work being done benefited from having a common visual display that was easy to build and edit on the fly. The software medium allowed the display to persist over time and made it possible to upload information to other formats, such as Word and HTML. During the team's first retreat, Steve and the other team members used the *Visual Explorer* technique (Chapter Five) to discuss their backgrounds and how they connected with this project. The VE image each person selected became part of the team's photo gallery.

Serious Play

At first, the task force's work was all serious and no play. Soon, however, the shared display became a playing field strewn with interesting objects. As in any sport, the artificial constraint of shared space provided useful boundaries. The visible ideas on the screen became something to bat around within reasonable and very real limits. The forms of play ranged from jovial participation to fitting text elements on the shared display as if they were parts of a puzzle or moves in a game of chess.

The *Visual Explorer* images selected by the group also provided humor and no end of jokes ("Hey, look at Marge's penguins"). In cases like this, jokes are especially good when they help people produce a brew of metaphors ("Penguins are sturdy little animals!"). Metaphors can become games, and these games can lead to positive connections. ("Why is a D4 switch like the sea urchin in that gull's mouth? Because it has a short life span but tons of siblings and children.")

Co-Inquiry

Putting something in the middle—in this case Compendium's shared display—can be a good way to start a dialogue. The role of the facilitator was to help participants structure the emergent thoughts of the dialogue and to make that structure available between meetings. The group members learned to have virtual meetings about their points of view or queries ("What are our top three priorities for the next four weeks?") by logging into specific discussion groups on an intranet site developed for this purpose. Thus the inquiry developed a foundation for persisting and progressing. The knowledge generated then provided structure and content for the subsequent work of other groups at XYZ.

Steve also observed that English was not the first language of many on this task force. Although company policy calls for English fluency, in practice, many cultural wires were being crossed in communications, adding to the noise level of the issues people on the team faced. The discipline of paraphrasing in writing the key ideas being expressed and then having the team modify that text as necessary helped clarify the spoken ideas.

Crafting

Crafting is the largely aesthetic endeavor of shaping things as you go along and then synthesizing them into a final form for users and other constituents. Steve's group made some fairly well-crafted products. It developed a protocol for D4 broadband switching that was accurate, clearly written, and well vetted. It produced a Web site with a searchable record of all team deliberations. And it produced a wealth of stories and metaphors about the experiences of people inside and outside the company with D4-related technology. Persistent searches for encompassing metaphors (asking, for example, What does this challenge we face look like as a whole?) helped the team make a scaffold of the knowledge resources at XYZ in order to face future challenges.

Case Study 2: Leadership in New Media

The Motley Fool is a media business organization that supports personal investing with books, radio shows, newspaper columns, and a popular Web site. Its stated mission is to "educate, amuse, and enrich" people worldwide on the topic of personal finance.[3] Although the organization has been buffeted by the dot-com shakeout, its experience is instructive.

The Motley Fool's name bespeaks an identity borrowed from the comment of one of Shakespeare's characters: "those that are fools, let them use their talents." The name derives, says the company's Web site, "from Elizabethan drama where only the court Jester (the 'Fool') could tell the King the truth without getting his head lopped off." This lowly wisecracker, dressed in motley attire, was paid to amuse the royal court. His acts of foolishness were also his ticket to freedom of speech, and his words often held wisdom. According to Tom and Dave Gardner, founders of The Motley Fool, "Everyone here is a leader." In other words, every fool in this place has a voice. Contrarians are, after all, a tradition in investing.

Paying Attention

The Fool brand offers a clever set of tools to help people pay attention to what's important in the complex world of personal finance. The company encourages two general modes of paying attention, the analytical (attention to details) and the synthetic (attention to patterns, trends, and meaning). The Fool's community is a vast network of people with diverse perspectives spurring each other on to look at the world, then look again. They are dedicated fact diggers, and the quality of information they offer is excellent even if the quantity is a bit overwhelming. But not to worry: The Fool provides plenty of lenses and filters to help the user pay attention to the right things. You can narrow your attention to the Dow Jones Index, or you can broaden your attention to how sunspots might affect the world economy. The Fool is a great example of how attention can be refined by co-inquiry.

Personalizing

Personalizing is a Motley Fool hallmark. A fool is a likable, wise, and playful person—and it could be you, if you want to join in the fun. The Motley Fool grew by establishing a strong "personality" with which its community members strongly identify.[4] The Fool's investment strategies also draw on the personal domains of its members: their personal needs, dreams, goals, and passions. The notion "who we are is how we invest" is a recurrent theme. You can make your tastes and biases do some work for you. If you think the company you buy your gardening tools from is really terrific, then consider buying its stock—but first apply some analytical criteria to check out where it is your heart has led you.

The Fool also personalizes its operations. Staff have on-line names, such as "TMF Mikey," and thus customer interaction is not anonymous. (In spite of the requisite "Hi, my name is so-and-so, how may I help you?" spoken by customer service representatives, most companies do not personalize customer interaction.) Members also can and do take on public personae in Fool discussion groups. Members begin to trust and respect other members from learning over time the kind of individuals they seem to be. For Fool members, personalizing means creating and evolving one's persona (image as a person).

Imaging

One of the playful devices encouraged by The Fool is the telling of *fribbles*. These are stories related by members of the on-line community that provide meaningful images for understanding the challenges of investing. Although as we write this fribbles are no longer being used, in their prime they were a way in which community members could connect and begin to educate one another. For example, one fribble began: "In frail condition, both physically and mentally, my elderly mother resides in a nursing home in Chicago. She can remember little of her present day activities or recent events. While hazy about time, place, and the identity of all but her closest relatives, she is able to recite from memory her stock portfolio. . . . The night nurse says Mother often prays her Rosary, then starts whispering her list of holdings before drifting off to sleep, usually before she hits Mattel in the middle of the alphabet."[5]

Personal investing is a subject that makes a lot of people nervous, and many people avoid the subject as a result. This fribble, and countless others like it, wove a fabric of community around difficult investment decisions. If you give one investor numbers only, then that investor must behave like a computer. If you give another investor the numbers and also *stories* of investment—about what investment means and how it fits in with lives like that investor's—then that investor can behave less mechanically because the story has imbued the process with meaning.

Serious Play

The Fool's core philosophy, "The 13 Steps to Foolish Investing," says truth plus questioning everything equals fun. "Clever, logical, imaginative: Those are the roots of Folly." Almost all the advice

The Fool offers is indeed quite logical, commonsense even, and shrewd. Management and staff cast themselves as wild and crazy people who are nonetheless very serious about what they do. All this makes lots of people want to participate, not merely to buy a product but to join in the daily fun.

The Fool's internal culture can be playful and upbeat. Employees' serious play fans and feeds the five values the company espouses: optimism, honesty, teamwork, innovation, and winning. In a speech to employees, one of the founders highlighted the etymology of the word *relevance* as it relates to *relief* and *levity*: The Fool aspires to be totally relevant to its customer community. It aims to offer relief from the chaos and confusion of investing. It seeks levity as the lightness that leads to and comes from relief. A sense of humor provides both—and thus The Fool becomes *relevant*.

Co-Inquiry

The Motley Fool founders say, "This stuff isn't rocket science; we all just need to learn together." The Motley Fool crosses the boundaries of "expertise" and creates dialogue. A vital part of The Fool's Web site is the discussion groups. Here people from all walks of life—day traders, house spouses, entrepreneurs, amateurs, and professionals—meet to share knowledge and ignorance. The Fool is an example of Helgesen's web of inclusion, an ever-changing network with a strong core and lots of room at the edges for coming and going.[6] All authority, even that of The Fool's resident experts, is open to searching questions. The Fool's corporate strategy includes increasing the influence of its community on how the company does business, what it focuses on, and what it means to be a Foolish Investor. The whole operation is in effect a sustained and collective inquiry into the changing nature of personal investment.

Crafting

The Motley Fool presents personal finance as an accessible craft. No formula will suffice. Technique helps but is not enough. Crafting is a deep expression of self, and personal investment, at its best, needs to be an expression of the whole person: goals, hopes, fears, history, and relationships. A successful investment portfolio is well crafted, with criteria that are aesthetic as well as rational and analytical.

The living, well-rounded, crafty corporate persona of The Motley Fool is itself an aesthetic achievement. Powerful questions for The Motley Fool are: How do we maintain our culture? How can we listen well to all our people? Will The Fool stay relevant? Can we bring our message to the whole world? We have fun, magic, and mystery—but what is this game we are playing?

Case Study 3: Individual Leadership Coaching

"It's like trying to survive a hurricane at sea." This is how *Bill* envisions the leadership challenge facing him as *Advent,* the company where he works, faces radical changes in the way it operates. Advent is a large international weather forecasting organization in the midst of its own hurricane—the turbulent forces of deregulation and increased competitiveness in target markets.

Bill manages Advent's customer services unit. The unit's major function is to respond to inquiries about the weather. Most of the inquiries seek information for civil and criminal litigation cases and ask about weather conditions at a particular time in the past. Computer databases offer fast access to data for the previous five years. Bill himself is frequently called on to appear in court as an expert witness or as an adviser in judicial inquiries. Recently, Bill has been investigating information technologies that provide proactive services. For example, such services might relate local and international weather conditions to economic, political, or environmental information. This information could help industries discover weather-related trends in the market performance of products such as newspapers or pharmaceuticals or predict events such as the future performance of various food crops, the climatic effects of deforestation, and so on.

Bill develops a hurricane metaphor for his challenge: "Should we risk remaining in the path of the hurricane and survive in the eye of it by turning all the power off? I've read somewhere that it's possible to survive a hurricane that way. Should I steer my ship to calmer waters in the quadrant least likely to be in the path of the hurricane? Perhaps we should abandon ship."

Expressing himself in this way hasn't come easily to Bill. Indeed, when David Horth first met him, he was reluctant to discuss either the organizational crisis or the impact it was having on his unit and him personally. Rather than discuss low morale in his organization, Bill talked about how productivity had decreased and spoke of his frustration in not being able to do anything about it. He felt he had an important role in resolving the crisis for his unit. What should it be? How should he go about it? What were the risks to him and his unit? Worst of all, Bill felt he was at the helm of a ship without a chart or a compass and was able to see and respond only to the next crashing wave.

Bill's frustration became the focus of David's work with him. Could his frustration be harnessed to help him lead his unit to increased productivity? What could Bill himself learn from the crisis? How could he unleash his own leadership potential in order to positively affect operational effectiveness both for his own unit and for the organization as a whole? David's initial focus was to help Bill help himself and thereby help the people he worked with. David asked him to complete several writing assignments. The first was a letter, written as though to an old friend, discussing some of the issues Bill was dealing with organizationally and personally. The objective for Bill at this point was not to analyze the organizational issues but to discover insights into the following:

- Who he is: his strengths and weaknesses and how he came to be this way. (Personalizing.)

- The extent to which he uses perceptions, logic, feelings, and intuitions when challenged. (Paying attention.)

- How he sees himself in the future. (Imaging.)

- How he draws others into the work of navigating the hurricane. (Co-inquiry.)

- What vision and plans he has for the development and implementation of his own leadership. (Crafting.)

Bill's first major discovery was a *root metaphor* (as discussed in Chapter Three), which became an internal mechanism guiding his future actions. Through successive writings, he realized that this root metaphor had guided him through previous crises in his life and career. His metaphor had a literal aspect: a compass given to him by his father many years before. This family heirloom had originally belonged to his great-grandfather, a navigator on the *Cutty Sark*, a tea clipper. The compass that guided his grandfather through perilous waters now became an internal compass guiding Bill through the metaphorical perils of his life and career. Bill adopted the compass metaphor to generate metaphorical imagery for the current crisis in his organization, a vision of the future resolution, and his own role in resolving the crisis. Along with this came renewed vigor and the courage to pursue the plans he was able to formulate.

Bill's choice was to set a course for a safe quadrant where he found a previously unknown harbor, a reinvigoration for his weary crew, and a new trading post for his cargo. From here trade winds were to blow him speedily but safely to his final destination. In more mundane language, Bill listened carefully to his marketing colleagues who steered him toward a new opportunity in the market, matching the capabilities of his unit. This new opportunity slowly but surely took off, providing work for his unit and a feeling among team members that they were doing something meaningful for the larger community while thoroughly engaging their own passions.

Case Study 4: Creative Product Innovation

Over a beer one evening, *Fred* shared with his colleague *John* an issue that had been gnawing at him for several weeks. Fred is a salesperson for *Techno Inc.*, and John manages the firm's software development team. The company had recently announced that it was developing a new series of computers with a new operating system. Fred had been carefully watching the customer response. On the one hand, customers were delighted with a new technology that promised to be faster, more efficient, and more user friendly. On the other hand, these customers had critical information systems that relied heavily on the existing technology. How could they reap the benefits of the new while safeguarding their investment?

Over the meal that followed, Fred sketched out the dilemma to John. Metaphors flowed along with their wine: "Have our cake and eat it too"; "Like the new generation of Volkswagen Beetle"; "Like a PT Cruiser." Everything was retro. Fred and John explored one of the metaphors a little more. The customers under Fred's care displayed the same kind of passion and loyalty for their existing systems as did owners of VW Beetles. How could the company engage this passion and loyalty? How could the new system be retro and still include the efficiencies? Where was the engine in the old Beetle?— in the back. They looked at each other in astonishment. Both had had the same idea at the same time. What if Techno developed an engine—an operating system—that behaved like the old one but was in fact driven by the new technology? The engine could use existing operating system interfaces and offer additional features that could be adopted over time. That evening Fred and John went their separate ways to reflect on the implications of the idea. A week later John phoned Fred: "My team is up for the challenge. It's feasible. But how do we get the funds to do this? Let's talk."

Meeting again in the evening in a restaurant, napkins and pens at the ready, Fred and John tackled the next phase of questions: What are the requirements? How do we design this hybrid? This time, their tool was *imaging*. "Try this," said Fred. "What if we wrote the sales brochure for this hybrid right here, right now? As if it were two years from now and already existed? What would be the benefits? What reference sales would we draw on? What quotes from satisfied customers? What features would provide the benefits?" The sales brochure on the napkin became the template for design of the new engine's code and implementation.

Their work, however, wasn't over yet. They had to make a case for this idea and then sell it in the organization. Techniques for *personalizing* and *co-inquiry* came to their rescue. Fred called on his network of peers, other salespeople, marketers, and managers at various levels of the organization. An influential customer offered to help Fred catch the ear of the senior executives by presenting the case in customer terms. The business case that Fred and John put together was compelling not only because it made sense financially but because the metaphors, the brochure, and their passion for the idea captured the imagination of influential executives. John and Fred also identified sponsors and champions for the proposal and folks who could run interference with influential naysayers. First, they received a budget to develop and test prototypes, then funds to launch a full-blown program of work that gave rise to a highly successful hybrid just in time for the launch of the new system.

Case Study 5: Executive Interdependence

Sterling Inc. is an old and very successful company providing financial services in the specialty insurance industry. Its marketplace is in a conservative arena that is facing rapid change. The company does "the technical work very well, always room for improvement, but we do know how to count beans, thank you." Sterling executes magnificently according to the rules of its game—but the game is changing. Competition is opening radically as the market is de- and re-regulated by U.S. government agencies. And of course the Internet is changing the meaning of insurance services; new players threaten established monoliths.

Samuel has been CEO of Sterling for twelve years and is ready to retire, with honors it would seem, because the company has done well during his tenure. *Joseph* is the senior vice president of operations and heir apparent to the CEO. Sam has mentored Joe, a much younger man, solid in operational knowledge, well versed in the industry. Sam and Joe are beginning to ask themselves, What is the industry? Where are we going? This is a question among some of their colleagues as well, but most others will have none of it. What they typically say is: "The industry is what we see from the center of where we are. The industry is the thing of which we are near the top. Momentum is direction."

Joe, recognizing he is soon to become the leader, frets that leadership is not his strongest aspect. How can he match Sam's strong and confident authority, his firm sense of direction? How, he asks himself, can the people in the company transfer their allegiance from Sam to him? He takes on the task of leadership development.

Sam and Joe hire an executive coach to work with them both individually and together on being more effective with the changes the company is facing. The coach solicits 360-degree feedback on their behalf from the rest of the company's executive forum and from a sample from the board of directors. Then he works with Sam and Joe on making sense of the feedback.

Creative leadership requires both self-development and community development. Focusing leadership energy on a complex challenge is a good way to do both. This foray into coaching seems successful, so Sam and Joe take what they've learned to Sterling's executive forum (EF, more an affiliation of fiefdoms than a council or a team). They propose a leadership development program for the EF in which forum members will work collectively on a major challenge, at the same time focusing on improving their individual and collective leadership abilities. The Center for Creative Leadership agrees to facilitate the process. As members of the EF begin individual coaching, they also talk about what they think the important challenges are for Sterling.

The first Sterling Executive Leadership Forum is a two-day retreat "in some serious woods"; as one participant observed, "We are not going anywhere." All phones are turned off during the sessions and short breaks. The purpose is to identify a challenge and begin work on it (or more likely, continue to work on it but in a different way). The purpose of this and subsequent gatherings is also, as Joe puts it, "to build muscle." The power wielded by the EF as a whole has been rather weak, apart from Sam's commanding rule. Says

Sam, "I want to see them work together and actually build something, not just squabble and rearrange the furniture."

Attending the opening afternoon and evening of the retreat is
like being in front of a firehose of information. Industry gurus and
key customers spell out their hopes and concerns. Headlines from
the EF interviews about key challenges are posted around the room:
"GE Attacks Sterling! No Prisoners!"; "The Internet Changes the
Way People Buy Insurance"; "The Hacker and Slacker Generation
Is Coming!" The next morning the group addresses the question,
"So what is happening to us and to the industry, and what does all
this mean?" Notes and the headlines from the day before are posted
round the room. A bunch of poster-sized, pen-and-ink cartoons are
hung there as well, courtesy of a roving artist turned loose the previous day. The cartoons earn some wry laughs and grimaces. The
participants sit in a circle, counsel-style.

The ensuing dialogue is tentative but fairly open. At some point
in the day the group agrees on ground rules for this kind of conversation. One person grumbles about "the kindergarten circle," and
there is some frank push-back about doing "this soft stuff." Several
people cite hopeful aspects of the conversation so far and are game
to experiment as long as it means getting some work done on the
big issues. A few people make reference to their coaching and how
it might link to the group's shared challenges.

Let's review Sterling's creative leadership activities to see where
its executives are developing individual and collective competency:

Paying Attention

These days it is healthy for work groups to get together and spend
time looking closely at the challenges they face. A *data dump*—
customer voices, industry trends, and other information—can work
if participants also have tools to make sense together of what they
see. Dialogue is a tool for focusing and holding attention on complexity. At Sterling, it used to be that Sam did most of the paying
attention at an industry level. Joe is committed to having the mem-

bers of the EF do more of this themselves and then check what they are seeing with each other. The members discovered they sometimes disagree on the most basic level—that is, about what they are actually observing—and that discovery is not at all a bad thing.

Personalizing

The EF members were in danger of becoming caricatures to each other. They guarded most of their positions and favored taking political action behind the scenes. In many ways (not all of them bad) Sam's personality was the order of the day, including his tastes, hunches, and biases. For these individuals, some simple acts of letting their guards down and getting to know one another were in order. The EF members held peer interviews regarding the challenge. They began peer coaching and also began group mentoring younger staff. Everyone brought in personal photos that represented the sources of his or her leadership values. As stacks of pictures emerged from briefcases, personal stories were shared and welcomed: "I didn't know Marty worked for the government for six years"; "His father was a coal miner, a union guy"; "She went to school with my sister"; "We have different values"; "We have the same values."

Personal 360-degree feedback helped individuals address their own strengths and weaknesses. Coaching helped them better see what their contributions could be and what participation in the leadership of Sterling meant.

Imaging

The EF spent some time constructing scenarios for the future (if we do this, this might happen; our competitors seem to be going over here). Its members did a movie-making exercise in which, using pictures clipped from trade magazines, they built scenarios rich with the stories they all had about what's changing and what's not. Sterling now has a *war room* with a big wall on which it pictures its competitors.

Serious Play

By most standards the EF members were not a playful bunch. Buttoned-down financial types, clubby without being close, they did not attract young blood to their group. As their serious play emerged, it looked less like fun and more like exploration and experimentation. It showed fresh curiosity and a letup in the members' usual know-it-all one-upmanship, as though they were saying, "We know all the old maps, and they are starting to fray. How do we rewrite the maps and build new compasses?" One of the young MBA hires said he liked the fact that the company was trying new things: "That new dress code is a good idea."

Co-Inquiry

The executives quickly converged on a challenge: "How do we make the annual strategy and resource allocation process more effective?" When they solved that one, they moved on to another one. Once the process of figuring out the business was opened up, there was less backroom bargaining. Together they uncovered some pretty scary scenarios for their business and learned to keep an open dialogue going rather than using events to jockey for position and favor. After the retreat a series of regular strategy meetings made solid ideas take shape. The EF became less insular as a group, frequently inviting customers to retreats and bringing in controversial speakers to stir things up.

Crafting

Sterling's craft is based in finance, but the tools and the rules are changing. The new craft of the Sterling of the future is not yet clear, but it will include a healthy dose of financial conservatism alongside a willingness to invent new services for new markets. This *community of crafts* will include Web designers and actuaries; it may also include marketers, anthropologists, and city planners. Handling all the complexities means looking closely at purpose, mission, and values. What is shaping the big picture? For some at Sterling the big picture is more captivating than quarterly earnings—both are plainly necessary, and it takes attention to both to craft an enterprise with both vision and strength.

Case Study 6: Inventing a New Manufacturing Paradigm

Xerox is reforming itself to focus on digital document processing systems. An R&D program called Lakes has been central to this effort.[7] "In effect, the mission of Lakes was to reinvent copying," says John Elter, vice president and chief engineer of new business development at the Xerox Office Document Products Group. Elter was the singular leader of this massive project, but the creative leadership of the project was a matter of how the entire group approached its work.

Historically, Xerox has been the innovator but not the executor of key aspects of the personal computer revolution. The self-conscious aim of the Lakes project has been to conceive *and* deliver. Lakes started with a blank-sheet assignment: to create all-new technology rather than increments to the status quo. Its goals are to make seamless the scanning, storing, reproducing, printing, and distributing of documents and to make real the concept of *zero to landfill*, meaning that every part of a product is designed for reuse or recycling. This latter notion, part of an ongoing *environmental leadership* movement within Xerox, perhaps best illustrates the Lakes team's radical commitment to superb *crafting*—that is, to advanced, meticulous design in service of functionality. *Design for remanufacturing* poses a complex challenge for Xerox, forcing it to rethink old ways of doing business and putting it into new relationships with suppliers and customers.

The Lakes project has culminated in a line of new products for Xerox. It has also deeply influenced the way the company works with customers and designs solutions. Here are some of the ways the Lakes team has practiced creative leadership.

Paying Attention

A challenging vision like zero to landfill is a means of making people start paying attention: everything is different, so they had better look at every detail in a new light. Nothing can be taken for granted. Attention is a group activity as well as an individual one. Everyone on the Lakes team—not just market research staff—has traveled the world talking to customers and watching them work. Lakes members spent their first six months together not designing anything but simply listening to what they called "the voice of the customer." The pilot document center itself was created with a kind of artificial intelligence designed to pay attention. The team created software, called Sixth Sense, that allows about six hundred data points in a Xerox machine to be monitored over phone lines. The machine knows what is wrong and alerts the service representative to what parts are needed.

Personalizing

The Lakes team members, according to Elter, "think they're on a mission from God." They are supremely passionate about their work—and not surprisingly so. They are engineers and technologists who have been asked to reinvent copying and told they can start with a blank slate—no preconceptions, existing platforms, or limitations.

Lakes has collaborated with LivingSystems, a consulting firm in Santa Fe, New Mexico, to create developmental experiences that will support the team in facing its enormous challenge. What LivingSystems created combined personalizing with serious play. About half of the eight hundred Lakes engineers and managers voluntarily attended four-day, small-group sessions to explore the vision of environmental leadership. The sessions were held in the western deserts and eastern mountains of the United States. They consisted of fieldwork and a vision quest. When asked if this was too much of a stretch for engineers, Elter replied, "Give us the undiluted stuff.

We can handle it." These sessions helped participants establish their own connections to the ecological values of the project. As a result, "the Lakes product meets or exceeds all EPA, Nordic Swan, Environmental Choice, and Blue Angel requirements."[8]

Imaging

Lakes people intently practice all three kinds of vision discussed in Chapter Three: direct, abstract, and imaginative. They integrate paying attention and imaging by creating L-mode maps of the emergent design—an abstract vision but rich in detail and theory. They also create imaginative visions, full of emotion and vivid pictures, that are responsive to the voices they are attending to (including their own voices). These are scenarios of the office of the future, "green" images of zero-to-landfill machines, and scenarios of the world inhabited by their own children.

Serious Play

There is an interplay of looseness and tightness in Lakes team behavior. The team is tight in employing robust design and analytical rigor. It is loose in its willingness to take risks and experiment. The Lakes philosophy is one of *emergence*: set the vision, values, principles, and general structures, and new forms of beneficial order will emerge. Play is necessary if individuals and communities are to begin to think in new ways. Play is what passionate people naturally do at the boundary between order and chaos.

Co-Inquiry

"Such an ambitious project," says Anne Stocum, manager of environmental market leadership at Xerox, "required intense partnership with suppliers." According to one Lakes systems engineer: "We brought in all of our external suppliers early on and explained our philosophy to them. We wanted them to understand the project and to support it. And we needed their help."[9]

Sustaining very good questions without answering them prematurely is a hallmark of co-inquiry. Among these questions are variations of: What is right for the customer? What is right for the future of the planet? How do we work with each other effectively? People whom some at Lakes have described as a "hodgepodge of talents and personalities" have come together and organized their behaviors in pursuit of these questions. A key issue in facing complex challenges is how the individuals involved treat each other. The Lakes team adopted an employee Bill of Rights. Among its tenets was the maxim "Even though you disagree with me, don't make me wrong."

Lakes has freely borrowed attitudes toward co-inquiry from among that competency's classic forms: science above all has imposed its rigors on the dialogue. Nonetheless, there is a kind of religion in all this, or at least the spiritual pursuit of a deeply shared vision at the intersection of technology and ecology. Some of the Lakes members are fanatic about this, and yet any possible excesses are apparently contained within the scrutiny of the community as a whole. Artistry done well is also a form of inquiry; the Lakes process is an example of artful work.[10]

Crafting

Some years ago, Xerox did not harvest the creative products of Xerox PARC—Steve Jobs, Steve Wozniak, and others reaped the benefits of PARC's innovation in designs ranging from the mouse to the desktop interface—and this illustrates a shortcoming of craft on the corporate level. Today's Lakes project is committed to actually putting tools in the hands of the *user*. Creativity is not crafting without this distinguishing trait. End-users are frequently the drivers of crafting. European green standards in particular are driving companies toward designing products intended from the beginning to be recycled, reused, or remanufactured.

Crafting organizes tangibles and intangibles into a whole and judges them as a whole. Crafting is not merely a summing of parts.

Crafting connects the most mundane elements with the subtlest and highest values. The Lakes project and its products appear, from this perspective, to have been well crafted. As a result of the Lakes experiment, the economic and engineering lessons of remanufacturing are spreading throughout the company. In 2000, Xerox saved an estimated $200 million through product remanufacturing and parts reuse, diverting nearly 150 million pounds of waste from landfills.[11]

According to Karl Weick, "Sensemaking is less about discovery than it is about invention." Moreover, "sensemaking is a process of making do with whatever resources are at hand."[12] It is our hope that *The Leader's Edge* has provided you with useful tools—insights, examples, exercises, and guidelines—for making the most of your own resources. Creative leadership is anything but a cookie-cutter activity. It is a unique, multifaceted, organic, evolving process.

As the people and companies described in this chapter illustrate, creative leadership is not a singular pursuit. Both creativity and leadership are communal enterprises. As you explore and expand your creative leadership abilities, you may discover a fundamental shift in your understanding of what it means to be an individual and what it takes to make a community.

Creative leadership requires you to have diligence, reflection, insight, and underneath it all, a passion for truth and a passion for the future. We have no doubt that the creative leaders of today are the people behind the innovations of tomorrow.

Appendix A:
The Leading Creatively Program

The Leading Creatively program (LCP) was first piloted in 1994 as an ongoing collaborative inquiry with participants, organizations, and colleagues in the field (see Appendix B for an overview of our research questions and methods). Although the program evolved in response to what we learned and was customized for specific contexts, the mission and key elements of the program persisted.

From its beginning the Leading Creatively program has had this mission statement: "Participants will discover their own aesthetic competencies, and learn how to apply these in order to revitalize themselves, their work and the communities they serve."

The program does this, over the course of a week, by engaging participants in experiences designed to help them perceive and make sense of a particular challenge each one faces as a leader and to help them uncover and strengthen innate competencies.

Our hypothesis has been that comprehensive processes for making sense of complexity are aesthetic in important ways and that individuals and groups can develop these processes for effective use. A goal of the LCP can be described as developing the capacity for what Eric Booth calls *everyday art* and putting this capacity at the service of creative leadership. We attempt to facilitate learning that stays with people, going beyond a set of recipes that would simply gather dust on the bookshelves once people have returned to their daily environments. We wish to tap into core competencies people bring with them so these competencies can be surfaced, owned, further developed, and valued. We conduct co-inquiry with our participants to assess and increase the efficacy of the LCP in their work and lives.

The Leading Creatively program has eight key elements:

Challenge statement. Participants come to the program with their principal complex challenge spelled out (this assignment is part of the program prework). During the program they have space to articulate and further explore their challenge. Moreover, when they go on an excursion (such as learning to draw), seemingly moving away from the problem and developing some new modes of looking at things, they then come back to the issue and say, "How might this apply to this challenge?"

Drawing. Everyone has the ability to draw complex images. We adapt Betty Edwards's methods of "drawing on the right side of the brain"—accessing right-hemisphere mode (R-mode) perception and cognition. What we call *paying attention* is a primary focus of this element. As Edwards says: "My students generally agree that learning to see by means of drawing makes a qualitative difference. They had never before realized how much more there was to see, how very different things could appear, and how radically this kind of seeing could affect their thinking."[1]

Collage. Selecting, altering, and composing disparate images into a new image was a dominant art form in the last century as well as a potentially powerful form of sense making. Participants make collages representing their challenges at the beginning and near the end of the program. These collages become objects in the middle of dialogue.[2]

Music making. Recognizing and producing musical sounds calls upon awareness of rhythm, harmony, silence, and voice. Participants practice the risk taking of improvising in public. They explore what such risk taking might mean with respect to their own leadership and for eliciting others' leadership.

Story writing and storytelling. Stories are one of the most common and potentially powerful forms of sense making in organizations, in cultures, and in each of our lives.[3] Participants explore their leadership challenges in stories they write.

Dream circle. Participants learn principles of dialogue in a context of personalized intuitions as volunteers put their dreams in the middle of a dialogue and explore connections to their challenges.[4]

Creativity assessment. Participants receive data from their own workplace about its climate for creativity, as measured by the CCL multirater feedback instrument KEYS® to Creativity. They also get feedback through the Kirton Adaption-Innovation Inventory (KAI), which measures creativity style.

Collaborative inquiry. Participants reframe and understand their leadership challenges in give-and-take with their cohorts in the program. The context of making art provides new options for communication, for questioning, and for feedback. Program participants are invited to join the Center for Creative Leadership in learning about the nature of sense making in the face of complex challenges. Healthy skepticism is frequent and welcome. The annual gathering for LCP alumni (the Airlie Conference) is a place for renewal and exchange of learnings about creative leadership.

Appendix B:
Our Research Methods

Our research methods have been to design, test, and deliver a five-day program for the development of creative leadership (the Leading Creatively program) and to embed that program and its development in a collaborative inquiry that includes CCL faculty and staff, program participants, organizational partners, and colleagues and scholars in the field.

Our high-level research questions are: What is the full range of competencies people in organizations use to face complex challenges? Where do these competencies come from, and how can they be further developed? What is the meaning and value of aesthetic competency in the service of leadership and in the face of complex challenges?

Collaborative inquiry as a research method is a version of what Kurt Lewin called *action research*, in which "researchers operate as collaborators with members of organizations in studying and transforming organizations."[1] Dalmar Fisher and William Torbert describe collaborative inquiry as "explicit, shared reflection about corporate mission; open interpersonal relations with disclosure, support and confrontation of apparent value differences; creative resolutions of paradoxes; [and] interactive development of unique, self-amending structures appropriate to this particular organization at this particular historical moment."[2]

We have conducted collaborative inquiry in these ways:[3]

- The Leading Creatively program was designed and piloted in collaboration with three different intact work groups at three different corporate sites. We have followed up at each site over many months to understand the effects of the program as well as to explore more broadly the nature of aesthetic competency.

- The program is designed to focus participants' experience on making sense of some complex challenge they face in the workplace. The milieu of the LCP is thus inquiry among staff and participants in perceiving, reframing, and understanding the issues each person brings to the program.

- Program alumni are invited to collaborate with us in various ways to critically test these ideas about creative leadership by trying them out in their work and in their lives. One forum for such collaboration is the annual Airlie Conference for alumni.

- Ninety-eight alumni completed a lengthy written survey regarding the impacts and implications of the program on work and life.

- We have conducted over two hundred interviews with LCP alumni regarding the competencies they use in addressing complex challenges in work and in life.

Appendix C:
A Reflective Assessment of C2 Competencies: Competencies for Making Sense of Complex Challenges

Your name:_____

Think about your key challenge, and then write it out as you currently frame it:

Using the scale shown, rate yourself on each of the following activities, *as it applies to this challenge*.
1 = Ineffective; I don't do much of this.
2 = Occasional use; limited success.
3 = A strength.

Section 1: Paying Attention	Rating
Sustain attention to the big picture(s), across boundaries.	___
Listen to weak or conflicting signals.	___
Use multiple channels or methods for paying attention.	___
Am aware of how my own biases affect my observations.	___
Temporarily suspend judgments or biases to see more.	___
Persevere in paying attention despite discomfort.	___
Concentrate attention when necessary, despite noise and overload.	___

Shift attention to the periphery, gray areas, or
    negative spaces.   —

Section 2: Personalizing   Rating

Connect my deepest values or passions to the workplace.   —
Help others connect their passions and their work.   —
Detach from personal passions as required for greater
    objectivity.   —
Explore and evolve my own personal identity.   —
Bring personal experiences, avocations, or interests to
    bear on a new situation.   —
Have the guts to be a whole person at work.   —
Operate out of a strong sense of *who I am*.   —
Get and use feedback from those around me.   —

Section 3: Imaging   Rating

Use stories to communicate or share ideas.   —
Create and use metaphors to portray ideas.   —
Create and use shared visual images.   —
Display data clearly and effectively.   —
Paint the picture of what the organization is trying to
    achieve.   —
Create and explore scenarios of the future.   —
Use a disciplined imagination to see things differently.   —
Respect, support, and challenge images *made by others*
    that portray ideas, imagine things differently, and
    so forth.   —

Section 4: Serious Play   Rating

Experiment intelligently.   —

Make fruitful mistakes.   ____

Use humor and levity effectively.   ____

Am self-effacing when appropriate.   ____

Explore with curiosity and a sense of fun.   ____

Rule bend and rule break effectively.   ____

Learn about complexity by trying things and getting
feedback.   ____

Explore connections between seemingly unrelated
domains.   ____

Section 5: Collaborative Inquiry   Rating

Invite and explore differences in perspective.   ____

Build new perspectives in collaboration with others.   ____

Express doubts or criticism in a constructive way.   ____

Hold a complex issue open to debate and deliberation
without rushing to an answer.   ____

Make room for quiet voices.   ____

Find ways to discuss the important undiscussables.   ____

Create shared understanding across community
boundaries.   ____

Foster an environment in which people can address
difficult issues with one another.   ____

Section 6: Crafting   Rating

Orchestrate or compose the parts of work, and life,
into worthwhile wholes.   ____

Master the tools of my trade(s).   ____

Make my own tools.   ____

Know the proper places for approximation and perfection.   ____

Know when to work within tradition and when to break
with tradition.   ___

Respect and engage the best in the craft of others.   ___

Am a connoisseur or able critic of creative work.   ___

Invest work with elegance, artistry, spirit, and beauty.   ___

Summarize the survey results in your own words under the following headings:

Strengths That Are Not Surprising or Are "Old News"	Strengths That Are Surprising or "News"
Developmental Needs That Are Not Surprising or Are "Old News"	Developmental Needs That Are Surprising or "News"

Appendix D:
The ORC Star-Mapping Process

To explore the notion of visual sense making with your group, you can conduct a simulation using the star-mapping process of the *Orion Research Center* (ORC). This can be a way of preparing the members of your group to invent their own methods to fit their own needs for making better sense of strategic data about a number of projects that must be prioritized.

Instructions

- Ask each person to fill out the scorecard (Exhibit D.1, at the end of the Appendix) as prework or at the time of the session. Note that each person is asked to rate *two* projects. It helps if the projects are personally meaningful to the person filling out the scorecards for them.

- Ideally, about seven to fifteen people will work with about twenty to thirty projects at a single table. Multiple tables can be run per session.

- (Optional.) Once the scorecards are completed, let the group spend ten to twenty minutes trying to select or prioritize projects using only the scorecards. Later the group can compare this experience to the experience of using star-mapping.

- (Optional.) Ask each person to briefly describe the projects he is submitting to the rest of the group.

- (Optional.) Ask each person to select a picture for each of her two projects from the deck of *Visual Explorer* images (described in Chapter Five). Each image should remind her of something essential in the project. Then, when she introduces the project to the group, she uses the picture to help describe it (typically as a metaphor for the project).

- Have the whole group transfer the data from the scorecards to star maps. Color each quadrant a different color (consistently using one color for the first quadrant, another color for the second quadrant, and so on across all the maps). See the illustration in Figure 3.2, showing the twelve *legs* that correspond to the twelve scorecard questions and the quadrants that correspond to the four scorecard categories (strategic fit, capability, risk, and reward). Each quadrant thus has a different meaning, and information is carried in the size and shape of the quadrants. Cut out the star shapes. Mark the top of each shape. Put a name or code number that identifies the project on the back of the star map.

- Lay out paper as large as a tabletop, about four feet by six feet or so.

- Draw a pair of x and y axes on the paper (and also draw the diagonal xy line for later use). X is "strategic fit," and y is "attractiveness." Attractiveness may be thought of as the sum of the dimensions of capability, risk, and reward, but it will have a high degree of subjectivity also. *A key point of this exercise is to allow personal subjectivity to be interspersed with the numbers and analysis.*

- Ask the group to place the star maps on the xy plot. Much discussion (and usually some elbowing) will ensue as people defend, ask questions, compare, wonder, and so forth.

- Observe that there are four groups of projects on the xy plot (projects that are high on one axis and low on the other, projects low on both axes, and projects high on both axes).

- Discuss each project group and its members and confirm placement (argue).

- (Optional.) Cut out the images previously chosen for each project and paste them on the backs of the appropriate star

maps. Turn each star map image side up, and repeat the placement discussion, now working from the idea and image of
each project instead of the numbers.

- (Optional.) Try other labels (risk or capability, for example)
  for one or both of the axes.

- Force each project to its nearest point on the *xy* line, in effect
  rank ordering the projects from high to low priority. No ties
  are allowed. Discuss the results again.

- Give each person ten mint chocolate patties, and ask people
  to vote on the projects that after all this discussion their gut
  says are good projects to do. The better the project, the more
  mint patties are stacked on it. Discuss the results again, especially any anomalies from the previous prioritization.

- If two different groups worked with the same data, each now
  visits the other's table to observe any differences in the
  priorities.

- Debrief the simulation: What was the experience like? How
  was it different from the group's typical way of processing
  information? How did emotions and intuitions enter the
  process? How did the group deal with the complexities in
  the information?

Exhibit D.1. R&D Strategic Planning Scorecard.

Please fill out the *R&D Strategic Planning Scorecard* twice—once for each of two different projects. Each will be an R&D project (broadly defined) within or shared by your operating area. One project should be more mainstream or already approved and the other more speculative or controversial.

Rate the project as best you can on each of the twelve dimensions on the scorecard. Try to avoid personal bias in your ratings. (Your teammates will have a chance to correct your biases.) You may estimate as necessary.

The ratings will be input for a simulation of the ORC strategic planning process. This is only a simulation, and the ratings you submit will not be used beyond it.

Name of the project. _____

Describe it in 12 words or less. _____

Check only ONE ITEM in EACH ROW, scoring the project from 1 to 5	5	4	3	2	1
Quadrant 1: Strategic Fit					
1. Strategic intent	One of the top 5 strategic initiatives ☐	One of the top 10 strategic initiatives ☐	High-visibility project positively reviewed by board of directors ☐	Board has expressed interest in project ☐	No current strategic link and no board interest ☐
2. Market plan	Game changer, new customers ☐	Game changer, existing customers ☐	Next generation, new customers ☐	Next generation, existing customers ☐	Line extension ☐
3. Life cycle position of product	Developing explosively ☐	Growing ☐	Embryonic ☐	Maturing ☐	Declining ☐
Quadrant 2: Reward					
4. Product lifetime before replacement	25 years ☐	15 years ☐	5 years ☐	3 years ☐	< 3 years ☐

5. Segment share versus all competitors	> 2.0× ☐	> 1.5× ☐	> 1.0× ☐	> 0.25× ☐	< 0.25× ☐
6. Profit potential (net)	> $5.0 MM/year ☐	> $2.0 MM/year ☐	> $1.0 MM/year ☐	> $0.5 MM/year ☐	< $0.5 MM/year ☐

Quadrant 3: Risk

7. Probability of technical success within time line	> 80% (We are sure we can do it) ☐	> 60% (We think we can do it) ☐	> 40% (We can probably do it) ☐	> 20% (We might be able to do it) ☐	< 20% (It will be really hard to do it) ☐
8. Probability of sales success given technical success	> 80% ☐	> 60% ☐	> 40% ☐	> 20% ☐	< 20% ☐
9. Patent protection	Protected against competitive patents for > 5 years ☐	Protected against competitive patents for 3–5 years ☐	Uncertain patent protection ☐	Competitive patents exist ☐	Superior patented product will be on the market when we go commercial ☐

Quadrant 4: Capability

10. Time to commercialization	< 3 months ☐	< 9 months ☐	< 12 months ☐	< 24 months ☐	< 36 months ☐
11. Technical knowledge	Our people are familiar with this technology ☐	Fairly new to most of our people, but familiar outside ☐	New to all of our people, but familiar outside ☐	New to all of our people and the technical field ☐	*Off the wall* to us and the technical field ☐
12. Market knowledge	Our people are familiar with this market ☐	Fairly new to most of our people, but familiar outside ☐	New to all of our people, but familiar outside ☐	New to all of our people and the market ☐	*Off the wall* to us and the market ☐

Notes

Preface

1. W. H. Drath and C. J. Palus, *Making Common Sense: Leadership as Meaning-Making in a Community of Practice* (Greensboro, N.C.: Center for Creative Leadership, 1994); C. J. Palus and W. H. Drath, *Evolving Leaders: A Model for Promoting Leadership Development in Programs* (Greensboro, N.C.: Center for Creative Leadership, 1995); C. J. Palus and D. M. Horth, "Leading Creatively: The Art of Making Sense," *Journal of Aesthetic Education,* 1996, 30(4), 53–68.

The question of how people create sense and meaning has been especially well addressed in the work of Karl Weick, Robert Kegan, and William Torbert and their colleagues, and their work is infused throughout this book. A good place to start (and where we started) is with Robert Kegan's seminal book *The Evolving Self: Problem and Process in Human Development* (Cambridge, Mass.: Harvard University Press, 1982).

The topic of successive stages in the development of human meaning making is an important one but beyond the scope of this book. Ken Wilber synthesizes and extends all that is known about developmental stages in several of his books. We recommend K. Wilber, *Integral Psychology* (Boston: Shambhala, 2000). In Wilber's terms, the practices in *The Leader's Edge* can be viewed as a contribution toward *integral leadership*—a stage beyond *postmodern leadership*.

Introduction

1. *Chemstar, Orion,* and *Johns River Station* are companies with which we have collaborated on leadership development as part of the Leading Creatively Project. In this book, we have not used real names for these companies or the individuals involved with them and have removed identifying details. This is standard policy at the Center for Creative Leadership because of the intimate and sensitive nature of work on individual and organizational development in a research context.

2. P. B. Vaill, *Managing as a Performing Art: New Ideas for a World of Chaotic Change* (San Francisco: Jossey-Bass, 1989), pp. 39–40. See also P. Mayer, "Introduction to the Special Issue: The Aesthetic Face of Leadership," *Journal of Aesthetic Education,* 1996, 30(4), 1–4; R. A. Smith, "Leadership as Aesthetic Process," *Journal of Aesthetic Education,* 1996, 30(4), 39–52.

3. W. H. Drath, *The Deep Blue Sea: Rethinking the Source of Leadership* (San Francisco: Jossey-Bass, 2001).

4. H. Cleveland, *Leadership and the Information Revolution* (San Francisco: World Academy of Art and Science, 1997), p. 43.

Chapter One

1. H. Cleveland, *Leadership and the Information Revolution* (San Francisco: World Academy of Art and Science, 1997), p. 58.

2. Our need to enhance the ways we pay attention in an increasingly cacophonous world is a subject that transcends the leadership issues discussed in this book. For a good review of the cognitive and social bases of attention, the business implications of attention deficit, and the antidotes to this deficit, see T. H. Davenport and J. C. Beck, *The Attention Economy: Understanding the New Currency of Business* (Boston: Harvard Business School Press, 2001).

3. D. N. Perkins, *The Intelligent Eye: Learning to Think by Looking at Art* (Santa Monica, Calif.: Getty Center for Education in the Arts, 1994).

4. A. de Geus, "Strategy and Learning," *Reflections*, 1999, *1*(1), 75–81.

5. The idea that attention, and intelligence more generally, is multiple rather than monolithic and that people can take advantage of these multiple modes is an idea most thoroughly explored by Howard Gardner at Harvard University. The Leading Creatively Project has been greatly informed by his work. See H. Gardner, *Multiple Intelligences: The Theory in Practice* (New York: Basic Books, 1993); *Frames of Mind: The Theory of Multiple Intelligences* (New York: Basic Books, 1983).

6. Edwards is unique in concentrating on practical methods for differentiating R-mode and L-mode; she draws on neurological studies to make an empirical case for the validity of these modes of perception. See B. Edwards, *Drawing on the Right Side of the Brain: A Course in Enhancing Creativity and Artistic Confidence*, rev. ed. (New York: Putnam, 1989). Jerome Bruner, a founder and pioneer of modern cognitive science, was also early in recognizing the importance of "the left hand" for understanding human achievement: "the scientist and the poet do not live at antipodes . . . the artificial separation of the two modes of knowing cripples." See J. S. Bruner, *On Knowing: Essays for the Left Hand* (New York: Atheneum, 1969), p. 2.

7. These modes, and certainly the hemispheres of the brain, work in an intertwined fashion in all but extreme conditions. One should aspire to enhance the collaboration of modes, not their separate or exclusive functioning. In his book *Dragons of Eden* (New York: Random House, 1977), scientist Carl Sagan concluded that the important creative achievements of civilization are the result of collaboration between the right and left hemispheres.

8. David Hurst attributes the notion of "values-based rationality" (as often clashing with "fact-based rationality") to the pioneering German sociologist Max Weber. See D. K. Hurst, "When It Comes to Real Change Too Much Objectivity May Be Fatal to the Process," *Strategy & Leadership*, 1997, *25*(2), 10–13; R. Brubaker, *The Limits of Rationality: An Essay on the Social and Moral Thought of Max Weber* (London: Allen and Unwin, 1984).

9. David Hurst, personal communication, Nov. 13, 1998. Hurst cites the work of organizational scientist Elliott Jaques who retells the Greek myth of Chronos and Kairos. These figures stand for the two basic and very different experiences of *time*. Chronos is the measured and abstract calendar, or *chronological*, time. Kairos is the perpetual now, the moment of opportunity and direct experience. See E. Jaques, *The Form of Time* (New York: Crane, Russak, 1982).

10. M. Csikszentmihalyi, *Flow: The Psychology of Optimal Experience* (New York: HarperCollins, 1990).

11. T. L. Friedman, "Cyber-Serfdom," *New York Times*, [www.nytimes.com], Jan. 30, 2001.

12. T. J. Peters and R. H. Waterman Jr., *In Search of Excellence: Lessons from America's Best-Run Companies* (New York: HarperCollins, 1982).

13. A. Damasio, *The Feeling of What Happens: Body and Emotion in the Making of Consciousness* (New York: Harcourt, 1999).

14. H. Mintzberg, *The Nature of Managerial Work* (New York: HarperCollins, 1973).

15. H. Mintzberg, *Mintzberg on Management: Inside Our Strange World of Organizations* (New York: Free Press, 1989), p. 336.

16. H. Lancaster, "Managers Can Use Their Leisure Time as Training," in "Managing Your Career," *Wall Street Journal Interactive Edition*, [www.wsj.com], Aug. 11, 1998.

17. M. Johnson, *The Body in the Mind: The Bodily Basis of Meaning, Imagination, and Reason* (Chicago: University of Chicago Press, 1992), p. xix.

18. W.I.B. Beveridge, *The Art of Scientific Investigation*, 3rd ed. (New York: Vintage Books, 1957), pp. 88–89.

19. For a deeper exploration of the physiology of the left and right brain, see R. Ornstein, *The Right Mind* (New York: Harcourt, 1997).

20. K. Mieszkowski, "Wild Cards: Report from the Futurist," *Fast Company*, [www.fastcompany.com/online/13/futuristpetersen.html], Feb. 1998; see also J. L. Peterson, *Out of the Blue: How to*

Anticipate Big Future Surprises (Arlington, Va.: Arlington Institute, 1997).

21. Mieszkowski, "Wild Cards."

22. D. L. Cooperrider, P. F. Sorensen, D. Whitney, and T. F. Yaeger (eds.), *Appreciative Inquiry: Rethinking Human Organization Toward a Positive Theory of Change* (Champaign, Ill.: Stipes, 2000).

23. A. F. Osborn, *Applied Imagination* (New York: Scribner, 1953).

24. The SCAMPER list has been adapted and used in all kinds of settings, including CCL's Targeted Innovation program. Educator Robert Eberle, *SCAMPER: Games for Imagination Development* (Buffalo, N.Y.: D.O.K., 1981), formed the SCAMPER acronym, as a mnemonic device, from the categories in Alex Osborn's original checklist. We have further adapted the questions for this book.

25. H. Lancaster, "Managers Can Use Their Leisure Time as Training."

26. E. Booth, *The Everyday Work of Art: How Artistic Experience Can Transform Your Life* (Naperville, Ill.: Sourcebooks, 1997); M. C. Bateson, *Composing a Life* (New York: Atlantic Press, 1989).

27. M. S. Wilson and P. Cartner, "Namaste," unpublished manuscript, June 30, 1999.

28. At CCL, the phrase "going against the grain" is typically employed to describe learning some behavior that runs against habit, style, and preference. This usage was first employed by K. A. Bunker and A. D. Webb, *Learning How to Learn from Experience: Impact of Stress and Coping* (Greensboro, N.C.: Center for Creative Leadership, 1992).

29. A group from CCL visited Xerox PARC on April 14, 1998. John Seeley Brown's remark is paraphrased from notes made by CCL faculty member Robert Ginnett during that visit.

30. C. Harris (ed.), *Art and Innovation: The Xerox PARC Artist-in-Residence Program* (Cambridge, Mass.: MIT Press, 1999). See also the excellent PAIR Web site [www.pair.xerox.com].

31. S. S. Gryskiewicz, *Positive Turbulence: Developing Climates for Creativity, Innovation, and Renewal* (San Francisco: Jossey-Bass, 1999).

32. Perkins, *The Intelligent Eye*, p. 41.

33. C. Argyris, *Overcoming Organizational Defenses: Facilitating Organizational Learning* (Upper Saddle River, N.J.: Prentice Hall, 1990).

34. R. Langreth and S. D. Moore, "Not Proud of It Right Now," *Wall Street Journal*, Oct. 27, 1999, p. A6.

Chapter Two

1. This is a paraphrase from our notes taken at David Whyte's presentation to alumni of the Leading Creatively program in March 1997. He also offers much on this point in D. Whyte, *The Heart Aroused: Poetry and the Preservation of the Soul in Corporate America* (New York: Currency/Doubleday, 1996).

2. Organizational creativity expert David P. Campbell (personal communication, Jan. 30, 2002) refers to a similar notion of secondary skills, saying: "The more secondary skills an individual has, the more doors will be open. The more employees with useful secondary skills that an organization has, the more effective it will be. Secondary skills include skills such as speaking a foreign language, playing the piano, sketching pictures, welding, knowing Morse Code, and so on. I am fond of saying that time spent learning a secondary skill is never wasted."

3. B. McCarthy, *About Learning* (North Barrington, Ill.: Excel, 1996), pp. 251, 273.

4. C. Wynett, presentation made at "The KEYS Conference," Airlie Conference Center, Warrenton, Va., Mar. 21, 1999.

5. *Assessment for development*, or A4D, is a core competency of the Center for Creative Leadership as well as a basic model that CCL offers participants in the Leadership Development Program (LDP)®. Our main source for this discussion of A4D is H. Browning and E. Van Velsor, *Three Keys to Development: Defining and Meeting Your Leadership Challenges* (Greensboro, N.C.: Center for Creative Leadership, 1999).

6. M. A. Dalton and G. P. Hollenbeck, *How to Design an Effective*

System for Developing Managers and Executives (Greensboro, N.C.: Center for Creative Leadership, 1996).

7. R. A. Heifetz, *Leadership Without Easy Answers* (Cambridge, Mass.: Harvard University Press, 1994).

8. I. Progoff, *At a Journal Workshop: The Basic Text and Guide for Using the Intensive Journal* (New York: G. P Putnam, 1982, p. 34).

9. R. D. Stacey, *Managing the Unknowable: Strategic Boundaries Between Order and Chaos in Organizations* (San Francisco: Jossey-Bass, 1992), p. 9.

10. B. Lopez, *Arctic Dreams: Imagination and Desire in a Northern Landscape* (New York: Scribner, 1986), pp. 279–280.

11. D. K. Hurst, *Crisis and Renewal: Meeting the Challenge of Organizational Change* (Boston: Harvard Business School Press, 1995).

12. T. M. Amabile, "Within You, Without You: The Social Psychology of Creativity and Beyond," in M. A. Runco and R. S. Albert (eds.), *Theories of Creativity* (Thousand Oaks, Calif.: Sage, 1990).

13. P. J. Hilts, *Scientific Temperaments: Three Lives in Contemporary Science* (New York: Simon & Schuster, 1982), p. 130.

14. R. Westrum, "Social Intelligence About Hidden Events," *Knowledge*, 1982, *3*(3), 381–400, cited in K. E. Weick, *Sensemaking in Organizations* (Thousand Oaks, Calif.: Sage, 1995), p. 2.

15. Hilts, *Scientific Temperaments*, p. 131.

16. B. Crandall, personal communication, Nov. 16, 1998.

17. W. Bridges, *Jobshift: How to Prosper in a Workplace Without Jobs* (Cambridge, Mass.: Perseus Books, 1994).

18. K. A. Bunker, "The Power of Vulnerability in Contemporary Leadership," *Consulting Psychology Journal*, 1997, *49*(2), 122–136.

19. Ortega y Gasset, cited in P. Warshall, "The Great Arsenic Lobster," *Whole Earth*, Fall 1999, p. 13.

20. Wynett, presentation made at "The KEYS Conference."

21. P. Orton, quoted in E. Weil, "Every Leader Tells a Story," *Fast*

Company, [www.fastcompany.com/online/15/rftf.html], June 1998.

22. N. M. Tichy, *The Leadership Engine: How Winning Companies Build Leaders at Every Level* (New York: Harper Business, 1997).

23. J. Campbell, *The Hero with a Thousand Faces* (Princeton, N.J.: Princeton University Press, 1949).

24. N. Goldberg, *Writing Down the Bones: Freeing the Writer Within* (Boston: Shambhala, 1986).

25. R. W. Hedin, *Married to the Church* (Bloomington: Indiana University Press, 1995).

26. H. Miller, *Henry Miller on Writing* (T. H. Moore, ed.), (New York: New Directions, 1964), p. 111.

27. "Make it strange"—see it fresh, push the limits, reinvent so it can be seen at all—was the dictum of the poet Ezra Pound.

28. J. H. Dobrzynski, "Online Pioneers: The Buzz Never Stops," *New York Times*, Nov. 21, 1999, sec. 3, p. 1.

29. C. Fishman, "Sabbaticals Are Serious Business," *Fast Company*, [www.fastcompany.com/online/05/hallmark.html], Oct. 1996.

30. L. Dackman, "An Interview with Robert Wilson," *Arts+Architecture*, 1984, 3(1), 60–77.

31. S. Helgesen, *The Web of Inclusion: A New Architecture for Building Great Organizations* (New York: Currency/Doubleday, 1995), p. 238.

32. D. M. Noer, *Healing the Wounds: Overcoming the Trauma of Layoffs and Revitalizing Downsized Organizations* (San Francisco: Jossey-Bass, 1993).

Chapter Three

1. "Making thought visible" is a central theme in the work of Betty Edwards (the phrase itself she borrows from George Orwell). She engages this theme through various kinds of drawing. See B. Edwards, *Drawing on the Artist Within: An Inspirational and Practical Guide to Increasing Your Creative Powers* (New York: Simon & Schuster, 1986).

2. B. McCarthy, *About Learning* (North Barrington, Ill.: Excel, 1996). McCarthy calls this learning cycle 4MAT. It has eight steps all together; the final four steps (we have adapted the names to our research) are *practice, play, refine, craft*. 4MAT works like this: the first four steps of the cycle culminate in formal concepts and rules. The next step is when people practice these concepts and rules to increase their understanding of the basics of whatever they are learning. They *play* with the mastered basics to extend their ability and gain flexibility and mastery. They take what they learn through play and *refine* it to update the formal concepts and rules. Finally, they *craft* the learning into the big picture of the person or organization, as, for example, a completed product or a mission statement. See the Web site [www.aboutlearning.com] for further information on this useful model.

3. J. Bronowski, *A Sense of the Future: Essays in Natural Philosophy* (Cambridge, Mass.: MIT Press, 1977), p. 26.

4. J. L. Gassée, *The Third Apple: Personal Computers and the Cultural Revolution* (Isabel A. Leonard, trans.), (New York: Harcourt, 1987), p. 30.

5. More of the groundbreaking work of Fred Kofman can be found at his *Leading Learning Communities* Web site [www.leadlearn.com]. A useful guide to visioning and many other topics in this book is the fieldbook of the Organizational Learning Center: P. M. Senge, C. Roberts, R. B. Ross, B. J. Smith, and A. Kleiner, *The Fifth Discipline Fieldbook: Strategies and Tools for Building a Learning Organization* (New York: Doubleday, 1994).

6. M. Parker, *Creating Shared Vision: The Story of a Pioneering Approach to Organizational Revitalization* (Clarendon Hills, Ill.: Dialog International, 1990).

7. P. Schwartz, *The Art of the Long View* (New York: Doubleday/Currency, 1991); K. van der Heijden, *Scenarios: The Art of Strategic Conversation* (New York: Wiley, 1996).

8. Stephen Jay Gould reports this from travels in Athens; see "Four Metaphors in Three Generations," in S. J. Gould,

Dinosaur in a Haystack: Reflections in Natural History (New York: Harmony Books, 1995). In the same chapter Gould argues that "Darwin . . . sensed that imagery and metaphor must be used as indispensable tools in the art of persuasion" (p. 450).

9. S. Levy, *Insanely Great: The Life and Times of Macintosh, the Computer That Changed Everything* (New York: Penguin Books, 2000), p. 100.

10. G. Lakoff and M. Johnson, *Metaphors We Live By* (Chicago: University of Chicago Press, 1980); J. Jaynes, *The Origin of Consciousness in the Breakdown of the Bicameral Mind* (Boston: Houghton Mifflin, 1976).

11. The model is adapted from Willy McCourt's interpretation of Morgan's work; see W. McCourt, "Using Metaphors to Understand and to Change Organizations: A Critique of Gareth Morgan's Approach," *Organization Studies*, 1997, *18*(3), 511–512. For Gareth Morgan's work on organizational metaphors and images, see G. Morgan, *Images of Organization* (Thousand Oaks, Calif.: Sage, 1986); *Imaginization: The Art of Creative Management* (Thousand Oaks, Calif.: Sage, 1993).

12. G. A. Kelly, *The Psychology of Personal Constructs* (New York: Norton, 1955); M. Mair, "Metaphors for Living," in A. W. Landfield (ed.), *Nebraska Symposium on Motivation, 1976: Personal Construct Psychology* (Lincoln: University of Nebraska Press, 1977).

13. For more information about Roger Nierenberg's work, see [www.themusicparadigm.com].

14. M. Mair, "Metaphors for Living," p. 280.

15. R. Zaltman and R. H. Coulter, "Seeing the Voice of the Customer: Metaphor-Based Advertising Research," *Journal of Advertising Research*, 1995, *35*(4), 35–51; see also D. H. Pink, "Metaphor Marketing," *Fast Company*, [www.fastcompany.com/online/14/zaltman.html], Apr. 1998.

16. D. Whyte, *The Heart Aroused: Poetry and the Preservation of the Soul in Corporate America* (New York: Currency/Doubleday, 1996).

17. M. Pandya, "They're in a Position to Mix Metaphors with Business," *New York Times*, Nov. 27, 1994, sec. 5, p. 1.

18. John F. Kennedy, remarks at Amherst College, Oct. 26, 1963. Frost was Kennedy's favorite poet; he had spoken at Kennedy's inaugural and dedicated a poem to him.

19. E. Booth, *The Everyday Work of Art: How Artistic Experience Can Transform Your Life* (Naperville, Ill.: Sourcebooks, 1997).

20. S. Helgesen, *The Web of Inclusion: A New Architecture for Building Great Organizations* (New York: Currency/Doubleday, 1995).

21. R. Dawkins, *Unweaving the Rainbow: Science, Delusion, and the Appetite for Wonder* (Boston: Houghton Mifflin, 1998), p. 282. Dawkins also distinguishes between good and bad "poetic science." Metaphors, he says, continue to play a vital role in scientific understanding, but even compelling poetry and clever metaphors can get things all wrong. An antidote for misguided poetry is the competency of co-inquiry, discussed in our Chapter Five, with which communities critically test new ideas.

22. In his autobiographical book *Speak, Memory*, rev. ed. (New York: Putnam, 1966), novelist, poet, and lepidopterist Vladimir Nabokov reports, "I discovered in nature the nonutilitarian delights that I sought in art. Both were a form of magic, both were a game of intricate enchantment and deception" (p. 125).

23. Mair, "Metaphors for Living," p. 254.

Chapter Four

1. P. B. Vaill, *Managing as a Performing Art: New Ideas for a World of Chaotic Change* (San Francisco: Jossey-Bass, 1989), pp. 37–38.

2. K. J. Gergen, *The Saturated Self: Dilemmas of Identity in Contemporary Life* (New York: Basic Books, 1991), pp. 193–196. Gergen cites the influence of philosopher Richard Rorty (*Contingency, Irony and Solidarity* [New York: Cambridge University Press, 1989]), who described the "playfulness . . . of [the] shared ability to appreciate the power of redescribing . . . which becomes

possible only when one's aim becomes an expanding repertoire of alternative descriptions." Although Gergen is known as a *postmodern* thinker, the notion of serious play is an example of his describing a later stage of meaning making, one called *integral* by Ken Wilber, *Integral Psychology* (Boston: Shambhala, 2000).

3. M. Schrage, *Serious Play: How the World's Best Companies Simulate to Innovate* (Boston: Harvard Business School Press, 2000), p. 2.

4. F. Kofman and P. M. Senge, "Communities of Commitment: The Heart of Learning Organizations," *Organizational Dynamics*, 1993, 22(2), 5–19.

5. Vaill, *Managing as a Performing Art*, p. 2.

6. This section of this chapter is adapted from C. J. Palus, "Permanent Whitewater: Playing with the Metaphor," *Issues & Observations*, 1995, 15(1), 7–9.

7. J. Gleick, *Chaos: Making a New Science* (New York: Viking Penguin, 1987).

8. P. F. Drucker, *Managing in Turbulent Times* (New York: Harper-Collins, 1980), p. 7.

9. S. S. Gryskiewicz, *Positive Turbulence: Developing Climates for Creativity, Innovation, and Renewal* (San Francisco: Jossey-Bass, 1999).

10. C. M. Christensen, *The Innovator's Dilemma: When New Technologies Cause Great Firms to Fail* (Boston: Harvard Business School Press, 1997).

11. C. Dahle, "Mind Games," *Fast Company*, [www.fastcompany.com/online/31/play.html], Jan.–Feb. 2000. All comments from Play employees and clients are taken from this article.

12. S. Helgesen, *The Web of Inclusion: A New Architecture for Building Great Organizations* (New York: Currency/Doubleday, 1995).

13. D. H. Gelernter, *Mirror Worlds: Or the Day Software Puts the Universe in a Shoebox . . . How It Will Happen and What It Will Mean* (New York: Oxford University Press, 1991), p. 224; see

also D. H. Gelernter, *Machine Beauty: Elegance and the Heart of Technology* (New York: Basic Books, 1997).

14. Science in the seventeenth century was highly influenced by the views of Francis Bacon, who viewed experimentation as a matter of curiosity-driven exploration, or what Bacon called *induction*. In the twentieth century the notion of scientific experimentation was formalized by Karl Popper and others as the testing of deductions derived from hypotheses. This should remind us that both forms of experimentation are vital: playful induction (R-mode in nature) and deductive hypotheses testing (L-mode). See P. Medawar, *Pluto's Republic: Incorporating the Art of the Soluble and Induction and Intuition in Scientific Thought* (New York: Oxford University Press, 1982).

15. M. Lewis, *The New New Thing: A Silicon Valley Story* (New York: Norton, 1999), p. 42, 43.

16. W.I.B. Beveridge, *The Art of Scientific Investigation*, 3rd ed. (New York: Vintage Books, 1957), p. 32.

17. L. Shlain, *Arts and Physics: Parallel Visions in Space, Time, and Light* (New York: Morrow, 1991), p. 178. Shlain cites T. Ferris, *Coming of Age in the Milky Way* (New York: Morrow, 1988), as his main reference for this story.

18. S. Smithers, "Magical Wars and Spirited Debates: Divine Play in Ancient India," *Parabola*, Winter 1996, p. 83.

19. J. Bronowski, *The Ascent of Man* (Boston: Little, Brown, 1974), p. 36.

20. Jim MacDonald, personal communication, Sept. 1998.

21. Helgesen, *The Web of Inclusion*, p. 67.

22. K. E. Weick and K. H. Roberts, "Collective Mind in Organizations: Heedful Interrelating on Flight Decks," *Administrative Science Quarterly*, 1993, *38*(3), 357–381. Weick and Roberts cite G. Ryle, *The Concept of Mind* (Chicago: University of Chicago Press, 1949), p. 136.

23. D. Jones, "Seeing the Ordinary as Extraordinary," [www.dewitt-jones.com/html/seeing_the_ordinary_cont_.shtml], 2001.

Chapter Five

1. A number of emerging research practices are also being described as *co-inquiry* and invoke a set of ideas similar to that put forth in this chapter. Leadership for complex challenges thus requires a kind of applied research leading to new, shared, and practical knowledge. Those wishing to deliberately build communities of inquiry focused on research, including what is often called *action research* or *action inquiry*, should consult the growing literature on best practices in this area. C2 Competencies encourage participation in leadership as a shared meaning-making activity and thus are beneficial for those wishing to practice this kind of transformative research. The following books are excellent places to start: J. N. Bray, J. Lee, L. L. Smith, and L. Yorks, *Collaborative Inquiry in Practice: Action, Reflection, and Meaning Making* (Thousand Oaks, Calif.: Sage, 2000); D. Fisher, D. Rooke, and W. Torbert, *Personal and Organizational Transformations Through Action Inquiry* (Boston: Edge Work Press, 2000); P. Reason and H. Bradbury (eds.), *Handbook of Action Research: Participative Inquiry and Practice* (Thousand Oaks, Calif.: Sage, 2001).

2. D. L. Cooperrider, P. F. Sorensen, D. Whitney, and T. F. Yaeger (eds.), *Appreciative Inquiry: Rethinking Human Organization Toward a Positive Theory of Change* (Champaign, Ill.: Stipes, 2000).

3. 3M, "3M Innovation Chronicles: Legacy of Innovation: Art Fry and the Invention of Post-it® Notes," [www.3m.com/about3M/pioneers/fry.html], Apr. 1998.

4. P. Gray, "The First Flight Didn't Happen in a Vacuum," *Greensboro News & Record*, Jan. 10, 1997, p. A10.

5. We worked with Willenius-Wilhelmsen Lines (when it was known as Wilhelmsen Lines) in a previous research project. The company has kindly given us permission to use its name.

6. Janetta M. McCoy, personal communication, Oct. 23, 2001. Also see J. M. McCoy, *The Creative Work Environment: The Relationship of the Physical Environment and Creative Teamwork at a*

State Agency—A Case Study, unpublished doctoral dissertation (University of Wisconsin-Milwaukee, 2000).

7. H. Gardiner, "In New Drug Labs, 'Porches' and 'Huddle Zones': Searching for Breakthroughs, Pharmaceuticals Industry Ignites a Building Boom," *Wall Street Journal,* Oct. 6, 1999, pp. B1, B12.

8. Smith Brothers Office Environments, Inc., "Workplace Research and Studies: Approach the Future," [www.sboe.com/Approach/20the/20future.htm], Sept. 13, 2000.

9. David Hills, professor emeritus, Wake Forest University, personal communication, June 24, 1999. Hills was reflecting on a CCL collaboration with the U.S. Army.

10. D. Overby, "In Aspen, Physics on a High Plane," *New York Times,* Aug. 28, 2001, pp. D1, D3; Aspen Center for Physics, "The Aspen Center for Physics," [http://andy.bu.edu/aspen/brochure/brochure03.html], Jan. 29, 2002.

11. Portions of this section are adapted from C. J. Palus and W. H. Drath, "Putting Something in the Middle: An Approach to Dialogue," *Reflections,* 2001, *3*(2), 28–39. We also draw on the following excellent resources for the practice of dialogue: W. Isaacs, *Dialogue and the Art of Thinking Together* (New York: Random House, 1999); N. M. Dixon, *Dialogue at Work: Making Talk Developmental for People and Organizations* (London: Lemos & Crane, 1998).

12. S. Helgesen, *The Web of Inclusion: A New Architecture for Building Great Organizations* (New York: Currency/Doubleday, 1995), pp. 103–122.

13. Cheryl De Ciantis, former faculty member and artist-in-residence at CCL, demonstrates the power of art, especially self-made art, when placed in the middle of dialogue. Her work with the Touchstone activity is especially revealing and practical. (Touchstones in this context are abstract personal sculptures, made from natural objects, representing one's sense of aspiration and purpose.) See C. De Ciantis, *Using an Art Technique to Facilitate Leadership Development* (Greensboro, N.C.: Center for Creative Leadership, 1995).

14. D. Abramson, "Wiring the Corporate Brain," *CIO Enterprise*, Mar. 15, 1999, pp. 30–36.

15. J. S. Brown, "Research That Reinvents the Corporation," *Harvard Business Review*, 1991, 69(1), 102–117.

16. Fast Company, "Unit of One Anniversary Book," *Fast Company*, [www.fastcompany.com/online/07/097one.html], Feb. 1997.

17. R. B. Leiber and J. E. Davis, "Storytelling: A New Way to Get Close to Your Customer," *Fortune*, Feb. 3, 1997, pp. 102–108.

18. David K. Hurst, personal communication.

19. P. L. Galison, *Image and Logic: A Material Culture of Microphysics* (Chicago: University of Chicago Press, 1997), p. 49.

20. Helgesen, *The Web of Inclusion*, p. 107.

21. The work of Ronald Heifetz is an essential resource for understanding leadership with less than full authority: see R. A. Heifetz, *Leadership Without Easy Answers* (Cambridge, Mass.: Harvard University Press, 1994).

Chapter Six

1. H. Mintzberg, *Mintzberg on Management: Inside Our Strange World of Organizations* (New York: Free Press, 1989), pp. 25–27.

2. D. A. Schön, *Educating the Reflective Practitioner: Toward a New Design for Teaching and Learning in the Professions* (San Francisco: Jossey-Bass, 1987), p. 11.

3. M. W. McCall and R. E. Kaplan, *Whatever It Takes: Decision Makers at Work* (Upper Saddle River, N.J.: Prentice Hall, 1985), p. 23.

4. Our colleague Stan Gryskiewicz called our attention to this lovely story.

5. The following section is adapted from C. J. Palus, "Creating Decisions," *Leadership in Action*, 1998, 18(5), 13–14.

6. R. Guzzo and S. Palmer, "Group Decision Processes and Effectiveness in Executive Selection," paper presented in J. J. Deal and V. I. Sessa's symposium *Choices at the Top: Learnings and*

Teachings on Selecting Executives, at the thirteenth annual meeting of the Society for Industrial and Organizational Psychology, Dallas, 1998.

7. D. Vaughan, "Risky Business," *Boston College Magazine*, Spring 1996, pp. 24–36; see also D. Vaughan, *The* Challenger *Launch Decision: Risky Technology, Culture, and Deviance at NASA* (Chicago: University of Chicago Press, 1996).

8. G. Klein, *Sources of Power: How People Make Decisions* (Cambridge, Mass.: MIT Press, 1998).

9. These two lists of decision-making factors are adapted from K. E. Weick, *Sensemaking in Organizations* (Thousand Oaks, Calif.: Sage, 1995).

10. R. A. Heifetz and R. Sinder, "Political Leadership: Managing the Public's Problem Solving," in R. Reich (ed.), *The Power of Public Ideas* (New York: Ballinger, 1988).

11. G. Klein and K. E. Weick, "Decisions: Making the Right Ones, Learning from the Wrong Ones," *Across the Board,* [www.conferenceboard.org], June 2000.

12. Klein, *Sources of Power*.

13. Some years ago the developmental psychologist L. S. Vygotsky used the term *scaffold* to describe a temporary framework of social, cognitive, and emotional support that teachers construct for learners. See L. S. Vygotsky, *Mind in Society* (Cambridge, Mass.: Harvard University Press, 1978). Although we use the term in a different context, our use is, we believe, complementary.

14. A. Koestler, *The Act of Creation* (London: Pan Books, 1964), pp. 670–671, 689.

15. H. Gardner, *Frames of Mind: The Theory of Multiple Intelligences* (New York: Basic Books, 1983), pp. 375, 377.

16. Adventure activities are thus part metaphor and part literal, what we might call *close metaphor* or a *scaffold*. See the exploration of the use of metaphor in this way in S. Bacon, *The Conscious Use of Metaphor in Outward Bound* (Denver: Colorado Outward Bound School, 1983).

17. D. H. Gelernter, *Machine Beauty: Elegance and the Heart of Technology* (New York: Basic Books, 1997), p. 2.

18. This section is adapted from C. J. Palus, "The Art and Science of Leadership," *Leadership in Action*, 1999, *19*(1), 12–13.

19. E. F. Keller, *A Feeling for the Organism: The Life and Work of Barbara McClintock* (New York: Freeman, 1993), p. 148.

20. B. Boyd, *Vladimir Nabokov: The American Years* (Princeton, N.J.: Princeton University Press, 1991).

21. L. Shlain, *Arts and Physics: Parallel Visions in Space, Time, and Light* (New York: Morrow, 1991).

22. B. M. Stafford, *Artful Science: Enlightenment, Entertainment, and the Eclipse of Visual Education* (Cambridge, Mass.: MIT Press, 1994).

23. P. J. Hilts, *Scientific Temperaments: Three Lives in Contemporary Science* (New York: Simon & Schuster, 1982).

24. S. Levy, *Insanely Great: The Life and Times of Macintosh, the Computer That Changed Everything* (New York: Penguin Books, 2000), pp. 138–139.

25. J. L. Gassée, *The Third Apple: Personal Computers and the Cultural Revolution* (Isabel A. Leonard, trans.), (New York: Harcourt, 1987).

26. Levy, *Insanely Great*.

27. D. Bayles and T. Orland, *Art and Fear: Observations on the Perils (and Rewards) of Artmaking* (Santa Barbara, Calif.: Capra, 1993), p. 117.

28. Bayles and Orland, *Art and Fear*, pp. 3–5.

29. E. Booth, *The Everyday Work of Art: How Artistic Experience Can Transform Your Life* (Naperville, Ill.: Sourcebooks, 1997).

30. Booth, *The Everyday Work of Art*.

31. M. C. Bateson, *Composing a Life* (New York: Atlantic Press, 1989).

32. Booth, *The Everyday Work of Art*.

33. I. Progoff, *At a Journal Workshop: The Basic Text and Guide for Using the Intensive Journal* (New York: Dialogue House Library, 1975).

34. The authors have heard David Whyte make this point in various presentations. Also see D. Whyte, *The Heart Aroused: Poetry and the Preservation of the Soul in Corporate America* (New York: Currency/Doubleday, 1996).

35. M. C. Bateson, *Peripheral Visions: Learning Along the Way* (New York: HarperCollins, 1994), p. 224.

36. R. Gold, (Rationale of the PAIR program, dated Sept. 1996), [www.parc.xerox.com/red/members/richgold/PAIRBOOK/pair5.html], Jan. 31, 2002.

37. M. Roskill (ed.), *The Letters of Vincent Van Gogh* (New York: Simon & Schuster, 1997), p. 152.

38. As mentioned previously, we borrow extensively from the concepts and techniques in Betty Edwards's books: *Drawing on the Right Side of the Brain: A Course in Enhancing Creativity and Artistic Confidence*, rev. ed. (New York: Putnam, 1989); *Drawing on the Artist Within: An Inspirational and Practical Guide to Increasing Your Creative Powers* (New York: Simon & Schuster, 1986). For a further rationale for this admittedly unusual leadership development exercise, see C. De Ciantis, "What Does Drawing My Hand Have to Do with Leadership? A Look at the Process of Leaders Becoming Artists," *Journal of Aesthetic Education*, 1996, 30(4), 87–98.

39. The question "What is your art?" is from D. Richards, *Artful Work: Awakening Joy, Meaning, and Commitment in the Workplace* (San Francisco: Berrett-Koehler, 1995).

40. J. Cameron, *The Artist's Way* (Los Angeles: Tarcher/Perigee, 1992); M. A. Bryan with J. Cameron and C. Allen, *The Artist's Way at Work* (New York: Morrow, 1998).

41. C. Harris (ed.), *Art and Innovation: The Xerox PARC Artist-In-Residence Program* (Cambridge, Mass.: MIT Press, 1999), p. 6.

42. Bayles and Orland, *Art and Fear*, p. 13.

43. Stafford, *Artful Science*, p. 134.

44. Stafford, *Artful Science*.

45. E. Dissanayake, *Homo Aestheticus: Where Art Comes From and Why* (Seattle: University of Washington Press, 1995).

Chapter Seven

1. K. E. Weick and D. K. Meader, "Sensemaking and Group Support Systems," in L. M. Jessup and J. S. Valacich (eds.), *Group Support Systems: New Perspectives* (New York: Macmillan, 1993), pp. 230–252.
2. Compendium enables groups of people to construct knowledge on the fly. It allows teams to combine informal, exploratory discussion with formal problem-solving frameworks. Compendium makes the resultant knowledge available for ongoing reuse and expansion via a relational database and a variety of display and reporting formats (for example, hyperlinked HTML pages, MS Word, and a visual map of nodes and links). Originally developed at Verizon as a methodology for cross-functional business process redesign and for addressing "wicked" problems in telephone operations (such as Y2K planning among diverse stakeholders), Compendium has been applied on more than seventy projects in a variety of organizations and is currently being developed for leadership applications in collaboration with CCL. See A. Selvin and others, "Compendium: Making Meetings into Knowledge Events," paper presented at Knowledge Technologies 2001, Austin, Tex., Mar. 4–7, 2001. This paper and more information about Compendium are available at [www.compendiuminstitute.org].
3. Information about The Motley Fool is from the company's Web site [www.fool.com].
4. Jim Rosenberg, personal communication.
5. Excerpted from M. E. Lyons, "A Mother's Portfolio," [www.fool.com/Fribble/1999/Fribble990727.html], July 27, 1999. Used with the permission of Mary E. Lyons.
6. S. Helgesen, *The Web of Inclusion: A New Architecture for Building Great Organizations* (New York: Currency/Doubleday, 1995).
7. This section is adapted from M. Hotchkiss, C. Kelley, R. Ott, and J. Elter, "The Lakes Story," *Reflections,* 2000, *1*(4), 24–31; J. A. Schofield, "Copy This," *Design News,* [www.manufacturing.net], Mar. 1, 1999; United States–Asia Environmental Partner-

ship, "Xerox Corporation: Design for Remanufacturing," case study, [www.usaep.org/scem/case2.html], Jan. 31, 2002. This case description is derived entirely from publicly available reports, as cited. Neither the authors nor CCL have worked with Xerox on any aspect of the Lakes Project.

8. Hotchkiss, Kelley, Ott, and Elter, "The Lakes Story."

9. United States–Asia Environmental Partnership, "Xerox Corporation."

10. D. Richards, *Artful Work: Awakening Joy, Meaning, and Commitment in the Workplace* (San Francisco: Berrett-Koehler, 1995).

11. Xerox Corporation, "Xerox Company Factbook," [www2.xerox.com//downloads/newsroom/XeroxFactbook.pdf], Oct. 24, 2001.

12. K. E. Weick, *Sensemaking in Organizations* (Thousand Oaks, Calif.: Sage, 1995), pp. 13, 145.

Appendix A

1. B. Edwards, *Drawing on the Artist Within: An Inspirational and Practical Guide to Increasing Your Creative Powers* (New York: Simon & Schuster, 1986), p. 40.

2. C. J. Palus and W. H. Drath, "Putting Something in the Middle: An Approach to Dialogue," *Reflections*, 2001, *3*(2), 28–39.

3. D. P. McAdams, *The Stories We Live By* (New York: Guilford Press, 1997).

4. M. Ullman, *Appreciating Dreams: A Group Approach* (Thousand Oaks, Calif.: Sage, 1996).

Appendix B

1. D. Greenwood, W. F. Whyte, and I. Harkavy, "Participatory Action Research as a Process and as a Goal," *Human Relations*, 1993, *46*(2), 177.

2. D. Fisher and W. R. Torbert, *Personal and Organizational Transformations: The True Challenge of Continual Quality Improvement* (New York: McGraw-Hill, 1995), p. 111.

3. For a full description of the process and results of our Leading Creatively research, see C. J. Palus and D. M. Horth, "Leadership Development as Building Capacities for Making Sense of Complexity: An Assessment of the Outcomes of the Leading Creatively Program," paper presented to the Professional Development Workshop: States of the Art: The Theory, Practice and Research of Artful Inquiry and Intervention, at the Academy of Management annual meeting, Washington, D.C., Aug. 4, 2001. (Available from the authors; journal version in preparation.)

Bibliography

Abramson, D. "Wiring the Corporate Brain." *CIO Enterprise*, Mar. 15, 1999, pp. 30–36.

Amabile, T. M. "Within You, Without You: The Social Psychology of Creativity and Beyond." In M. A. Runco and R. S. Albert (eds.), *Theories of Creativity*. Thousand Oaks, Calif.: Sage, 1990.

Argyris, C. *Overcoming Organizational Defenses: Facilitating Organizational Learning*. Upper Saddle River, N.J.: Prentice Hall, 1990.

Aspen Center for Physics. "The Aspen Center for Physics." [http://andy.bu.edu/aspen/brochure/brochure03.html]. Jan. 29, 2002.

Bacon, S. *The Conscious Use of Metaphor in Outward Bound*. Denver: Colorado Outward Bound School, 1983.

Bateson, M. C. *Composing a Life*. New York: Atlantic Press, 1989.

Bateson, M. C. *Peripheral Visions: Learning Along the Way*. New York: HarperCollins, 1994.

Bayles, D., and Orland, T. *Art and Fear: Observations on the Perils (and Rewards) of Artmaking*. Santa Barbara, Calif.: Capra, 1993.

Beveridge, W.I.B. *The Art of Scientific Investigation*. (3rd ed.) New York: Vintage Books, 1957.

Bohm, D. *On Dialogue*. Ojai, Calif.: David Bohm Seminars, 1990.

Bohm, D., and Peat, F. D. *Science, Order and Creativity*. New York: Bantam Books, 1987.

Booth, E. *The Everyday Work of Art: How Artistic Experience Can Transform Your Life*. Naperville, Ill.: Sourcebooks, 1997.

Boyd, B. *Vladimir Nabokov: The American Years*. Princeton, N.J.: Princeton University Press, 1991.

Bray, J. N., Lee, J., Smith, L. L., and Yorks, L. *Collaborative Inquiry in Practice: Action, Reflection, and Meaning Making*. Thousand Oaks, Calif.: Sage, 2000.

Bridges, W. *Jobshift: How to Prosper in a Workplace Without Jobs*. Cambridge, Mass.: Perseus Books, 1994.

Bronowski, J. *The Ascent of Man*. Boston: Little, Brown, 1974.

Bronowski, J. *A Sense of the Future: Essays in Natural Philosophy.* Cambridge, Mass.: MIT Press, 1977.

Brown, J. S. "Research That Reinvents the Corporation." *Harvard Business Review,* 1991, 69(1), 102–117.

Brown, J. S., and Duguid, P. *The Social Life of Information.* Boston: Harvard Business School Press, 2000.

Browning, H., and Van Velsor, E. *Three Keys to Development: Defining and Meeting Your Leadership Challenges.* Greensboro, N.C.: Center for Creative Leadership, 1999.

Brubaker, R. *The Limits of Rationality: An Essay on the Social and Moral Thought of Max Weber.* London: Allen and Unwin, 1984.

Bruner, J. S. *On Knowing: Essays for the Left Hand.* New York: Atheneum, 1969.

Bryan, M. A., with Cameron, J., and Allen, C. *The Artist's Way at Work.* New York: Morrow, 1998.

Bunker, K. A. "The Power of Vulnerability in Contemporary Leadership." *Consulting Psychology Journal,* 1997, 49(2), 122–136.

Bunker, K. A., and Webb, A. D. *Learning How to Learn from Experience: Impact of Stress and Coping.* Greensboro, N.C.: Center for Creative Leadership, 1992.

Cameron, J. *The Artist's Way.* Los Angeles: Tarcher/Perigee, 1992.

Campbell, J. *The Hero with a Thousand Faces.* Princeton, N.J.: Princeton University Press, 1949.

Christensen, C. M. *The Innovator's Dilemma: When New Technologies Cause Great Firms to Fail.* Boston: Harvard Business School Press, 1997.

Cleveland, H. *Leadership and the Information Revolution.* San Francisco: World Academy of Art and Science, 1997.

Cooperrider, D. L., Sorensen, P. F., Whitney, D., and Yaeger, T. F. (eds.). *Appreciative Inquiry: Rethinking Human Organization Toward a Positive Theory of Change.* Champaign, Ill.: Stipes, 2000.

Csikszentmihalyi, M. *Flow: The Psychology of Optimal Experience.* New York: HarperCollins, 1990.

Dackman, L. "An Interview with Robert Wilson." *Arts+Architecture,* 1984, 3(1), 60–77.

Dahle, C. "Mind Games." *Fast Company,* [www.fastcompany.com/online/31/play.html], Jan.–Feb. 2000.

Dalton, M. A., and Hollenbeck, G. P. *How to Design an Effective System for Developing Managers and Executives.* Greensboro, N.C.: Center for Creative Leadership, 1996.

Damasio, A. *The Feeling of What Happens: Body and Emotion in the Making of Consciousness.* New York: Harcourt, 1999.

Davenport, T. H., and Beck, J. C. *The Attention Economy: Understanding the New Currency of Business.* Boston: Harvard Business School Press, 2001.

Dawkins, R. *Unweaving the Rainbow: Science, Delusion, and the Appetite for Wonder.* Boston: Houghton Mifflin, 1998.

De Ciantis, C. *Using an Art Technique to Facilitate Leadership Development.* Greensboro, N.C.: Center for Creative Leadership, 1995.

De Ciantis, C. "What Does Drawing My Hand Have to Do with Leadership? A Look at the Process of Leaders Becoming Artists." *Journal of Aesthetic Education,* 1996, *30*(4), 87–98.

de Geus, A. "Strategy and Learning." *Reflections,* 1999, *1*(1), 75–81.

Dissanayake, E. *Homo Aestheticus: Where Art Comes From and Why.* Seattle: University of Washington Press, 1995.

Dixon, N. M. *Dialogue at Work: Making Talk Developmental for People and Organizations.* London: Lemos & Crane, 1998.

Dobrzynski, J. H. "Online Pioneers: The Buzz Never Stops." *New York Times,* Nov. 21, 1999, sec. 3, p. 1.

Drath, W. H. *The Deep Blue Sea: Rethinking the Source of Leadership.* San Francisco: Jossey-Bass, 2001.

Drath, W. H., and Palus, C. J. *Making Common Sense: Leadership as Meaning-Making in a Community of Practice.* Greensboro, N.C.: Center for Creative Leadership, 1994.

Drucker, P. F. *Managing in Turbulent Times.* New York: HarperCollins, 1980.

Eberle, R. *SCAMPER: Games for Imagination Development.* Buffalo, N.Y.: D.O.K., 1981.

Edwards, B. *Drawing on the Artist Within: An Inspirational and Practical Guide to Increasing Your Creative Powers.* New York: Simon & Schuster, 1986.

Edwards, B. *Drawing on the Right Side of the Brain: A Course in Enhancing Creativity and Artistic Confidence.* (Rev. ed.) New York: Putnam, 1989.

Fast Company. "Unit of One Anniversary Book." *Fast Company,* [www.fastcompany.com/online/07/097one.html], Feb. 1997.

Fisher, D., Rooke, D., and Torbert, W. *Personal and Organizational Transformations Through Action Inquiry.* Boston: Edge Work Press, 2000.

Fishman, C. "Sabbaticals Are Serious Business." *Fast Company,* [www.fastcompany.com/online/05/hallmark.html], Oct. 1996.

Friedman, T. L. "Cyber-Serfdom." *New York Times,* [www.nytimes.com], Jan. 30, 2001.

Galison, P. L. *Image and Logic: A Material Culture of Microphysics.* Chicago: University of Chicago Press, 1997.

Gardiner, H. "In New Drug Labs, 'Porches' and 'Huddle Zones': Searching for Breakthroughs, Pharmaceuticals Industry Ignites a Building Boom." *Wall Street Journal,* Oct. 6, 1999, pp. B1, B12.

Gardner, H. *Frames of Mind: The Theory of Multiple Intelligences.* New York: Basic Books, 1983.

Gardner, H. *Multiple Intelligences: The Theory in Practice.* New York: Basic Books, 1993.

Gassée, J. L. *The Third Apple: Personal Computers and the Cultural Revolution.* (Isabel A. Leonard, trans.) New York: Harcourt, 1987.

Gelernter, D. H. *Mirror Worlds: Or the Day Software Puts the Universe in a*

Shoebox . . . How It Will Happen and What It Will Mean. New York: Oxford University Press, 1991.

Gelernter, D. H. *Machine Beauty: Elegance and the Heart of Technology.* New York: Basic Books, 1997.

Gergen, K. J. *The Saturated Self: Dilemmas of Identity in Contemporary Life.* New York: Basic Books, 1991.

Gleick, J. *Chaos: Making a New Science.* New York: Viking Penguin, 1987.

Goldberg, N. *Writing Down the Bones: Freeing the Writer Within.* Boston: Shambhala, 1986.

Gould, S. J. *Dinosaur in a Haystack: Reflections in Natural History.* New York: Harmony Books, 1995.

Gray, P. "The First Flight Didn't Happen in a Vacuum." *Greensboro News & Record,* Jan. 10, 1997, p. A10.

Gryskiewicz, S. S. *Positive Turbulence: Developing Climates for Creativity, Innovation, and Renewal.* San Francisco: Jossey-Bass, 1999.

Guzzo, R., and Palmer, S. "Group Decision Processes and Effectiveness in Executive Selection." Paper presented in J. J. Deal and V. I. Sessa's symposium *Choices at the Top: Learnings and Teachings on Selecting Executives,* at the thirteenth annual meeting of the Society for Industrial and Organizational Psychology, Dallas, 1998.

Harris, C. (ed.). *Art and Innovation: The Xerox PARC Artist-in-Residence Program.* Cambridge, Mass.: MIT Press, 1999.

Hedin, R. W. *Married to the Church.* Bloomington: Indiana University Press, 1995.

Heifetz, R. A. *Leadership Without Easy Answers.* Cambridge, Mass.: Harvard University Press, 1994.

Heifetz, R. A., and Sinder, R. "Political Leadership: Managing the Public's Problem Solving." In R. Reich (ed.), *The Power of Public Ideas.* New York: Ballinger, 1988.

Helgesen, S. *The Web of Inclusion: A New Architecture for Building Great Organizations.* New York: Currency/Doubleday, 1995.

Hilts, P. J. *Scientific Temperaments: Three Lives in Contemporary Science.* New York: Simon & Schuster, 1982.

Hotchkiss, M., Kelley, C., Ott, R., and Elter, J. "The Lakes Story." *Reflections,* 2000, *1*(4), 24–31.

Hurst, D. K. *Crisis and Renewal: Meeting the Challenge of Organizational Change.* Boston: Harvard Business School Press, 1995.

Hurst, D. K. "When It Comes to Real Change Too Much Objectivity May Be Fatal to the Process." *Strategy & Leadership,* 1997, *25*(2), 10–13.

Isaacs, W. *Dialogue and the Art of Thinking Together.* New York: Random House, 1999.

Jaques, E. *The Form of Time.* New York: Crane, Russak, 1982.

Jaynes, J. *The Origin of Consciousness in the Breakdown of the Bicameral Mind.* Boston: Houghton Mifflin, 1976.

Johnson, M. *The Body in the Mind: The Bodily Basis of Meaning, Imagination, and Reason*. Chicago: University of Chicago Press, 1992.

Jones, D. "Seeing the Ordinary as Extraordinary." [www.dewittjones.com/html/seeing_the_ordinary_cont_.shtml]. 2001.

Kegan, R. *The Evolving Self: Problem and Process in Human Development*. Cambridge, Mass.: Harvard University Press, 1982.

Kegan, R. *In Over Our Heads: The Mental Demands of Modern Life*. Cambridge, Mass.: Harvard University Press, 1994.

Keller, E. F. *A Feeling for the Organism: The Life and Work of Barbara McClintock*. New York: Freeman, 1993.

Kelly, G. A. *The Psychology of Personal Constructs*. New York: Norton, 1955.

Klein, G. *Sources of Power: How People Make Decisions*. Cambridge, Mass.: MIT Press, 1998.

Klein, G., and Weick, K. E. "Decisions: Making the Right Ones: Learning from the Wrong Ones." *Across the Board*, [www.conferenceboard.org], June 2000.

Koestler, A. *The Act of Creation*. London: Pan Books, 1964.

Kofman, F., and Senge, P. M. "Communities of Commitment: The Heart of Learning Organizations." *Organizational Dynamics*, 1993, *22*(2), 5–19.

Lakoff, G., and Johnson, M. *Metaphors We Live By*. Chicago: University of Chicago Press, 1980.

Lancaster, H. "Managers Can Use Their Leisure Time as Training." In "Managing Your Career," *Wall Street Journal Interactive Edition*, [www.wsj.com], Aug. 11, 1998.

Langreth, R., and Moore, S. D. "Not Proud of It Right Now." *Wall Street Journal*, Oct. 27, 1999, p. A6.

Leiber, R. B., and Davis, J. E. "Storytelling: A New Way to Get Close to Your Customer." *Fortune*, Feb. 3, 1997, pp. 102–108.

Levy, S. *Insanely Great: The Life and Times of Macintosh, the Computer That Changed Everything*. New York: Penguin Books, 2000.

Lewis, M. *The New New Thing: A Silicon Valley Story*. New York: Norton, 1999.

Lopez, B. *Arctic Dreams: Imagination and Desire in a Northern Landscape*. New York: Scribner, 1986.

Mair, M. "Metaphors for Living." In A. W. Landfield (ed.), *Nebraska Symposium on Motivation, 1976: Personal Construct Psychology*. Lincoln: University of Nebraska Press, 1977.

Mayer, P. "Introduction to the Special Issue: The Aesthetic Face of Leadership." *Journal of Aesthetic Education*, 1996, *30*(4), 1–4.

McCall, M. W., and Kaplan, R. E. *Whatever It Takes: Decision Makers at Work*. Upper Saddle River, N.J.: Prentice Hall, 1985.

McCarthy, B. *About Learning*. North Barrington, Ill.: Excel, 1996.

McCourt, W. "Using Metaphors to Understand and to Change Organizations: A Critique of Gareth Morgan's Approach." *Organization Studies*, 1997, *18*(3), 511–512.

McCoy, J. M. *The Creative Work Environment: The Relationship of the Physical Environment and Creative Teamwork at a State Agency—A Case Study.* Unpublished doctoral dissertation, University of Wisconsin-Milwaukee, 2000.

Medawar, P. *Pluto's Republic: Incorporating the Art of the Soluble and Induction and Intuition in Scientific Thought.* New York: Oxford University Press, 1982.

Mieszkowski, K. "Wild Cards: Report from the Futurist." *Fast Company,* [www.fastcompany.com/online/13/futuristpetersen.html], Feb. 1998.

Miller, H. *Henry Miller on Writing.* (T. H. Moore, ed.) New York: New Directions, 1964.

Mintzberg, H. *The Nature of Managerial Work.* New York: HarperCollins, 1973.

Mintzberg, H. *Mintzberg on Management: Inside Our Strange World of Organizations.* New York: Free Press, 1989.

Morgan, G. *Images of Organization.* Thousand Oaks, Calif.: Sage, 1986.

Morgan, G. *Imaginization: The Art of Creative Management.* Thousand Oaks, Calif.: Sage, 1993.

The Motley Fool. [www.fool.com]. Dec. 2001.

Nabokov, V. V. *Speak, Memory.* (Rev. ed.) New York: Putnam, 1966.

Nissley, N. "Art-Based Learning in Management Education." In B. DeFillippi and C. Wankel (eds.), *Rethinking Management Education.* Greenwich, Conn.: Information Age Press, forthcoming.

Noer, D. M. *Healing the Wounds: Overcoming the Trauma of Layoffs and Revitalizing Downsized Organizations.* San Francisco: Jossey-Bass, 1993.

Ornstein, R. *The Right Mind.* New York: Harcourt, 1997.

Osborn, A. F. *Applied Imagination.* New York: Scribner, 1953.

Overby, D. "In Aspen, Physics on a High Plane." *New York Times,* Aug. 28, 2001, pp. D1, D3.

Palus, C. J. "Permanent Whitewater: Playing with the Metaphor." *Issues & Observations,* 1995, *15*(1), 7–9.

Palus, C. J. "Learning Scaffolds." *Issues & Observations,* 1997, *17*(1), 15.

Palus, C. J. "Creating Decisions." *Leadership in Action,* 1998, *18*(5), 13–14.

Palus, C. J. "The Art and Science of Leadership." *Leadership in Action,* 1999, *19*(1), 12–13.

Palus, C. J., and Drath, W. H. *Evolving Leaders: A Model for Promoting Leadership Development in Programs.* Greensboro, N.C.: Center for Creative Leadership, 1995.

Palus, C. J., and Drath, W. H. "Putting Something in the Middle: An Approach to Dialogue." *Reflections,* 2001, *3*(2), 28–39.

Palus, C. J., and Horth, D. M. "Leading Creatively: The Art of Making Sense." *Journal of Aesthetic Education,* 1996, *30*(4), 53–68.

Palus, C. J., and Horth, D. M. "Leading Creatively." *Leadership in Action,* 1998, *18*(2), 1–8.

Palus, C. J., and Horth, D. M. *Visual Explorer: Picturing Approaches to Complex Challenges.* Greensboro, N.C.: Center for Creative Leadership, 2001.

Pandya, M. "They're in a Position to Mix Metaphors with Business." *New York Times*, Nov. 27, 1994, sec. 5, p. 1.

Parker, M. *Creating Shared Vision: The Story of a Pioneering Approach to Organizational Revitalization.* Clarendon Hills, Ill.: Dialog International, 1990.

Perkins, D. N. *The Intelligent Eye: Learning to Think by Looking at Art.* Santa Monica, Calif.: Getty Center for Education in the Arts, 1994.

Peters, T. J., and Waterman, R. H., Jr. *In Search of Excellence: Lessons from America's Best-Run Companies.* New York: HarperCollins, 1982.

Peterson, J. L. *Out of the Blue: How to Anticipate Big Future Surprises.* Arlington, Va.: Arlington Institute, 1997.

Pink, D. H. "Metaphor Marketing." *Fast Company*, [www.fastcompany.com/online/14/zaltman.html], Apr. 1998.

Progoff, I. *At a Journal Workshop: The Basic Text and Guide for Using the Intensive Journal.* New York: G. P. Putnam, 1992.

Reason, P., and Bradbury, H. (eds.). *Handbook of Action Research: Participative Inquiry and Practice.* Thousand Oaks, Calif.: Sage, 2001.

Richards, D. *Artful Work: Awakening Joy, Meaning, and Commitment in the Workplace.* San Francisco: Berrett-Koehler, 1995.

Rorty, R. *Contingency, Irony and Solidarity.* New York: Cambridge University Press, 1989.

Roskill, M. (ed.). *The Letters of Vincent Van Gogh.* New York: Simon & Schuster, 1997.

Ryle, G. *The Concept of Mind.* Chicago: University of Chicago Press, 1949.

Sagan, C. *Dragons of Eden.* New York: Random House, 1977.

Schofield, J. A. "Copy This." *Design News*, [www.manufacturing.net], Mar. 1, 1999.

Schön, D. A. *Educating the Reflective Practitioner: Toward a New Design for Teaching and Learning in the Professions.* San Francisco: Jossey-Bass, 1987.

Schrage, M. *Serious Play: How the World's Best Companies Simulate to Innovate.* Boston: Harvard Business School Press, 2000.

Schwartz, P. *The Art of the Long View.* New York: Doubleday/Currency, 1991.

Selvin, A., and others. "Compendium: Making Meetings into Knowledge Events." Paper presented at Knowledge Technologies 2001, Austin, Tex., Mar. 4–7, 2001. Available at [www.compendiuminstitute.org].

Senge, P. M. *The Fifth Discipline: The Art and Practice of the Learning Organization.* New York: Currency/Doubleday, 1990.

Senge, P. M., Roberts, C., Ross, R. B., Smith, B. J., and Kleiner, A. *The Fifth Discipline Fieldbook: Strategies and Tools for Building a Learning Organization.* New York: Doubleday, 1994.

Shlain, L. *Arts and Physics: Parallel Visions in Space, Time, and Light.* New York: Morrow, 1991.

Shlain, L. *The Alphabet Versus the Goddess: The Conflict Between Word and Image.* New York: Viking, 1998.

Smith Brothers Office Environments, Inc. "Workplace Research and Studies: Approach the Future." [www.sboe.com/Approach/20the/20future.htm]. Sept. 13, 2000.

Smith, R. A. "Leadership as Aesthetic Process." *Journal of Aesthetic Education*, 1996, 30(4), 39–52.

Smithers, S. "Magical Wars and Spirited Debates: Divine Play in Ancient India." *Parabola*, Winter 1996, pp. 77–83.

Springer, S. P., and Deutsch, G. *Left Brain, Right Brain*. New York: Freeman, 1981.

Stacey, R. D. *Managing the Unknowable: Strategic Boundaries Between Order and Chaos in Organizations*. San Francisco: Jossey-Bass, 1992.

Stafford, B. M. *Artful Science: Enlightenment, Entertainment, and the Eclipse of Visual Education*. Cambridge, Mass.: MIT Press, 1994.

Stein, M. I. *Simulating Creativity*. New York: Academic Press, 1974–1975.

3M. "3M Innovation Chronicles: Legacy of Innovation: Art Fry and the Invention of Post-it® Notes." [www.3m.com/about3M/pioneers/fry.html]. Apr. 1998.

Tichy, N. M. *The Leadership Engine: How Winning Companies Build Leaders at Every Level*. New York: Harper Business, 1997.

United States–Asia Environmental Partnership. "Xerox Corporation: Design for Remanufacturing." Case study. [www.usaep.org/scem/case2.htm]. Jan. 31, 2002.

Vaill, P. B. *Managing as a Performing Art: New Ideas for a World of Chaotic Change*. San Francisco: Jossey-Bass, 1989.

Vaill, P. B. *Spirited Leading and Learning: Process Wisdom for a New Age*. San Francisco: Jossey-Bass, 1998.

van der Heijden, K. *Scenarios: The Art of Strategic Conversation*. New York: Wiley, 1996.

Vaughan, D. *The Challenger Launch Decision: Risky Technology, Culture, and Deviance at NASA*. Chicago: University of Chicago Press, 1996.

Vaughan, D. "Risky Business." *Boston College Magazine*, Spring 1996, pp. 24–36.

Vygotsky, L. S. *Mind in Society*. Cambridge, Mass.: Harvard University Press, 1978.

Weick, K. E. *Sensemaking in Organizations*. Thousand Oaks, Calif.: Sage, 1995.

Weick, K. E., and Meader, D. K. "Sensemaking and Group Support Systems." In L. M. Jessup and J. S. Valacich (eds.), *Group Support Systems: New Perspectives*. New York: Macmillan, 1993.

Weick, K. E., and Roberts, K. H. "Collective Mind in Organizations: Heedful Interrelating on Flight Decks." *Administrative Science Quarterly*, 1993, 38(3), 357–381.

Weil, E. "Every Leader Tells a Story." *Fast Company*, [www.fastcompany.com/online/15/rftf.html], June 1998.

Westrum, R. "Social Intelligence About Hidden Events." *Knowledge*, 1982, 3(3), 381–400.

Whyte, D. *The Heart Aroused: Poetry and the Preservation of the Soul in Corporate America.* New York: Currency/Doubleday, 1996.

Wilber, K. *Integral Psychology.* Boston: Shambhala, 2000.

Wilson, M. S., and Cartner, P. "Namaste." Unpublished manuscript, June 30, 1999.

Xerox Corporation. "Xerox Company Factbook." [www2.xerox.com//downloads/newsroom/XeroxFactbook.pdf]. Oct. 24, 2001.

Zaltman, R., and Coulter, R. H. "Seeing the Voice of the Customer: Metaphor-Based Advertising Research." *Journal of Advertising Research,* 1995, *35*(4), 35–51.

Index

A

ACS model (Center for Creative Leadership), 41, 45–46
Action research, 221
Adaptive challenges, 47
Advent, 202–204
Airlie Conference (Center for Creative Leadership), 219, 222
Amabile, T. M., 50–51
Aman, J., 114
Amateur, passion of, 52–53
Analytic sandwich, 165–168
Angstrom Inc., 143, 146
Apple Computer, 22, 73, 176–177; Macintosh, 91, 119, 176–177
Appreciation, definition of, 30
Appreciative inquiry, 129–131
Approach Inc., 134
Argyris, C., 35
Arlington Institute, 25
Art: constructive and reconstructive, 191; definition of, 173; everyday, 179–180, 217; developing leadership as, 172–177; and learning from artists, 177–184; and responsible artistry, 189–190; and transportable laws of artistry, 180–184
Artist's Way at Work, The (Bryan, Cameron, and Allen), 186
Artist's Way, The (Cameron), 186
Aspen Center for Physics, 135
Assessment, 41–46. See also under Personalizing
Athens, Greece, 91
Attention: continuous partial, 16–17; deep, 30; definition of, 30; overload, 29
Attention, paying: and asking powerful questions, 17–19; cautions concerning, 34–36; as community competence, 31–34; developing, as personal competence, 30–31; five components of, 12; kinesthetic, 17–19; left-mode and right-mode, 14–17; to negative space, 19–21; shifting between modes of, 12–13
Authority, confronting, 157
Avery Dennison Inc., 46, 135

B

Barr, J., 95
Bateson, M. C., 30, 179, 181
Bayles, D., 177, 178, 189
Beauvais Cathedral, 176
Beveridge, W., 20, 118
Black-market complexity, 49, 53–54
Bollon, A. P., 18
Booth, E., 30, 97, 118, 179–180, 217
Bridges, W., 54
Bronowski, J., 72, 122
Brown, J. S., 32, 150
Bryan, M. A., 186
Bubnow, V., 153
Bunker, K. A., 55
Bunsen, R., 118–119

C

Cameron, J., 186
Campbell, J., 59–60
Carpenter, C., 65
Center for Creative Leadership (CCL), 11, 19, 29, 37, 114, 143, 219; ACS model, 41–46; Peak Selection Simulation, 165
Centrality fallacy, 52
Challenge: in ACS model, 44; adaptive versus technical, 47; oneself as part of, 47–48

Challenger (space shuttle), 166
Chaos, 110; nonrandom, 111–112; patterns within, 112
Chemstar, Inc. (fictional), 1, 9, 13, 21, 35, 55, 93–94, 119, 120, 153, 154, 157
Chouinard, Y., 151
Christensen, C. M., 112–113
Clark, J., 118
Cleveland, H., 8, 11
Coaching, individual leadership, 202–204
Cohen, L., 56
Co-inquiry: cautions regarding, 156–159; and community competence, 155–156; and creative leadership communities, 130–133; and crossing boundaries, 149–153; definition of, 129–130; and dialogue, 136–142; and group work spaces, 133–136; personal competence in, 153–155; and putting something in middle, 142–149
Collage, 73–75. *See also under* Imaging
Collateral skills, 38
Compendium (software), 194–197
Complex Challenge (C2) Competencies, 11, 35; and collaborative inquiry, 129–159; and crafting, 161–191; and imaging, 71–106; and paying attention, 11–36; and personalizing, 37–70; reflective assessment of, 223–226; and serious play, 107–127
Complex challenges: making sense of, 4–8; navigating, 1–10
Complexity: creating maps and compasses to navigate, 49–50; as hallmark of age, 11; poetry in face of, 95–104
Composing a Life (Bateson), 30
Conceptualization, 72
Connection, personal, 39–40, 72
Continuous partial attention, 16–17
Crafting: community competence in, 187–189; decisions, 164–169; definition of, 161–162; and developing leadership as science and art, 172–177; and learning from artists, 177–184; personal competence in, 184–187; scaffolding for learning, 169–172; and thinking in wholes, 162–164
Crandall, B., 53–54
Creating Shared Vision (Parker), 86
Creative leadership communities, 130–133
Creative leadership competencies worksheet, 186

Csikszentmihalyi, M., 16
Customer gap, 150–151. *See also* Language gap
Cutty Sark (clipper ship), 204
Cytoclonal Pharmaceuticals, 18

D

Damasio, A., 17
Darwin, C., 174
Dawkins, R., 104
Dayton, Ohio, 131
de Geus, A., 13
Deutsch, G., 15
Develop, meaning of, 30
Dhahran, Saudi Arabia, 60
Dialogue, 136–142. *See also* Co-inquiry
Dickey, J., 71
Dirtbags, 151
Discipline, 57
Diversity, 67
Dow Jones Index, 199

E

Edwards, B., 14, 182, 218
Einstein, A., 169–170
Ellis, C., 124
Elter, J., 211–213
Everyday art, 179–180, 217
Everyday Work of Art, The (Booth), 30
Executive interdependence, 206–211
Experimentation, 119–121
Exploration, for development, 46–50

F

Fabrication, 163, 190
Fast Company, 115
Fermi National Accelerator Laboratory (Fermilab), 66, 176
Fisher, D., 221
Flow state, 16
Fosdick, H. E., 95
Free agents, 67
Free-writing, 60
Fry, A., 131

G

Galison, P. L., 152
Game, definition of, 117
Gardner, D., 198
Gardner, H., 170

Gardner, T., 198
Gassée, J. L., 73
Gelernter, D. H., 117, 172
General Motors (GM) Nova, 104
Gergen, K. J., 107
Geteway, Inc., 151
Geus, A. de, 13
Gianella-Borradori, A., 35
Giotto, 175
Gogh, T. van, 181–182
Gogh, V. van, 181–182
Gold, R., 181, 188
Goldberg, R., 139, 143
Gray, P., 131
Gryskiewicz, S. S., 33, 112
Guzzo, R., 165

H

Haiku, 96–97
Hallmark Cards, Inc., 65
"Hand That Held the Flag, The" (Young),
    61
Harvard University, 52; Business School,
    50–51, 94; Graduate School of Educa-
    tion, 13
Healtheon, 118
Hedin, R. W., 63–64
Heifetz, R. A., 47, 167
Helgesen, S., 104, 115, 137, 138, 201
Hewlett, B., 104, 117
Hewlett Packard, 92, 104, 117, 135
High-gear attention, 12–13
HMS *Beagle*, 174
Holmes, O. W., 34
Horth, D. M., 20, 53, 101, 110, 203
HTML, 196
Hurst, D. K., 16, 50

I

IBM, 58, 177
Identity, 68–69
Image and Logic (Galison), 152
Imagination: making, tangible, 72–84;
    and misuse of images, 104–105
Imaging: cautions about, 104–106; and
    collage, 73–75; as community compe-
    tence, 102–104; developing, at per-
    sonal level, 99–102; and making
    imagination tangible, 72–84; and
    making poetry, 95–104; and metaphor,
    91–95; and organizational vision,

84–87; and pictorial language, 75–79;
    and scenarios, 87–91; and star-map-
    ping, 79–84
Improvisation, 113, 115–116
Inclusion, webs of, 104
Indiana University, 63–64
Industrial Age, 11
Innovation: fundamental, 112; increasing
    velocity of, 83–84; and serious play,
    108. *See also* Product innovation,
    creative
Integrated Systems Group, 195
Intel, 123–124
Internet, 73, 93
Intuition, 82
Inuits, 18
iVillage, 65

J

Jacksonville Symphony, 92
Jobs, S., 21–22, 176–177, 214
Johns River Station (fictional), 2, 9, 54,
    96–98, 120, 129, 149, 153
Johnson, M., 18
Jones, D., 126
Joyce, J., 105
Jung, C. G., 108

K

Kaplan, R. E., 163
Karate, 18
Kennedy, J. F., 95–96
Kennedy School of Government, 47
KEYS® to Creativity (CCL), 219
Kinesthetic attention, 17–19
Kirchhoff, G., 118–119
Kirton Adaption-Inventory (KAI), 219
Klein, G., 166, 169
Knowledge networking, 150
Koestler, A., 170
Kofman, F., 85, 109

L

Language gap, 151–152. *See also* Customer
    gap
Lawrence, D., 137
Leadership and the Information Revolution
    (Cleveland), 11
Leading Creatively program (LCP),
    217–219, 221–222
Learning: beginning of, in personal

connection, 39–40; in turbulence, 109–114
Left Brain, Right Brain (Springer and Deutsch), 15
Left-mode attention, 14–17
Letting-go, 56–58
Lewin, K., 221
Lewis, M., 118
LivingSystems, 212
Lopez, B., 50
Low-gear attention, 13

M

Magellan, F., 101
Mair, M., 93
Management: by walking around, 18; widespread leadership in addition to good, 187–188
Managing as a Performing Art (Vaill), 109
Managing the Unknowable (Stacey), 49
Massachusetts Institute of Technology (MIT) Media lab, 108
Maxwell, J. C., 169–171
McCall, M. W., 163
McCarthy, B., 39, 71–72
McClintock, B., 174
McDonald, J., 123
Me, Inc., 54
Meader, D., 195
Metaphors: as invitations, 92–93; making and using, 91–95; in practice, 93–95; root, 100–102; tyranny of, 93. *See also under* Imaging
Miami Herald, 137, 153
Microsoft Corporation, 17; Excel, 79–80; PowerPoint, 103
Miller, H., 64
Milne, G. M., Jr., 133
Mintzberg, H., 18, 161, 165
MIT Media Lab, 108
Morgan, G., 91–92
Motley Fool, The, 103, 198–202
Movie-making, 87–90
MS-DOS, 119
Myers-Briggs Type Indicator, 43

N

Nabokov, V. V., 174
National Geographic, 126
Nationwide, 114
Nature of Managerial Work (Mintzberg), 18

Negative space, 19–21, 83
Netscape, 118
New media, leadership in, 198–202
New York Times, 64
Newton, I., 174–175
Nicholson, G., 131
Nickelodeon, 68, 93
Nierenberg, R., 92
Nietzsche, F., 156
Nova (General Motors), 104
Novartis AG, 150

O

Open dialogue, 82–83
Orion, Inc. (fictional), 1, 9, 75; Orion Research Center (ORC), 75–84, 99, 102, 103, 105, 116, 143, 150, 152, 154, 163, 227, 230
Orland, T., 177, 178, 189
Ortega y Gasset, J., 58
Orton, P., 58
Osborn, A. F., 28

P

Packard, B., 104
Palmer, S., 165
Palus, C. J., 109
PARC. *See* Xerox Palo Alto Research Center (PARC)
Parker, M., 86
Passion, tapping into, 50–56
Patagonia, 151
Pattern finding, 82
Peak Selection Simulation (Center for Creative Leadership), 165
Perkins, D. N., 12, 33
Permanent whitewater, 109
Personal connection, 39–40
Personal investment, leadership in, 198–202
Personalizing: assessment in, 41–46; community competence in, 67–68; individual competence in, 58–66; and practicing exploration for development, 46–50; key ideas for, 38–39; and letting go, 56–58; and passion, 50–56; and personal connection, 39–40
Peters, T. J., 112
Petersen, J., 25–26
Pfizer, 133
Pictorial language, 75–79. *See also under* Imaging

Pidgin, 152
Plato, 190
Play. *See* Serious play
Play (company), 114–115
Poetry: and creative leadership, 95–96; in face of complexity, 95–104; as tool, 96–98
Post-it Notes, 131
Powerful questions: and appreciative questions, 27–28; asking, 21–29; definition of, 22–23; L-mode and R-mode, 23–25; and SCAMPER questions, 28–29; and so-what questions, 26–27; and what-if questions, 25; and wild cards, 26
Procter & Gamble, 39
Product innovation, creative, 204–206. *See also* Innovation
Progoff, I., 48
Ptashne, M., 52, 180

R

Ramey, J., 131
Reflection, 72
Reisinger, S., 137–138, 153
Re-vision, 35
Right-mode attention, 14–17
Robert Frost Library, 95–96
Roberts, K., 126
Royal Dutch Shell, 13
Ryle, G., 126

S

Sabbaticals, 65–66, 115. *See also* Personalizing
San Francisco Bay Area, 32, 188
Sandoz, 35
SCAMPER questions, 28–29
Scenarios, exploring, 87–91. *See also under* Imaging
Schrage, M., 108, 125
Science: connections between, and art, 173–176; definition of, 173; developing leadership as, 172–177
Self-assessment, 41–43
Self-evolution, 69
Senge, P. M., 109
Sense-making loop, 6, 193
Serious play: as community activity, 114–117; and community competence, 123–125; concept of, 97, 107–109; as heart of science and technology, 117–121; and learning amid turbulence, 109–114; personal competence in, 121–123
Serious Play: How the World's Best Companies Simulate to Innovate (Schrage), 108, 125
Shared horizon, 85
Shared imagery, 103
Silicon Graphics, 118
Silver, S., 131
Sinder, R., 167
Sixth Sense (software), 212
Sony, 93
Spider diagram, 79–80. *See also* Star-maps
Springer, S. P., 15
Stacey, R., 49
Stafford, B. M., 189–190
Star-mapping, 79–84, 227–229. *See also under* Imaging
Stefanovich, A., 114
Sterling Inc. (fictional), 206–211
Stocum, A., 213
Stone, L., 16
Storytelling, 58–65; institutionalizing, 67; six guidelines for effective, 64–65. *See also* Personalizing
Stranahan, G., 135
Support, in ACS model, 44
Suzuki method, 170, 171

T

Task force collaboration, 194–198
Taylor, J., 151
Teamwork, 82–83
Techno Inc. (fictional), 204–206
3M, 131
Thus Spake Zarathustra (Nietzsche), 156
Tichy, N. M., 59, 63
Torbert, W., 221
Trucking Company (TC; fictional), 115–117
Trust, 103–104, 116–117
Turbulence, learning amid, 109–114
Type III Problems, 167

U

Undiscussables (Argyris), 35
United Kingdom, 56
United States Air Force, 60
United States Army, Future Groups, 135
University of Michigan Business School, 59

V

Vaill, P. B., 4, 24, 107, 109
Values-based rationality, 16
van Gogh, V., 181–182
Vaughan, D., 166
Vernon, J., 134
Vision: abstract, 84; direct, 84–85; imaginative, 85; organizational, 84–87
Visual analysis, 103
Visual capture, 105
Visual Explorer (VE), 143–146, 149, 196, 197, 227
Visual verbal journals (VVIs), 99–100
Vulnerability, 55–56, 68

W

Wallenius-Wilhelmsen Lines, 132, 135–136
Web of Inclusion, The (Helgesen), 115
Weick, K. E., 126, 195, 215
Westrum, R., 52
Whatever It Takes (McCall and Kaplan), 163

X

Xerox, 135; Artist-in-Residence program (PAIR), 32, 188; Lakes Project, 211–215; Office Document Products Group, 211; Palo Alto Research Center (PARC), 31–32, 150, 181, 214
XYZ (fictional), 194–198

Whyte, D., 37–38, 95, 181
Wilson, R., 65–66, 176
World Academy of Art and Science, 8
Wozniak, S., 214
Wright Brothers, 131
Wynett, C., 39

Y

Young, D., 60

Z

Zaltman Metaphor Elicitation Technique (ZMET), 94
Zaltman, R., 94

About the Center for Creative Leadership

Founded in 1970, the Center for Creative Leadership® (CCL®) is one of the world's largest institutions focusing on disseminating practical leadership knowledge for individuals and organizations. CCL's mission of advancing the understanding, practice, and development of leadership for the benefit of society worldwide has led to international recognition of its portfolio of programs, assessments, and publications. They are regarded among the best offered by any institution anywhere. The portfolio is supported by CCL's five practice areas—Leadership for Complex Challenges, Leading in the Context of Difference, Individual Leader Development, Sustainable Leadership Capacity, and Team Development.

Funding is derived primarily from tuition, sales of products and publications, royalties, and fees for service. In addition, CCL also seeks grants and donations from foundations, corporations, and individuals in support of its educational mission.

Open-Enrollment Leadership Programs

CCL's open-enrollment leadership programs focus on individuals and may be used within the context of an organization's leadership development efforts. These programs help participants achieve specific developmental goals.

- The *Leadership Development Program (LDP)®, Foundations of Leadership,* and *The Looking Glass Experience* enable growth through developing personal awareness of one's leadership style and through identifying key areas of strength and weakness.

- *The African-American Leadership Program* and *The Women's Leadership Program* combine personal awareness of one's leadership style with research-based insights to show how leadership is affected by race and gender issues.

- The *Leading Creatively* program helps to understand how business performance and individual effectiveness relate to creativity.

- *Leadership at the Peak* and *Developing the Strategic Leader* use simulations and assessments to gain knowledge about how to lead and inspire change and revitalization.

- *Leadership and High-Performance Teams* shows how to develop and lead teams, turning average performers into a highly effective work group.

- *Coaching for Results* affirms the value of one-on-one developmental assistance, showing how it can be used to enhance individual and organizational effectiveness.

In October 2001, for the second consecutive time, CCL was ranked #1 for Leadership in *BusinessWeek* magazine's Executive Education Special Report. And CCL was the only non-degree business school to appear in *BusinessWeek's* top 20 providers of non-degree programs for executives. Please visit www.ccl.org/programs.

Custom-Designed Leadership Development Initiatives

On request, CCL can design and implement a leadership development initiative for your organization, designed specifically to meet its needs. Initiatives vary from redesigned versions of one of CCL's open-enrollment programs to unique events that build an organization from the ground up. Please visit www.ccl.org/custom.

Coaching

CCL has long understood the importance of honest, insightful, and confidential coaching in developing strong leaders. Our programs are distinct, and all include a reliance on quality assessment; rigorously trained coaches, ethics, and confidentiality; emphasis on the individual's development; and use of best practices throughout. For information on *Follow-on Coaching* (follows leadership programs), *Executive Coaching* (a venue for organizations that want a designed program without the classroom experience), and *Awareness Program for Executive Excellence (APEX)*® (for the most senior-level executives), please visit www.ccl.org/coaching.

Products

CCL pioneered the use of 360-degree assessment and feedback to help individuals, teams, and organizations learn about themselves. Assessments are an effective and necessary starting point for learning, growth, and change. Critical tools in both CCL and clients' development programs, they are also used on a stand-alone basis. CCL can provide facilitation services or train your trainers and facilitators in the use of these resources:

- *360 BY DESIGN*ᔆᴹ, a customizable, Internet-based 360-degree survey with on-line development planning and available support services.
- *Benchmarks*®, CCL's flagship 360-degree assessment tool that focuses on leadership skills and perspectives but also includes insights into potential flaws that can derail a career.
- *Prospector*®, for assessing ability to learn and willingness to take advantage of growth opportunities.
- *SKILLSCOPE*®, for assessing skills necessary for managerial effectiveness.

- *KEYS® to Creativity*, for organizations that want to enhance the environment for creativity and innovation.

Please visit www.ccl.org/assessments.

Publications

Through its publications, CCL aims to improve the current understanding, practice, and development of leadership by disseminating the latest practical knowledge gained in the course of CCL's research and educational activities. In addition to copublishing books and a magazine with Jossey-Bass, a Wiley company, on a variety of leadership topics, CCL also publishes independently through CCL Press.

Of particular interest to many leaders is the CCL Press *Ideas Into Action Guidebook* series. Geared to the practicing manager, these accessible and concise publications offer proven advice for carrying out a specific developmental task or solving a specific leadership problem. Ideas Into Action titles include:

Feedback That Works: How to Build and Deliver Your Message
Keeping Your Career On Track: Twenty Success Strategies
Reaching Your Development Goals
Learning from Life: Turning Life's Lessons into Leadership Experience

Please visit www.ccl.org/publications.

For more information on CCL's practice areas or special research that may help you in developing solutions for your organization's issues, please call CCL Client Services, (336) 545-2810, e-mail to info@leaders.ccl.org, or visit www.ccl.org.

More About Leadership for Complex Challenges

The Leadership for Complex Challenges group is one of five practice areas at the Center for Creative Leadership. The work of this group focuses on developing capacities for leadership in an increasingly complex world, where unfamiliar, chaotic, and fast-changing contexts are the norm. This book addresses the leadership needs of managers and professionals who are confronted daily with such challenges and are looking for creative and effective ways to confront them.

Additional activities of this group that relate to this book include:

Publications (available at www.ccl.org/publications)

- Wilfred H. Drath. *The Deep Blue Sea: Rethinking the Source of Leadership*.
- Wilfred H. Drath and Charles J. Palus. *Making Common Sense: Leadership as Meaning-Making in a Community of Practice*.
- Charles J. Palus and Wilfred H. Drath. *Evolving Leaders: A Model for Promoting Leadership Development in Programs*.
- Charles J. Palus. "The Art and Science of Leadership." *Leadership in Action*.
- Charles J. Palus and David M. Horth. "Leading Creatively." *Leadership in Action*.

Leadership Tool (Available at www.ccl.org/publications)

Visual Explorer: Picturing Approaches to Complex Challenges (co-developed by Charles J. Palus and David Magellan Horth). Designed for practicing leaders and managers, *Visual Explorer* is meant to help group members collectively explore a complex topic from a variety of perspectives. Each person selects from over 200 interesting and provocative images (photographs, reproductions of artworks, and so forth) that he or she wishes to explore in connection with a particular leadership topic. As they relate the connections between the topic and the image, each person tells stories or creates metaphors from their own point of view. This brings about shared understanding, which can lead to further action. This activity helps groups understand more fully the context and perspectives that surround the decisions they make and the actions they take.

Open-enrollment Program (Call 336-545-2810 or see www.ccl.org/programs for more information)

The *Leading Creatively* Program is a five-day experience that equips managers and executives with the creative competencies needed to make sense of, and deal more effectively with, the complexity and ambiguity of leadership in contemporary organizations. Attendees of this program have supplied much of the content for the development of the C2 Competencies that comprise the substance of this book.

Custom Programs (call 336-545-2810 or see www.ccl.org/programs for more information)

Facing and Solving Complex Challenges is an experience in which groups explore urgent challenges by learning and applying the C2 Competencies. The program can be applied to intact teams or cross-functional groups and tailored to timeframes from two-to-five days. Action-learning projects tackle the challenge back in the workplace under the sponsorship of senior executives.

The Artistry of Leadership™ is a keynote event and interactive musical experience that integrates original, contemporary piano music with individual reflection to explore leadership as an art. This event explores the importance and use of emotional intelligence with supervisors, managers, and executives as a tool for enhancing interpersonal effectiveness, creativity, visioning, and insight. Using a combination of facilitated discussion, small-group work, and interactive musical experience, participants will be able to identify pathways for meaningful communications with others in the workplace.

Further Research (contact Chuck Palus at palusc@leaders.ccl.org or David Horth at horthd@leaders.ccl.org for more information)

Research in conjunction with the *Facing and Solving Complex Challenges* custom program is currently being conducted. It studies middle managers from across functions in organizations as they collaborate in action-learning projects while they use the C2 Competencies discussed in this book. The research questions being investigated are first, What are the complex challenges currently being faced by leaders? and second, What forms of leadership are most effective in solving these challenges?